Rising Son

By

Charles R. Scott

THIRD WHEEL PRESS

THIRD WHEEL PRESS

New York, New York

First Edition: December 2012

ISBN-13: 978-1480272231
ISBN-10: 148027223X

Library of Congress Cataloging-in-Publication Data
Scott, Charles R.
Rising Son / Charles R. Scott
Summary: A father and eight-year-old son travel the length of Japan on
connected bicycles to raise environmental awareness.

To my wild and wondrous son, Sho.

Cape Soya

Sapporo

HOKKAIDŌ

JAPAN

HONSHŪ

Japanese Alps

Tokyo

Kyoto

Hiroshima

SHIKOKU

KYŪSHŪ

Cape Sata

Legend
Bicycle
Ferry

100 ml.

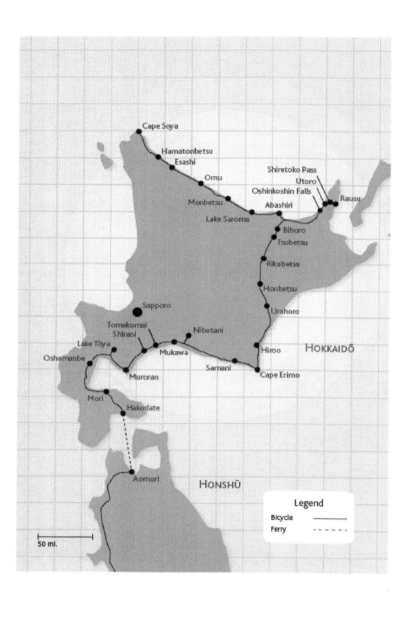

Cape Soya
Hamatonbetsu
Esashi
Omu
Monbetsu
Lake Saroma
Shiretoko Pass
Utoro
Oshinkoshin Falls
Abashiri
Rausu
Bihoro
Tsubetsu
Rikubetsu
Honbetsu
Urahoro
Sapporo
Tomakomai
Shiraoi
Nibutani
Lake Tōya
Mukawa
Oshamanbe
Samani
Muroran
Hiroo
Cape Erimo
HOKKAIDŌ
Mori
Hakodate
Aomori
HONSHŪ

Legend
Bicycle
Ferry

50 mi.

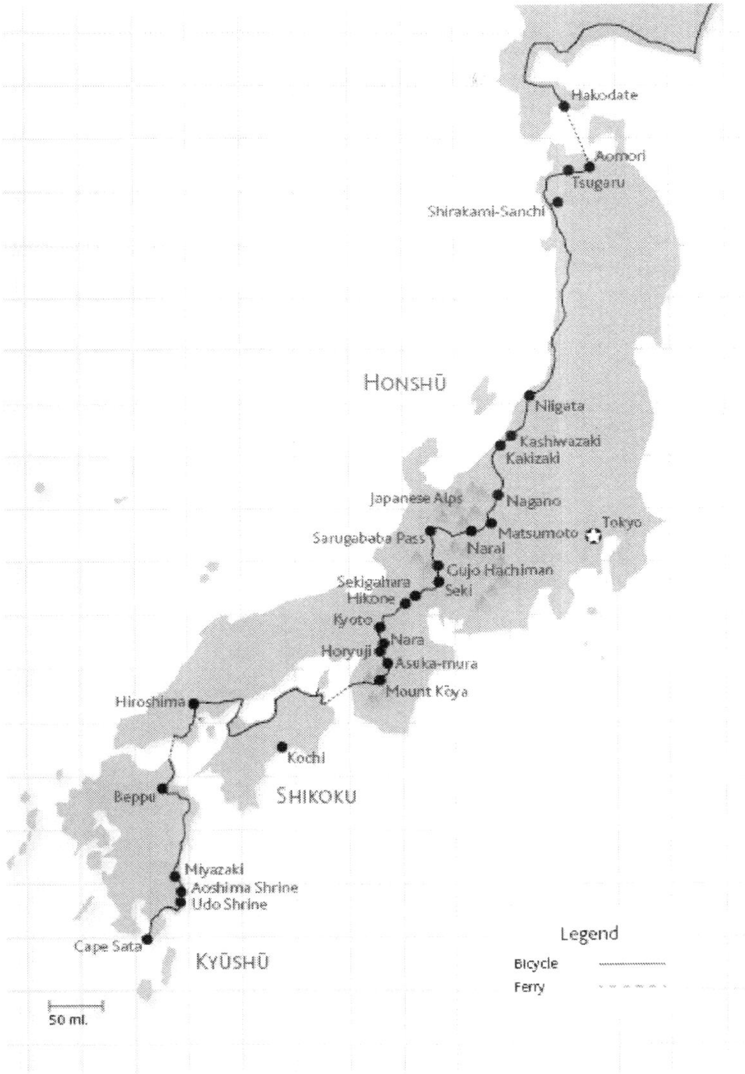

HONSHŪ

Hakodate

Aomori
Tsugaru

Shirakami-Sanchi

Niigata

Kashiwazaki
Kakizaki

Japanese Alps
Nagano

Sarugababa Pass
Matsumoto
Narai
Tokyo

Gujo Hachiman
Sekigahara
Seki
Hikone
Kyoto
Nara
Horyuji
Asuka-mura
Mount Kōya

Hiroshima

Kochi

SHIKOKU

Beppu

Miyazaki
Aoshima Shrine
Udo Shrine

Cape Sata
KYŪSHŪ

Legend

Bicycle
Ferry

50 ml.

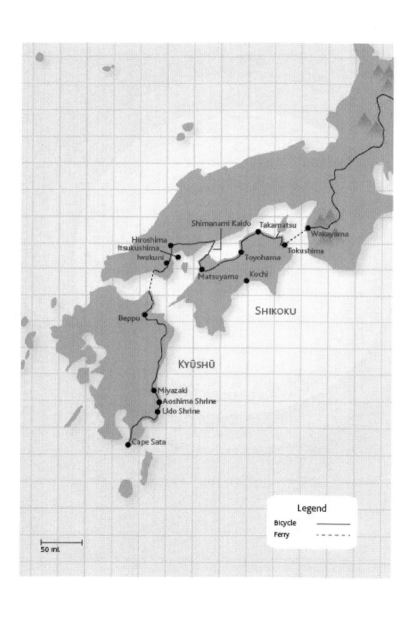

Shimanami Kaido

Hiroshima
Itsukushima
Iwakuni

Takamatsu

Wakayama

Tokushima

Toyohama

Matsuyama

Kochi

SHIKOKU

Beppu

KYŪSHŪ

Miyazaki
Aoshima Shrine
Udo Shrine

Cape Sata

Legend

Bicycle
Ferry

50 mi.

CONTENTS

Chapter 1

A Father-Son Adventure

THREE WEEKS IS TOO LONG TO BE APART FROM YOUR WIFE and infant son. After bounding through Asia with my boss—presenting products to demanding customers in eight countries over twenty days—I was back. Jet lag weighed on me like a monkey perched on my shoulders pounding at my head. My wife, our six-month-old son cradled in her arms, waved enthusiastically as I entered the crowded airport arrivals lobby. I kissed her and looked down at my son. "Sho has changed. I can already see a difference in him from when I left."

"He's happy to see you back," she said with a smile, bobbing him several times, which drew a giggle. His eyes, excited brown lights atop puffed up cheeks, searched mine for a moment. Then he reached out with his fat arms, fingers splayed open.

As I pulled him to my chest, I whispered, "I won't stay away from you that long again."

Seven years later, Sho and I were settled next to one another on a couch in our seventh floor apartment in New York City,

Pokemon cards spread all around. It was after his bedtime, but I had agreed to his plea for a few more minutes to play. I was making a list of life goals and didn't mind spending a little more time on it before putting him to bed.

Sho was carefully categorizing, analyzing and memorizing the cards as I sat beside him, a black pen in hand and a new white, lined pad of paper propped in my lap. The lights of the Empire State Building filled the middle of our apartment's three large windows, surrounded by the jagged, brightly lit spires of Manhattan's skyline. A few faint stars shone weakly above, unable to match the brilliance of the competing urban constellation.

My wife, Eiko, and two-year-old daughter, Saya, were next door in our bedroom, snuggled up beside one another in bed. Earlier, I had heard Saya's giggles and excited commentary carry through the wall, as my wife read out loud from a *Dora the Explorer* book. But now it was quiet. Eiko, exhausted from working all day, often fell asleep while reading to one of our children, usually waking up a few hours later and stumbling into our bed. Perhaps she was asleep now.

Frowning over my list, I wrote, "Run a sub-three-hour marathon." Then: "Create something of lasting value and social significance." I paused, considering what else to add. I was forty years old, married, with two kids and a cat. I had worked at Intel Corporation for eleven years, and my wife was in her thirteenth year at the United Nations. We owned two cars, a 3,100 square foot house in Westchester County, and rented an apartment in New York City next to our son's private international school. Our financial commitments were high, a never-ending treadmill, but our incomes, as long as we both remained employed, were enough to meet the demands. Thanks to years of study, professional focus, and good fortune, we were stable, happy and secure.

Yet I could feel some barely discernible psychic movement. Not exactly dissatisfaction, but a kind of push or call. As if I had been unconscious and needed to wake up. I had felt this for some time—years really—but turning forty prompted me to revaluate the hectic cycle of my work and family commitments. I decided to create a list of goals that reflected who I wanted to be and what I hoped to accomplish in the rest of my life.

I glanced at Sho, who was hunched over perhaps one hundred cards he had organized as if he were some kind of Pokemon scientist in search of a new discovery. He was wearing blue shorts and a Star Wars shirt, which hung loosely on his slender body. A combination of Caucasian and Japanese, he had my wife's soft brown eyes and her father's distinctive protruding ears. I had contributed his lean body type and the dimples in his cheeks.

The seven years since Sho's birth had passed quickly. When I held him on his first day of life, he fit the length of my forearm, his puffy squinting unfocused eyes staring up toward me, his mouth puckered as if he were trying to make a spit bubble. Soon he was a boy actually making spit bubbles for me, playfully showing off how long he could keep one formed before it burst. I often sang Harry Chapin's "Cats in the Cradle" to him as he fell asleep, a song that laments how quickly a child grows, told from the perspective of a busy father who realizes too late what he missed. I knew that the next decade would disappear in an accelerating blur of business trips and rushed mornings. And then my children would fly away.

Tapping the pen against my chin, I wondered if there might not be a way to interrupt the hectic routine of our daily lives, create a space to slow down and appreciate more fully the precious and fleeting moments of Sho and Saya's brief childhoods. I saw how easily I could spend the next ten years of my life settled into a kind of status quo existence—comfortable, but resigned to the limits created by our many financial commitments and the self-perceived need to maintain the accoutrements of successful professionals. Somehow, that path did not feel quite right.

I wanted to spend less time responding to an overwhelming flow of work and family demands and more time creating lasting memories. I wanted to seek out experiences that encouraged in my kids a love of adventure and a fearless openness to challenge and growth. I wanted them to gain an orientation toward life as something to nurture and savor, and to consider each day something to treasure, not just to get through.

Finally I wrote, "Dream up adventures with my kids." Staring at the list, I said, "Now that's a good one."

"What Daddy?" Sho asked, not looking up from the Dialga card he studied.

"We need to come up with an adventure to do together."

"What kind of adventure?" he responded, looking up from his cards.

"Well, it could be anything, and could be anywhere. But it needs to be fun, and it needs to be a challenge."

"Let's do something in Japan!" he replied. Since he was a baby, we had visited my wife's family in Tokyo annually for New Year's celebrations. Our trips lasted a week or two at most and were filled with socializing, visits to game rooms, Tokyo Disneyland and other family destinations. Sho's relatives treated him like a rock star whenever he came to town. No wonder he loved Japan.

"I'm fine with Japan. But it can't be the same old stuff we usually do. It's got to include some kind of challenge."

"We could swim there," Sho said. "That would be a challenge."

"Swim to Japan from New York City?" I asked, pretending to mull over the suggestion. "Let's do something that doesn't involve sharks and allows us to visit parts of the country we've never been to before."

"We could ride our bikes to new places. I'm really good at riding now."

I liked where he was going. I thought he was too young to ride the streets of Japan on his own, but I recalled a friend telling me about an attachment that allowed a child to ride safely behind his parent. If I remembered correctly, he'd called it a "trailer cycle." It looked like a kid's bike, but instead of a front wheel, a curved bar extended out the front, connecting to the adult's seat post. The child could change gears and, unlike a tandem bike, pedal at his own pace. I could imagine cycling with Sho like that through Japan's countryside. With enough advanced planning, I could easily take off a week or two from work for such an adventure.

A week or two would be fun, but why not make it something more challenging?

I recalled a period of time in my childhood when I was just a few years older than Sho. My father, a university professor who regularly cycled fourteen miles round trip to campus, had begun running in the late 1970's. He sprinkled our home with issues of *Runner's World* magazine. Jim Fixx's *The Complete Book of Running* seemed to be a permanent fixture on a side table in our family room. The book's distinctive cover had a deep red background with a simple snapshot of a man's legs in the midst of a stride. He wore a pair of red running shorts and racing flats, his beautifully toned, powerfully muscled legs making a satisfying figure four shape as he ran. I imagined that, some day, I might have legs that looked like that.

Starting around age ten, I jogged occasionally with my dad and gradually began to think of myself as a runner. I completed a few one-mile "fun runs" and ten-kilometer (6.2 miles) races over the next few years. One warm Saturday morning in the spring of 1981, when I was thirteen years old, I was walking around my home in Nashville, Tennessee, bored and looking for something to do. Spying a *Runner's World* magazine, I plopped down on our couch to flip through it. Inside I found an article on the history of the marathon, a 26.2-mile race that was part of the original Olympic Games in Ancient Greece. As I read, an idea began to form.

Later that morning, my father and I were jogging together on a familiar three-mile route along a quiet suburban road near our home. Magnificent flowering magnolia trees and powerful oaks stood guard over lush green one-acre lots surrounding modest middle class ranch houses tucked back at a uniform distance from the street.

"Dad," I said, as our feet tapped the pavement in syncopation. "Would it be okay with you if I ran a marathon?" Running twenty-six plus miles would be a big leap, more than four times longer than I had ever run before. I knew that my mother would worry that it was not healthy for a thirteen-year-old to attempt such a feat, but my father might let me do it. He was forty-six years old and had never run that far either, but I could see he was intrigued.

"A marathon?" he said, cocking his head to the side to look down at me as we ran.

"I want to try one," I explained. "I think it would be a cool thing to do and make me a better runner."

"I bet it would," he said with some excitement, adding, "I might even join you. I don't know if either of us can run that far, but it would be a good experience to try, wouldn't it?"

I smiled back at him, thinking with pride, "I'm going to be a marathoner." Of course, setting the goal was easy, but accomplishing it would be another thing altogether. And I didn't have the experience to realize just how much of a stretch this was going to be.

Now, nearly three decades later, I was still dreaming up crazy goals, only this time I was the father. I felt a surge of vitality at the idea of a long bike ride in Japan with Sho. And I imagined that the adventure offered a chance for him to begin to discover his tremendous physical potential, to experience the deep satisfaction of working toward a difficult goal, and to learn to accept discomfort as part of growth. At the same time, we could celebrate his Japanese heritage and learn more about the country of his mother's birth. I imagined visiting many of Japan's most famous cities and historical sites with him, cycling past farms, over mountains, and exploring parts of the country we had never visited. What a great way to slow down time and create lasting memories.

I thought about "The Call," a poem I loved by Nadya Catalfano, written when she was 94 years old:

Something soft and gentle
Glides through your fingers
And it seems to grab your hand and lead you
On to something greater
If only you had the sense to follow it

And I thought about the internal push that had become more insistent recently. I did not want simply a challenging vacation with my son. I wanted an extended break and some breathing room to reflect on whether corporate life was still right for me. I appreciated the prestige and salary, but I felt that something was amiss. I was often exhausted and irritable from business travel and work demands. I didn't seem to have enough time and energy left over for my kids, my wife and my interests outside of work. I had no right to complain about my job, which was interesting and rewarding, but somehow it did not feel like a fit anymore. I hoped that getting away for two months might give me a chance to analyze this more deeply. Did I simply need a break or was it time to make a professional change?

"You know what would be really cool?" I asked, excitement growing in my voice. "We could cycle from one end of the country to the other. You could ride a trailer cycle attached to my bike to stay safe and help with the pedaling."

"Sounds great. Let's do it!" Sho said with a nod of his head, as if it were as simple as that. He returned his concentration to the cards spread out in front of him, mumbling, "Now where did I put Empoleon . . ."

I tapped my pen on the list, mulling over what we had just decided. I'd never attempted anything like it. No one I knew had. My family and friends would certainly consider it foolhardy, potentially dangerous and probably a sign of a midlife crisis. I didn't know how many miles it would be or how long it would take. But I knew a trip like that would last more than my four weeks of annual vacation. It was possible that I would be fired from my job at Intel. What if my son were hurt or killed in an accident? Or declared that he wanted to quit one week into the trip? What if the bikes broke down in the middle of nowhere, or if I injured my knee and couldn't continue? The "what if's" kept coming but could not dampen the excitement I felt at the prospect of doing something so crazy and challenging with my son.

Chapter 2

Reactions and Fears

MY WIFE'S LOOK CHANNELED GENERATIONS OF WOMEN WHO had to check their husband's poor judgment. It was the day after Sho and I had come up with our grand plans, and I had waited until after dinner to tell my wife.

"You want to do *what*, exactly?" Her head was cocked to the side, as if she was having difficulty understanding what I had just said. Standing over the sink with a half-washed plate in her hand, she stopped cleaning for a moment, suds dripping from her hands, and turned to look me squarely in the face.

I was drying a drinking glass with a thin blue kitchen towel, a slight humming squeak coming from the motion, as if the glass were purring from the attention. Sho and Saya were sunk next to one another on our couch in front of the TV in the next room, bellies full, mesmerized by "Shrek." Our affectionate cat, Boo Boo, snuggled in between them, a black bundle of fur luxuriating in domestic bliss.

"Sho and I want to ride bicycles from one end of Japan to the other. I've calculated that it should be about 2,500 miles and take us a couple of months. We can do it over Sho's summer vacation." Earlier in the day, I had practiced what I planned to say, distilling the complex set of motivations and trip details to a few key points I thought Eiko would appreciate. Seeing her eyebrows arch, I continued bravely, "This is actually a good idea. I want to introduce our son to living life as an adventure. I want to be a role model and show him what amazing things he can accomplish. I want him to feel the excitement of pushing physical limits and to learn more about his Japanese heritage."

Eiko resumed cleaning the plate and listened patiently, choosing not to interrupt my enthusiastic sales pitch. Recognizing that I wasn't joking, she replied simply, "Okay, I get it. What are the risks?"

I'd practiced a response to this question too. "I've been researching it, and it's not too bad. I mean, you always have to be careful about cars, but he will ride a trailer cycle attached to my bike. And most of the time, we'll be in the countryside with little traffic. I found out that there are wild brown bears in Hokkaidō, but we should be able to avoid them. I don't know what else . . . We'll probably get wet. And tired of course. But it will be awesome, because it will teach Sho how to deal with adversity. And we'll be together, so it will be fun."

"Not all of us," my wife corrected, handing me the now clean, dripping plate, and starting to wash another. "Sho will be apart from his mother and sister, and you'll be apart from your wife and daughter. For how long did you say—two months?"

"I know, I know. It's not ideal. Saya's still too young to go, but maybe in two years, when she's four, I'll take her on Adventure Number Two. You could come on that one, too!"

"You want to do more of these?" She gave me the look. I glanced nervously at the slippery plate that she started to rub a bit too aggressively.

"I don't know," I answered. "I just feel like life is short, you know? It's like I have this precious gift right now, this brief period of time when Sho is old enough to go on some incredible adventures, and young enough to want to go with me.

Before we know it, he'll be a teenager and won't give a crap about spending time with either of us. I want to do the same thing with Saya when she's a little older. Show her how to turn life into an adventure."

As if on cue, we heard giggles from the other room and Saya yell out, "Silly Donkey!" Eiko's look softened, and she smiled at my enthusiasm. I saw affection and empathy in her eyes. "What about your job?"

"I still have to figure that one out. But I think I can pull it off." I did not yet know how. I also did not know that within a few months, the world would plunge into the worst recession in recent memory. And Intel, along with many other corporations, would commence layoffs.

We stared at one another in silence. Then Eiko smiled and gave me a kiss on the cheek. "Well, you're not afraid to be different—I'll give you that. That's one of the things I like about you, actually. And I trust your judgment. I don't know if you were asking my permission exactly, but I see that you've made up your mind. And I'll support you. Just keep our son safe, okay?"

"I promise." I said, a broad grin growing on my face. "You know, you're one in a million."

"Thank you," Eiko replied, rolling her eyes. "You can stop selling now. And how about finishing up the dishes while I get the kids' bath ready?"

I began telling other people about our trip. Some were enthusiastic, seemingly drawing energy from our plans. They confided their own dreams of adventure, their fantasies of taking a sabbatical from work, their desire to spend more time with their children. Despite enjoying lives of material comfort, they felt something was missing. One email made me especially happy. "Being a conservative, career-oriented, money-minded couch potato, I think that you both are crazy. But even the thought of doing something one 1000th of what you are doing excites me. You certainly inspired me to spend some time playing chess or badminton with my son, which we both love very much. Thank you."

Others, often people who knew me through work, were bewildered by the project. They offered tepid acknowledgment of the adventure with politely puzzled expressions. It was clear that this endeavor was not going to augment my professional reputation.

Still others, concerned about Sho's safety, focused on the risks and obstacles in the endeavor. A colleague introduced me to an acquaintance living in Japan. I sent him a brief e-mail with a description of our plans and asked if he had any suggestions of resources we might consult to help us prepare. "It will be much more complicated than you realize," he responded. "There are at least two books recently written by people who have crossed Japan on bikes. One had almost 400 flat tires during his trip. I hope you will have a good support team, because you will need it. As you know, Japan is quite mountainous and the roads are not as wide as they are in the U.S. You should have at least one vehicle trailing you, hazards flashing, as protection and to carry your supplies. A tire repair kit with lots of patches and spare tubes is highly recommended. Cash, lots of it, is also highly recommended, because you'll find that there aren't that many places to pitch a tent and *minshukus* [Japanese Inns] don't readily take credit cards. You should also plan where you want to spend nights beforehand, because many places don't take walk-ins, because they need to prepare the meals for boarders."

He went on, "I don't know if it's a good idea to plan your trip during the Japanese summer, unless you are okay with 95F temps and 90%+ humidity . . . You may also want to allocate a good-sized time cushion, because the route you have planned has many mountain passes to cross. Most highways that traverse mountains here are two-laners only, about 8ft wide— not much room for vehicles, especially trucks to go around. You should probably also research the traffic regulations in the cities, since a new law, put into effect in June of this year, requires bicycles to ride on the streets in cities, which is a scary undertaking. It should be fun, though, maybe not during the trip, but afterwards when you look back on it. Sorry if I may sound negative."

May sound negative? My stomach churned. The list of obstacles seemed overwhelming, but I felt a competitiveness rising within me. I was going to make sure that we had fun, not just when we "looked back on it," but during the ride. And I made a commitment to figure out how to address each of the problems he pointed out.

A week later, while flying to California from New York on a business trip, I happened to sit next to a Japanese woman from Tokyo vacationing in the U.S. After some small talk, I excitedly told her my plans and showed her the route my son and I planned to ride. "Wow, that's amazing!" she said with an approving nod of her head. She then added with absolute conviction, "You know, a Japanese mother would never let her child do such a thing." I had to smile.

Sho's attitude was carefree: if my dad thinks I can do it, then I'm sure I can. This was the most disturbing realization I had during moments of self-doubt. What if I was wrong? What if this was a terrible idea, an unrealistic and potentially dangerous result of my yearning for adventure? As I contemplated the risks, read the concerned e-mails and observed the anxious body language of friends, I shuddered at the thought that this could turn into a sad object lesson and a source of disillusionment for Sho. A negative voice inside my head anticipated the failure and sneered, "You've set up your son for a big disappointment. Nice job, idiot."

Chapter 3
Layoffs Looming

I WAS SETTLED INTO AN AISLE SEAT ON A CHINA AIR FLIGHT to Beijing, my laptop resting precariously on a stumpy tray table. It had been over a month since Sho and I had decided to cycle across Japan, and still I had not told my boss. The timing never felt right, and I rationalized that with nine months before the departure, I could put off the uncomfortable discussion a while longer. Although I had begun to piece together the trip details in snippets of time stolen from work and family, I felt pressure from preparation I still needed to do.

The seat was cramped and typing was awkward. But I wasn't complaining. Having nodded politely to my seatmate, I did not initiate conversation. I needed the time, over thirteen uninterrupted hours, to prepare for my meetings in China and work on the Japan ride. A fully charged spare battery ensured I could work throughout the entire flight.

I was headed to China to evaluate a potential multi-million dollar investment in a local tech company that was envisioning an initial public offering. I had reviewed much of the material in advance and only needed to go over a few documents and make a list of key issues to cover with the company. I could accomplish this in an hour. The rest of the time on the flight would be reserved for planning the Japan ride.

My neighbor was a heavy-set, middle-aged white guy wearing a crisp charcoal suit. His sideburns were cut neatly into gray-speckled mutton chops, like sentries guarding his pudgy face. His eyes contained the expectant look of a person ready to engage in hours of idle chit chat, but he read my body language and left me alone. Our neighbor in the window seat was another well-dressed, white business man reading the *Wall Street Journal.*

Middle Seat Man, glancing at the front page headline, said, "Can you believe what happened to Lehman Brothers? They let the firm die, just like that. I wonder which Wall Street domino is going to fall next."

Focused on my laptop, I tuned out their conversation, opened an Excel spreadsheet, and titled it, "Trip Prep." I closed my eyes for a moment and thought, "I need a plan. Where to start?" There were significant gaps in my knowledge, and I had to get this right to keep my son safe and complete the trip.

I named a tab in the spreadsheet: "Equipment," wondering what we should bring besides our bikes. Tab Number Two: "Training." We needed to be ready for the physical demands of cycling hours at a time, day after day. Next tab: "Bike Details." I needed to become more proficient at bike repair. I could change a flat but had little experience truing a wobbly wheel, replacing a broken spoke or chain, and other repairs I might have to perform beside a rural road in the middle of Japan. Tab Number Four: "Route and Itinerary." I had only a rough idea of the path we would take through the country. And where would we stay each night? Tab Number Five: "Resources." I wondered about the unknowns, things I didn't even know I should anticipate. I needed a broader set of knowledge to understand the risks and challenges that came with traveling thousands of miles by bike. It would be good to create a list of books to read and websites to study.

The final tab: "Dangers."

I was familiar with the general risks of cycling and knew something could go wrong. But I had raced in many triathlons, cycled thousands of miles on crowded, congested and cramped roads, and only had two bike accidents of any significance in the previous twenty years. In both cases, I was going a little too fast for the conditions. Once, I slipped on a patch of oil while turning. The other time, I slid off the road after braking on wet leaves at the top of a hill. I suffered bruises and scrapes in each crash and gained a deeper understanding of how to minimize the chances of an accident: pay close attention to road conditions and don't ride too fast.

I knew people who had suffered more serious bike accidents. A teenage driver talking on a cell phone knocked my buddy Martin off his bike and broke his neck. He was lucky not to have been paralyzed, and after about a year of dedicated rehabilitation, he recovered fully. The accident had occurred at dusk, and Martin sent out safety lights to every cyclist he knew, warning us not to ride in the dark and to make ourselves "idiot-proof visible."

And there was Dana, a classmate in graduate school. As students, we often jogged together, talking about our shared interest in Japan and plans for life after school. A few years after graduating, I attended her wedding. Not long after, she was riding in the bike lane on Massachusetts Avenue in Boston. The narrow lane funneled bikes in between a line of parked cars on the right and moving traffic on the left. The design meant that an open driver's side door would block the bike lane. Just before Dana reached the side of his car, a driver who didn't think to check the side mirror opened his door. She instinctively swerved sharply to the left and was killed instantly by a passing bus. Wearing a helmet did not protect her.

I often thought about Dana, and I miss her still. I took away an important lesson from her death: if someone opens a car door in front of your bike, slam on your brakes and hit the door, if you can't stop in time. Don't swerve. In cycling, like driving, sudden swerves greatly increase the odds of a bad accident.

And that's what it came down to: odds.

I grieved for Martin and Dana, but I could come up with a longer list of car crash incidents among people I knew. And I didn't think twice about strapping my children into a car nearly every day. Was cycling really more dangerous than driving a car? Possibly, but I didn't want to work only from anecdotal evidence. I wanted to quantify the risk and knew that in order to do so I was going to have to get geeky. I read report after report on bike safety statistics. Some said driving was more dangerous; others concluded the opposite. But they all agreed on one simple fact: speed kills.

I closed my eyes to rest for a minute and became conscious of my seatmates' conversation. They were still discussing the looming financial crisis that was creating worldwide panic. The man with the mutton chops was talking with passion, and his neighbor in the window seat nodded with a furrow in his brow. "You can see what's coming. More banks are going to go under. Panic will set in. And the economy will tank. The next year will be ugly. A lot of people are going to be out of work."

He reached up to stroke a side burn, as if warding off bad luck from the impending mayhem. After a pause, he added, "We'd all better hold on to our jobs as tight as we can."

There it was. Fear. The worst financial crisis in decades was beginning. Layoffs loomed. And I was planning to take a flippant two-month sabbatical to ride bikes with my kid? The prudent course would be to postpone the ride until the economic turmoil subsided. Hunker down. Avoid risky behavior and try not to lose my job.

It would be easy to postpone the bike trip through Japan, but pushing it out a year or two didn't feel right. The noise in my life could overwhelm the gentle call I was trying to hear. I knew that if I postponed the trip, I might never do it.

And then I made a decision: ignore the fear. I understood and could manage the risks of cycling. There was a remote chance that Sho and I might be hurt or killed while riding across Japan, but we could greatly decrease the odds through our actions. And we could just as easily be hurt or killed if we stayed in New York and followed our normal routine.

I opened my eyes and returned to the spreadsheet, writing down the following rules:

- Put lights on the bikes
- Do not cycle at night
- Ride at a safe speed

And I decided it was time to break the news to my boss. I knew that my boss would not think this was a good idea, but I thought she might agree if I made it clear how determined I was. I would also tell her at least six months in advance, so that we would have plenty of time to plan how to cover my work while I was gone. Imagining the conversation gave me chills. What would I do if she simply said no? Was I willing to be fired in order to take this trip?

Chapter 4

Training

THE TOWERING OAK AND SUGAR MAPLE TREES IN OUR BACK yard had shed their leaves. Sho and Saya stomped through them, kicking up flying plumes of swirling brown and red and orange, tackling one another and rolling through soft, damp leaf mounds. I smiled at the sound of my children's laughter as I pushed out my bicycle onto the driveway. The early afternoon sun helped to counter the fall chill, and I leaned the bike next to Sho's trailer cycle, which was resting against the side of my house in a spot warmed by the sun's rays.

Sho and I planned to leave soon on a two-day training ride to a state park, sleeping in our tent at a campsite. This would be our most ambitious effort to date, our inaugural overnight outing, and the first time we would ride with a full assortment of gear stuffed into a handlebar bag and four saddlebags (sometimes called "panniers," from the French "baskets"). I had intended to leave in the morning to give us plenty of time to make it to the park before dark, but it was already 1 p.m. In the morning, Saya and Sho had begged me to play with them outside, and after I finally extricated myself from the fun, it had taken longer than I had anticipated to prepare the bikes and assemble our gear. Packed into the saddlebags were a tent, tarp and rain cover, two sleeping bags and rolled up sleeping pads, a change of clothes for Sho and me, rain jackets, hooded ponchos, toiletries, a first aid kit, four spare inner tubes for my tires and two spare tubes for the smaller tire on Sho's trailer cycle, tire levers, a pump, a bike tool, a patch kit, flash lights, a map, a camcorder, sunscreen, insect repellent, snacks, my wallet, and more. The total weight of our equipment came out to an astonishing seventy-five pounds.

I examined my maroon Trek 520 touring bike and wondered if the screws that secured the saddlebags into eyelets on the front and rear forks would hold up under so much weight. I had purchased this model, paying about $1,500, precisely because it was designed for long-distance touring. Its chromoly steel frame was a combination of chromium and molybdenum alloying elements that made the bike sturdy and relatively light. This was the same family of steel used in race car roll cages to protect drivers from injury in a roll-over accident. I hoped that the bike lived up to the marketing hype and could handle the amount of gear I loaded onto it.

I attached Sho's trailer cycle to the Trek's seat post, ensuring that the front bar was securely locked in place and able to swivel to either side as the bikes made turns. I hopped on my bike and took a quick test ride to the end of the driveway and back, the empty trailer cycle following smoothly behind on its single rear wheel. I was unsteady at first, not used to riding with the unwieldy, fully-loaded saddlebags, but with just a little momentum, I found that the bikes were relatively easy to manage. Sho saw me riding and abandoned Saya, who was lying on a thick pile of leaves in the yard and flapping her arms and legs back and forth.

"What's she doing?" I asked, coming to a stop, as he ambled up to the edge of the driveway.

"Making a leaf angel."

"That sounds like fun. Are you ready for our big ride?"

"Oh, yeah!"

"Today will be the longest we've ever ridden together."

"How far are we going again?"

"We'll ride about forty miles today, sleep in our tent at a campsite in Fahnestock State Park, and return tomorrow, coming back the same way."

"That's eighty miles!"

"You got it," I said, glancing up at the sky and realizing that we needed to get under way immediately. Daylight would begin to fade in about five hours. I could ride forty miles in two and a half hours comfortably on my race bike, but it would probably take twice that long on a steel frame touring bike loaded down with seventy-five pounds of gear and Sho attached on his trailer cycle.

I called to Eiko, who came outside and gave us both hugs. "Stay safe, okay?" she counseled with a stern look as she mussed Sho's hair.

"We will. Don't worry," Sho and I said in unison.

"Are you sure you'll be warm enough?" Eiko asked, looking at Sho as he strapped on his helmet.

He wore gloves and two sweatshirts. Grinning up at her, he said, "I'm fine."

"I've packed an extra coat if he needs it," I assured her.

Saya bounded toward us from the yard carrying a huge pile of leaves and, squealing with laughter, tried to dump the entirety onto us. Her small hands were not up to the task, however, and she ended up tossing most of the leaves onto her own head. I could still hear her giggling as we pulled away from our house.

We cycled on rolling, lightly trafficked, tree-lined back roads, enjoying the gorgeous fall day. Sho hummed happily behind me, pedaling easily, and excitedly pointed out two stunning silently floating swans as we passed by the radiant waters of Teatown Reservoir. As he did so, the bikes swerved out to the left, even though I was gripping the handlebars tightly. "Careful buddy. Don't shift your weight so much. It makes it hard for me to control the bikes."

"I didn't do anything, Daddy."

"When you pointed at the swans, did you notice how we veered out to the left?"

"I hardly moved," he persisted.

As we continued to ride, I paid close attention to this issue. I was still becoming accustomed to cycling with a heavy load of gear and thought that maybe I just needed some more practice to keep our bikes under control. A few minutes later, Sho shifted his weight, causing me to veer off a straight line again. It wasn't by much, maybe three or four inches, but I worried that we wouldn't have much margin of error when cycling next to traffic on a narrow Japanese road.

We soon merged onto the North County Trailway, a "rails to trails" project that would take us to within about six miles of Fahnestock State Park. The paved bicycle and pedestrian path was uncomfortably bumpy at times, sturdy tree roots pushing up through the concrete path. But it offered us a safe route to gain experience and confidence with our bike set-up. I asked Sho to experiment with changes in his body position to see how much it would affect my ability to keep the bikes going in a straight line. He didn't have to do much to cause me to swerve slightly, and I wasn't able to do much to keep it from occurring. I made a mental note to look for a solution to this potential danger.

Over the next few hours, Sho asked to take several short breaks, and by the time we reached the town of Carmel, our jumping off point to leave the comfortable safety of the paved trail, the sun was ominously low in the sky. I calculated that we had an hour and a half before sunset, enough time to cover the final six miles to the park campsite before it became too dark to ride safely. We turned on Highway 301, a two-lane route with only a narrow shoulder that wound past rolling, tree-covered hills and glistening reservoirs. We stayed far to the right as cars passed us every few minutes. I kept a tight grip on the handlebars and tensed up any time I heard a vehicle approach, worried that Sho might cause me to swerve out. The terrain was hilly, but I pedaled at an aggressive pace in a desire to get this trafficked section over with as quickly as possible and to beat the setting sun. I was soon panting heavily from the effort. Just as we began to climb a long hill, Sho came up with an inspired game, in which he asked me a series of questions by spelling out every word.

"D-a-d-d-y space a-r-e space y-o-u space h-a-v-i-n-g space f-u-n question mark."

It was a challenge to pay close enough attention to understand what he was spelling, with wind rushing by, my heart pounding, and my legs burning from the exertion.

"What?" I yelled over my shoulder.

"D-a-d-d-y space a-r-e space y-o-u space h-a-v-i-n-g space f-u-n question mark." Sho repeated with some annoyance.

"Yeah, sure," I answered in a short gasp of air.

"D-a-d-d-y space w-h-y space a-r-e space y-o-u space p-a-n-t-i-n-g space l-i-k-e space a space d-o-g question mark."

"Can't . . . talk . . . now."

"W-h-y question mark."

"Hmph."

"W-h-a-t question mark."

Pant. Grunt.

"Daddy, you're not very good at this game."

"Grrr . . ." I felt like throwing the little smart alec off the bike.

A steady flow of traffic continued to zoom by us, keeping us hemmed in at the edge of the right lane. And to make matters worse, I began to see long shadows spreading across the road. It was getting dark.

"I thought we had at least an hour before sunset," I mumbled. I glanced up to see the sun already disappearing behind the tree line at the top of a nearby hill and realized my amateurish mistake. If the terrain had been flat, the sun wouldn't set along the horizon for another hour, but the high hills in this area brought on an early dusk. I thought about my friend Martin who had been hit by a car while cycling at this time of day, looked back at the single tiny blinking light I had affixed to Sho's seat post, and made a decision. It was time to get off the road now.

A minute later, I turned onto a small side road, dotted with houses, but mostly surrounded by forest.

"What are we doing, Daddy?"

"We ran out of sunlight and are not gonna make it to the campsite today. So we get to practice free camping."

"What does that mean?"

"It means we look for a free spot to set up our tent."

I saw a dirt path off to the right and asked Sho to dismount. We rolled our bikes onto the path, walked past a house and followed the route for a few dozen yards into the surrounding forest. We emerged into a clearing, and I gave Sho the honors.

"Choose the spot, buddy. This is where we're spending the night."

We leaned our bikes against a tree, had the tent up in about twenty minutes, and crawled inside. It was already dark, and we nibbled sandwiches and fruit by flashlight while recounting the day's adventures.

By 8:00, we were yawning. Turning off the flashlight, we crawled into sleeping bags and lay on our backs. The night sky spread open far above, shaky stars winking at us through the filter of the mesh tent roof.

"Daddy, will you sing me a song?" Sho asked, snuggling up close and closing his eyes.

I began to sing Ben Folds' "Still Fighting It" about a father talking to his son about how weird it is to grow up, and lamenting that one day his son would fly away. Sho was soon asleep and as I lay in the tent listening to his soft rhythmic breath, I felt the weight of his trust. I was far from ready to ride across Japan with him. I still hadn't figured out some basic issues, like keeping the heavily laden bikes on a straight line while riding in traffic. The muscles in my legs twitched from the day's exertion, and I knew that I would need to train a lot more to be able to pull so much weight day after day for over two months.

Sho and I woke early the next morning and nibbled on some dried fruit and bagels. As we began to break down the tent, a boy not much older than Sho rolled into the clearing on a mountain bike and came to an abrupt stop.

"Hi there," I said with a wave, and he spun around and disappeared the way he'd come.

Within a few minutes, the boy was back with his father in tow, a tall middle-aged man wearing jeans and a flannel shirt. His dark hair matched dark eye brows that were furrowed in concern, bordering on anger. We had obviously "free camped" on his property.

I stepped out to meet him.

"I'm sorry if we trespassed on your property. We were trying to make it to Fahnestock, but the sun went down before we got there, and I thought it was too dangerous to ride with my son in the dark," I explained, pointing to our bikes. "We tried to find a place out of the way to put up a tent."

He looked at me, then at Sho and our bikes, and the stern look on his face faded.

"I passed you boys when you were riding on Highway 301 yesterday. Hard not to notice a set-up like the one you got. Well, no harm done. Take your time."

"Thank you, sir. I appreciate your understanding. It'll just take us a few more minutes to load up our tent, and we'll be off your property . . ."

As we rode back home along the same route we had taken the day before, I said to Sho, "Hmm, our first two-day ride wasn't exactly a success. But I think we learned a few important lessons that will help when we try this again."

"Like you need to work on your spelling!"

Life was too hectic to schedule another overnight ride for the next few weeks, but Sho and I got in some shorter training sessions. Several times, I left work early to pick him up from his school in New York City. I brought the bikes, and we rode for an hour or two at a time on a crowded pedestrian path along the East River. As we looped around Battery Park, the southern tip of Manhattan, Sho waved to the Statue of Liberty and to tourists who snapped pictures of our unusual bike set-up. We often heard people exclaim, "That's so cool!" as we rode past.

I researched the veering problem and learned about the Burley Piccolo, a trailer cycle that attached to a custom rear rack, instead of the seat post. This design gave greater control over the bikes and allowed the kid on the trailer cycle to move more freely without throwing the adult rider off a straight line. I ordered the bike in time for our next major outing. It cost $275, but it was money well spent to keep us safe.

Four weeks had passed since our failed attempt to reach Fahnestock Park, and it was time to try again. We had to wear more layers than before to counter the cold November air, and Sho loosened his helmet straps just enough to allow him to keep his sweatshirt hood pulled over his head.

We had packed our bags the night before and were rolling out of our driveway at 9:00 on a Saturday morning. This time, the bikes did not veer out when Sho pointed out the swans in Teatown Reservoir. And we had many hours of light left when we merged onto Highway 301. The lakes we rode past were partially covered with ice, and we tucked our heads against the frigid wind blowing off the water.

It was mid-afternoon when we pulled into the campsite at Fahnestock State Park. Over 14,000 acres of protected wilderness surrounded us, and I drew in a deep, satisfying breath of crisp, clean air. We found an open site and leaned our bikes against a tree. Several other campers already had tents up, and I noticed that we were the only ones who had not arrived in a car.

"Let's get our tent set up," I said to Sho. "First thing we need to do is make sure the ground is clear." Sho kicked away sticks and rocks as I unrolled the tent tarp, snapping it in the air and letting it float down to settle over the cleared ground. We had the two-person tent set up in ten minutes.

"Now that's more like it," I said with a confident nod. "We did a lot better getting here this time around, didn't we?"

"Yep," Sho agreed. "Now what?"

"Now, let's go hike!"

We were back before dark and ate a cold but satisfying dinner in our tent. The temperature was dropping quickly, and our words began to turn into steam. After eating, I noticed Sho beginning to shiver and suggested, "Let's snuggle up in our sleeping bags and read."

As the light faded, we read Jack London's *The Call of the Wild* by flashlight. By 7:30, Sho was snoring, and I closed the book. I considered reading a bit longer, but felt the weariness of a full day of exercise and decided to close my eyes. I was remarkably sleepy and marveled at the immediate change in our body clocks, once we were away from bright rooms and televisions.

But it was cold. Our sleeping bags were designed for temperatures down to forty degrees, but it was probably twenty. Sho began shivering in his sleep, and I unzipped my sleeping bag, wrapped it over his, and squeezed in next to him. Our combined body heat helped warm both of us, but my exposed face was still cold. I was glad we'd be traveling to Japan in the summertime.

Chapter 5
Planet Earth

JOSEF WAS A GERMAN ENTREPRENEUR WHO HAD COME UP with an innovative approach to reduce a company's energy consumption. He was making his sales pitch as we waited for our food at Union Square Cafe in New York City, surrounded by well-dressed business people socializing and making deals. We were both comfortably casual, in jeans and untucked button-down dress shirts. But we were playing prescribed, formalized roles. As a venture capitalist at Intel Capital, Intel Corporation's venture investment group, my job was to invest in promising technology companies. And Josef was looking for an investor willing to put millions of dollars into his business.

"Most companies have no idea how much electricity they are consuming," said Josef. "Our software gives a senior executive the ability to get a snapshot of the total energy consumption and amount of money spent on electricity, by device, across an entire enterprise."

I thought about how this might help Intel and observed, "So a company could easily compare the energy costs of a rack of four-year-old servers in their data center to a recently installed rack of the latest generation servers and see how much more energy-efficient the newer technology is?"

Joseph nodded. "Absolutely! Giving key decision makers this information will show them that it makes sense to upgrade, which will increase server processor sales for Intel."

The waiter arrived with our food, a yellowfin tuna burger with cabbage slaw for me, spaghettini with flaked cod and broccoli rabe for Joseph. As the waiter topped off our waters, Joseph continued, "Companies can use our product to set rules, automatically turning on and off devices to reduce their use of electricity. For example, you could have all printers turn themselves off automatically at 11 p.m. and turn back on at 7 a.m. It saves a bunch of money over time. Of course, business people I talk with are most intrigued by our ability to help them save money, but they are also bothered when we show them how much energy they are simply wasting. It's amazing how people will change their behavior, once they have data and can track the waste."

In the previous three years, I had invested in a range of companies developing technologies for everything from improved healthcare to low latency grid software to intelligent traffic automation. I wanted to invest in a sector that was not only making money, but solving a difficult challenge of social significance. I'd begun to get interested in "clean technology" solutions that attempted to address environmental problems. The sector was rapidly becoming a darling of the venture community, which saw it as one of the next big waves of information technology spending.

Josef and I finished lunch, and I promised to be in touch.

Soon after I returned to my desk, my black Lenovo T61 laptop emitted a gentle three-note progression that softly echoed away into the ether. Simultaneously, an Outlook calendar reminder popped up on my screen: "Cleantech Software Strategy Review. Due In: 15 minutes." My stomach tightened. I had worked for weeks to put together this analysis, which I would present for the first time to the president of

Intel Capital and several other managing directors. Cleantech software was a new area of potential investment, and I did not know if the group would support it.

I reviewed my notes until it was time to dial into the conference call. A beep indicated that someone had joined the line.

"Lisa here." It was my boss, calling in from Intel's headquarters in California.

"Hey Lisa. It's Charles. Just the two of us so far."

Beep. Another participant joined.

Beep. Beep. Another two. Then more.

Three minutes after the scheduled start of the meeting, there was a final beep on the line. It was Intel Capital's president, the ultimate arbiter on all deals and investment strategies. He said, "Let's get started."

I took a calming breath and began, "This is the cleantech software investment strategy. It's a new area for us, so I'll spend some time up front on the problem statement and relevance to Intel, then recommend several categories of companies I think we should consider investing in.

"Let's start with the graph on the first slide. This is known as the Keeling Curve, which tracks the concentration of carbon dioxide in Earth's atmosphere. The graph shows remarkably steep and steady growth in CO_2 concentrations. Most of the growth comes from human activity, things like vehicles and coal fired power plants. In 1958, Keeling found a mean atmospheric CO_2 concentration of 315 parts per million by volume. By 2008, that number had grown to 385. Analysis of CO_2 concentrations taken from ice cores showed remarkably stable numbers over the previous 10,000 years, roughly between 270—280. But starting around the time of the industrial revolution, the numbers began to increase markedly. And the curve becomes alarmingly steeper beginning in the second half of the twentieth century, when Keeling started his measurements."

I paused for a breath, wondering if my audience was still with me. It was impossible to tell on the phone, and I didn't want to interrupt the flow to ask for questions yet. I pressed on.

"This curve is the basis for the climate change debate we hear so much about. Jim Hansen at NASA's Goddard Institute for Space Studies estimates that the safe upper limit of CO2 concentration is 350 parts per million, a number we blew past in the late 1980's. The UN Intergovernmental Panel on Climate Change tracked a rise in average surface air temperature on Earth of 0.74 degrees Celsius over the past century. In the near term, this is expected to lead to more widespread flooding and droughts, more severe storms, and an increase in plant and animal extinctions. Left unchecked, in a couple of centuries the trajectory will take Earth back to a phase last seen about forty million years ago, when there were no ice caps on the planet. That period came about because of volcanic eruptions spewing massive amounts of greenhouse gasses into the atmosphere and was a phase NASA describes as 'not compatible with a planet on which civilization developed and to which life on Earth is adapted.' Simply put, the Earth is getting too hot."

The president interrupted, "We get the problem statement. I'm interested in the part of your presentation where you explain how we can make money off it."

I moved to Slide Two. "The scale of the problem is massive, but so is the opportunity. There is something like $430 billion in government subsidies worldwide to encourage the development of clean technology. Global energy demand is growing at approximately 2.4 percent per year, which means that by the year 2030, utilities will need to produce twice the amount of electricity they generated in 2004. The utility industry is embracing the need to develop a 'smart grid' to better manage this growth, and I've seen predictions that this segment alone will generate $20 billion a year in projects in the next five years. Also, volatility in oil and natural gas prices are driving demand for alternatives and making wind and solar increasingly price competitive, assuming generous government subsidies continue.

"There are lots of options for us to consider in this segment. I see the most compelling near-term venture investment opportunity in capital-efficient business models, and I think we should target energy efficiency software in particular."

"That's more like it," the president observed, and we spent the rest of the hour talking about how we could make money from climate change. I mentioned Josef's product, and the president told me to investigate further.

My boss called after the meeting. "Nice job in the presentation," Lisa said. "Too verbose at the start, but you recovered nicely. We've got ourselves a new investment category. Now we just need to find good deals. Some of the companies you mentioned sounded promising."

"Thanks Lisa. By the way, while I've got you on the phone, I wanted to give you a heads up about my plans for next summer."

"Next summer? As in, seven months from now?"

"Yeah. I wanted to give you plenty of advance notice. I'm planning to take off two months to do a 2,500-mile bike ride across Japan with my son."

She didn't respond for a moment. I had obviously caught her by surprise. Finally, she said, "I don't know, Charles. It's not good timing. I mean, have you been reading the newspapers? The financial world is falling apart. Intel's revenues, along with everyone else's, will take a hit. You've been around the company long enough to know what that means: we're gonna have layoffs. If I were you, I'd want to be around and productive when that's going on. And you know our president. He'll want you to stay focused on making money for the corporation, not taking bike rides with your kid."

Lisa continued, "Why don't you put this off for another year or two. Wait until we're all not so vulnerable."

I remembered the conversation of my seatmates on the earlier flight to China, how fear seemed to dictate their decisions. And I thought about a refrigerator magnet my sister Becky had given me when I told her my plans to go ahead, even if the timing wasn't perfect. The magnet said, "The Time Is Now."

I shook my head into the phone. "Lisa, if I don't go for it now, I'm afraid I'll never do it. I've thought about this a lot, and I've already made up my mind. You and I have plenty of time to arrange for someone to cover for me while I'm gone. I hope I don't get laid off, but I'm willing to take that chance."

"Okay, Charles. It's your life. Thanks for the heads up."

That night, Eiko, Sho, Saya and I ate dinner together in our apartment. The glow of New York City's brightly lit buildings filled up the windows behind us, the spires' hulking forms shooting off hundreds of tiny incandescent beams into the evening sky, as if battling the dark canopy. The artificial rays flooded into our apartment, spreading ethereal flickering shadows on the windowsill.

We were eating one of our favorite meals: roll-your-own sushi. That morning before leaving for work, Eiko had placed two cups of rice in a cooker with two and a half cups of water, a tablespoon of rice wine and a strip of kelp. She set the timer so that the rice would be ready when we returned from work at the end of the day. The secret to tasty sushi rice is to let it steam until fluffy in a cooker for at least an hour after it's cooked. Then sprinkle in rice vinegar mixed with salt and sugar, while gently rolling the heated rice with a flat spoon and fanning away the steam. After that, the meal is as simple as cutting up squares of dried nori seaweed and laying out strips of sushi grade raw fish. Tonight we had tuna, yellowtail, salmon, smelt roe, avocado and sea urchin.

Sho took a large dollop of rice and dropped it onto a thin piece of seaweed.

"Not too much rice," Eiko counseled. "If you put on too much, it will spill out when you try to roll it up. Plus you'll get full too quickly." Sho obediently scraped off some of the rice with one chopstick and tenderly draped on a fat piece of tuna. He added a slice of avocado, rolled it up and dipped the end into a dish of soy sauce, before stuffing the entirety into his mouth.

Saya giggled as she spread rice on her plate with her fingers, and I gave her a stern look. "Don't play with your food," I warned and rolled up a piece of salmon sushi for her.

"Daddy, I want to watch the polar bears!" Sho said, mouth full.

"Huh? Oh, you mean the *Planet Earth* DVD?" I gave Eiko an inquiring look, and she nodded. I said, "Sure. Let's just finish dinner first, okay?"

Planet Earth was a five-DVD collection of a nature program series produced by the BBC. It was one of our family favorites. We often watched selected sections at night before bedtime.

After we had eaten our fill of sushi and cleaned up the dishes, the four of us settled on our couch in front of a thirty-six inch flat panel TV. Sho placed "Ice Worlds," one of the *Planet Earth* DVDs, into the player and navigated to the section he wanted. We watched a mother polar bear emerge from five months of hibernation in a den dug into the steep side of a mountain of snow in the Arctic. She playfully snow-plowed on her belly down the hill, relishing the spring, as two young cubs followed her unsteadily.

"The cub that just fell on its butt looks like you, Saya," Sho teased.

"Oh yeah? You look like poop!"

I lifted up Saya and settled her on my lap. She curled up her knees and snuggled back into my chest, sucking on the index and middle fingers of her left hand, a self-comforting habit formed when she was a newborn.

The scene then cut to a male polar bear staggering across rapidly melting ice. "Each year, as the climate warms, the Arctic holds less ice," the narrator intoned. "This is a disaster for polar bears. Without its solid platform, they can't hunt the seals they need in order to survive." We watched the bear struggle to crawl across a slushy expanse, a sad reminder of an all-too-real future that is already upon us. The bear eventually plunged into the Arctic waters and swam in search of seals lounging on the quickly melting ice fragments. He found no seals, however, and swam through the sea for several days. He finally emerged upon a landmass populated by a walrus colony. Exhausted and famished, the bear began to attack the group, increasingly desperate in his hunger. But the walrus's massive weight, thick skin and dangerous tusks were too much. After a number of failed attempts, the bear, now suffering wounds that made it difficult for him to walk, retreated in defeat, collapsed nearby and starved to death.

Over the image of the dead bear lying among the walruses, the narrator commented, "If the global climate continues to warm, and the Arctic ice melts sooner each year, it is certain that more bears will share this fate."

Saya did not understand what had occurred, but Sho did. He turned to me with a concerned look and asked, "Can't we help the bear?"

I smiled gently and pulled him close. "No, we can't. The increase in melting ice is actually a problem not just for polar bears, but for humans too. But you've given me an idea. You know how we talked about raising money for a charity when we ride across Japan? Let's find one that is trying to protect the environment."

The next day, I contacted Georgios Kostakos, a friend who worked in the United Nations Secretariat. When he heard about our plans to ride across Japan, Georgios asked if I would be open to using attention from the ride to promote the UN's environmental work, especially their efforts to coordinate a worldwide governmental response to the threat of climate change.

"Sho and I are at your service. Let me know what you think we could do to help."

I then contacted Maaike Jansen, whose daughter went to school with Sho. Maaike worked at the UN Environment Programme (UNEP), the group with responsibility for coordinating the UN's environmental work. She loved the idea of linking the ride to an environmental cause and said, "Let me see what I can do." Maaike was one of those people who simply got things done, and with her support, I was soon fully engaged with UNEP.

Sho and I decided to raise money for the UN's Billion Tree Campaign. In the months leading up to our summer departure, we gave speeches at schools and to local environmental groups in New York City, made videos encouraging governments to take action to address climate change, and were named "Climate Heroes" by the UN.

Our plans were featured in newspapers and magazines around the world. Achim Steiner, the Executive Director of UNEP, published an opinion piece in the *Asahi Shimbun* newspaper in Japan about our ride. *Al-Bia Wal-Tanmia*, a Beirut-based pan-Arab environment and nature magazine featured our plans in an article, as did *BizMode Magazine* in China and the *Express Newspaper* in India.

To celebrate Earth Day, Sho and I spoke to an assembly at the United Nations International School in New York City, where Sho was in second grade. As the principal introduced our talk, we stood off to the side of the stage in the school's split-level auditorium. About 500 kindergarten through fourth grade students surrounded us, excitement showing on their faces.

Nothing material was riding on this presentation. Unlike my cleantech software strategy pitch at work, this audience wasn't interested in making money: most of all, they wanted be entertained. As the principal finished her introduction, I took a deep breath to calm my nerves and wrapped my arm around Sho's shoulders. Because his friends would be listening, I felt more pressure to perform well than I did at work. I glanced down at Sho, who was smiling, apparently not nearly as bothered by public speaking as I. We walked on to the stage, rolling our connected bicycles alongside, and the children let out appreciative oohs and ahs.

"Hi. I'm Charles Scott," I said into a microphone that the principal handed me.

"And I'm Sho Scott," Sho added, pulling the microphone a little too close to his mouth.

One of his classmates yelled out, "We know who you are!" to giggles from the audience.

Sho blushed and soldiered on. "This summer, my dad and I are going to try to ride these connected bikes all the way across Japan!"

The audience applauded.

I added, "We don't know if we can do it, but we're going to try. And we're working with the United Nations to use the ride to try to help the environment. We're raising money for a worldwide tree planting campaign that is trying to plant one tree for every person on the planet. That's seven billion trees."

Sho and I split the fifteen-minute presentation between us, describing our plans in more detail and showing a video of a practice ride. Finally, we asked if anyone had questions. About thirty hands went up.

Sho called on a student in the front row.

"What will you do if your brakes give out when you're riding down a mountain?"

Sho looked up at me to answer that one.

"That's a great question. We've come up with a list of all the risks we can think of. And that's one of them. We plan to ride over something like ten mountains. Because we will carry about seventy-five pounds of gear on the bikes, the brakes will wear down faster than usual. Our solution is to check the brake pads regularly and put on a fresh pair just before we start to ride through the Japan Alps mountain range. We'll bring two sets of spare pads."

Another student asked, "What will you do when you get tired?"

Sho answered that one. "We'll take a break! My dad promised that we can stop at game rooms and other fun places."

A teacher asked, "Are you sure riding 2,500 miles, including over mountains, isn't too hard for an eight-year-old?"

We would hear this question many more times in the coming months. I was tempted to go into an opinionated critique of our increasingly sedentary modern society and give a lecture on the value of discomfort. But I overcame my tendency toward verbosity and answered simply, "You know, a kid can do a whole lot more than most adults think."

New York's brutal winter came and went. After months spent mainly training indoors in a gym, I began to ride outside again with Sho in the pleasant spring weather, usually along the paths that encircled much of the island of Manhattan. I mixed in as much strength and endurance training as I could. I trained for and ran the Boston Marathon, took spin and yoga classes, lifted weights, did several one hundred-mile bike rides with some local Ironman triathletes, and rode my bicycle up and down steep climbs in nearby Bear Mountain.

Sho joined me on several two to three-hour rides on a bike path along the perimeter of Manhattan. We rode at an easy pace and took breaks along the way, stopping to eat a hot dog or pretzel from a street vendor. I did not make Sho do any other specific training. His typical day included lots of physical activity with his friends, and requiring him to follow a formal training regimen seemed like a bad idea. I wanted him to look forward to our trip as an exciting adventure, not as drudgery. I felt strong, and Sho never faltered on our long training rides, but I had no way of knowing if we were doing enough.

Chapter 6
Fired?

THE COOL, DAMP SPRING SLOWLY YIELDED TO SULTRY SUMmer days and, before I knew it, we were on our way to Tokyo. Eiko and I spent the thirteen-hour flight excitedly going over plans. Saya curled up in her seat and watched kids' movies while clutching her stuffed animal Lamby and sucking on two fingers. Sho listened to the soundtrack from the Broadway musical *Billy Elliot* over and over until my iPod battery died. We had seen the show a few weeks earlier, and Sho had been amazed by the incredible dance moves of Kiril Kulish, the fifteen-year-old dancer who played the lead role. Within a few days of seeing the performance, Sho had memorized all the songs.

The plane approached Tokyo's Narita Airport on a warm, sun-drenched summer afternoon, and as we descended, I looked out at rice paddies, farms and forests giving way to the sprawling airport infrastructure. Runways, terminals, parking lots, elevated train tracks, warehouses and miles of concrete covered what only a few decades earlier had been farmland. In the 1960's and 1970's, thousands of local residents and others had protested the government's expropriation of their land, sometimes violently. But in the end, they had to yield to progress.

Our luggage—two large rectangular boxes holding the parts of our disassembled bikes and three suitcases stuffed with the saddlebags, a handlebar bag, clothes and gear for over two months of cycling and camping—filled two carts as we entered the bustling main airport terminal. Throngs of travelers jostled around us, and we settled for a moment next to a side wall to take stock of our next move.

A few feet away, a Japanese business man in a formal suit was talking excitedly into his cell phone. "*Hai! Hai! Kashikomarimashita. Hai!*" Yes, yes! I understand. Yes! As he spoke, he bowed low several times, as if the person listening on the other end could see the gesture. I glanced down with a raised eyebrow at Sho, who also had been watching. He giggled and whispered, "Maybe it's a camera phone?"

Eiko located a baggage delivery service counter, and we happily relieved ourselves of three suitcases and two bike boxes. They would be delivered later that evening to our hotel. We rented a cell phone for the bike ride and bought tickets for a bus into the city.

The bus arrived, and the four of us scrambled aboard. As it rumbled out of the airport and into the countryside toward Tokyo's massive urban sprawl some thirty-five miles away, I worked through a mental checklist. We planned to spend the next five days in Tokyo before flying to Sapporo, the capital city of the northern island of Hokkaidō. From there we would drive a rental van to Cape Sōya, the northernmost point of Japan. Eiko and Saya planned to track us in the van for the first week of our ride before returning to the U.S. After that, Sho and I would be on our own.

While in Tokyo, I opened a bank account, so that I would have an ATM card to withdraw cash during the ride. I went to a bike shop to buy some spare tubes and get some practice using bike repair terminology in Japanese. We had a lunch meeting with some TV producers who wanted to profile our ride, and I spent a day working in Intel's Tokyo office. Many in Intel had responded to our plans enthusiastically. In fact, the general manager of a mobile computing business unit had offered to sponsor the trip and arranged for us to receive a lightweight laptop that used an energy efficient Intel Atom processor. Some employees in Japan would provide us with technical support, and the Intel PR team planned to make a video about how we used the computer on the ride. That video would be shown in the Intel keynote speech at a large mobile computing conference in Tokyo.

Nonetheless, the president of my group still did not know about the trip. The general manager sponsoring the ride was in a separate business unit. And my manager had given verbal approval already, so I never explicitly told the president about my plans. Intel's HR system required me to fill out an official request for an unpaid leave within two weeks before departure. I submitted the online form to my manager while in Tokyo, assuming it was simply a formality.

After five days in Tokyo, we flew to Sapporo. A light rain was falling as we loaded our gear into a mini van in front of Toyota Rental. After settling Sho and Saya into the back seat and squeezing in our suitcases and the bike boxes, Eiko and I stood at the rear of the van, looking skeptically at the storage capacity.

"You sure this is big enough?" she asked. "The luggage barely fits, and we'll need even more space when you take the bikes out of the boxes and assemble them tomorrow."

I jogged back through the rain into the rental center, returning a few minutes later. "They have a bigger van, but it will cost another $900."

We had already spent many thousands of dollars on equipment and travel, and I was about to take a two-month unpaid leave from Intel. I did not want to add any more expenses to the trip. "I'll make it work," I declared, and we set off for the Sapporo Prince Hotel.

"Stay to the left, stay to the left, stay to the left," I mumbled to myself as we pulled out of the parking lot.

Sho laughed from the back seat. "Why do you keep saying that, Daddy?"

"People drive in the left lane in Japan, but I am used to driving in the right lane. I'm just making sure I don't forget."

Sapporo's tree-lined roads were broad and the traffic was light, a remarkable contrast to the crushing urban mess we had just left behind in Tokyo. As I made a right turn at a large intersection, I instinctively headed to the far right directly into oncoming traffic. Sho and Eiko simultaneously chorused, "Stay to the left!" as I jerked the car back into its proper lane.

That evening, we walked from our hotel down a pleasant avenue bustling with pedestrians and full of local restaurants and small shops selling household wares, trinkets, clothing, etc. I carried Saya on my shoulders, and Sho held Eiko's hand. As they walked, he jerked it back and forth aggressively.

"Ouch. That hurts. Please don't be so rough, Sho," Eiko admonished. He did not answer. After a few minutes, he jerked her hand hard again.

This time I intervened. "Sho, Mommy asked you not to do that. I don't expect to see it again." He didn't answer, and I said with an edge to my voice, "Did you hear what I said?"

Sho mumbled, "Yes" and flashed me an unhappy look.

"Oh, here's the ramen noodle place the concierge told us about," Eiko said, adding, "It looks quaint." It was a small shack with decorated cloth drapes hanging from the top of the entrance down to about waist level. I lifted Saya off my shoulders and pushed my way through the drapes. Inside was a simple counter with eight seats, two of which were occupied by a young couple scooping up noodles with their chopsticks and slurping loudly and unselfconsciously.

"*Irasshai!* Welcome!" An elderly woman in an apron called out from behind the counter, her hair wrapped under a handkerchief.

I set Saya down on a tall stool and settled beside her. Behind the counter, I could see several deep pots filled with hot water surrounded by small containers with various ingredients to add to the noodles. A stack of large porcelain bowls stood off to the side, ready to be filled.

"What do you want?" I asked, turning to Eiko. But she was not sitting on the neighboring stool. I glanced behind me and could see Eiko and Sho's legs still outside beyond the drapes. "*Sumimasen.* Excuse me," I said to the woman behind the counter as I stood up.

"Don't fall," I said pointing my finger with a serious look at Saya, leaving her sitting on the tall stool as I stepped outside.

Sho had his arms crossed and a stubborn look on his face. Eiko was leaning down talking with him. "I've asked you twice now to come inside."

"I want sushi!" Sho demanded, staring back at her intensely.

Realizing this would take more than a few seconds, I darted back inside. I was not going to leave my two-year-old daughter sitting by herself on a tall stool for more than a very brief moment. "Excuse me again. One second," I said in Japanese to the woman behind the counter, who gave me a bored look. I scooped up Saya and returned outside.

"What's the problem buddy?" I asked, gently stroking Sho's hair. He pulled his head away and repeated obstinately, "I don't want noodles. I want sushi!"

Eiko gave him a weary look and said, "Sho, we already decided that we would have noodles. Please stop making a fuss and come inside with us."

"No!" he yelled, stamping his feet.

Eiko and I exchanged looks, and I kneeled down so that I was eye level with Sho. I sympathized with how exhausting an international trip must be for an eight-year-old. And I wondered if he was feeling the pressure of expectations from our plans. Maybe it was all too much, and he only knew how to express it with a temper tantrum.

"You must be really tired from the jet lag and all the traveling. It's not easy, I know. And you've done a great job dealing with everything. Let's just have dinner, and we'll go back to the hotel afterward and get some good rest."

"I'm not eating ramen! I want sushi!"

I stood up and turned to Eiko. "I'm not interested in a power struggle. Let's just eat our food and get back to the hotel."

As Eiko, Saya and I walked back into the noodle shop, I turned to Sho and said, "We're eating noodles. You may join us or wait outside until we're done." He turned his back on me and sat down on the ground, staring off into the night.

"*Gomen nasai.* Sorry about that," I said to the apron-clad woman as Eiko, Saya and I took our places at the counter. I noticed the young couple surreptitiously glance at us, no doubt interested in the family drama. From where I sat, I could look out beyond the entrance to see Sho's seated form in the shadows. As Eiko, Saya and I ate three delicious steaming bowls of ramen, he sat hunched over on the ground, picking up small rocks and lethargically tossing them aside, over and over.

He went to bed hungry that night, and I worried that the entire ride across Japan might turn into a series of temper tantrums. Maybe he was trying to tell me something I did not want to hear: that I was expecting too much of him.

The hotel room was dark, as I slipped quietly out of bed and tiptoed past my sleeping wife and children. The glowing red digits of the alarm clock read 4:00. Heavy curtains kept out any early morning light, and I felt my way across the room through the darkness. Jamming my toe into a suitcase, I cursed under my breath. I gently pulled the bathroom door shut behind me and sat down on the edge of the bathtub, unfolding a map of Hokkaidō on the floor. I was bringing along a GPS unit, but wanted to have paper maps as backup. Consulting a spreadsheet I had printed out before leaving, I took out a yellow highlighter pen to trace our planned route on the map.

We had a reservation to spend the night at a traditional Japanese *minshuku* inn a few hundred yards from Cape Sōya, the northernmost point of Japan and the start of our bike ride. I had fantasized about beginning the ride at sunrise on the longest day of the year in mid-June, hoping to connect this personal challenge to the deeper rhythms of nature. But work and school schedules pushed out our start date a few days past the solstice, and I learned that at such northern latitude, the sun rose at 4:15 a.m. Wanting to be well rested on our first day, I'd reluctantly dismissed the idea of a sunrise departure.

For the next twenty minutes, I carefully highlighted our route from Cape Sōya around Japan's northern island. I had allocated eighteen days to cycle in Hokkaidō and was looking forward to its dramatic ocean views, peaceful rolling farmland, challenging mountains, and dense wilderness.

After I highlighted the final section ending in Hakodate, a large town on the island's southern tip, I stood up to stretch my back. I shook out one of my legs, which had gone numb as I worked in the cramped bathroom, and laid the map on the sink counter. Reaching my arms overhead, I grunted with satisfaction as I heard soft cracking sounds emanate from my shoulders and back.

Finished with the map, I pulled open my laptop to check e-mail. Settling back on the cold edge of the bathtub and resting the computer precariously on my legs, I scrolled through new messages. One was from Lisa, my manager, entitled, "Your PLOA." Or: Personal Leave of Absence.

> Charles, the PLOA system requires two levels of management approval. I need to get the president's approval and I can guess that he will not be supportive of a leave of this type.

Please send me an email detailing the purpose of the trip and all of the "Intel PR goodness" you're creating and the support you have from other execs. You'll need all of those folks backing you to get the president's approval. He's not supportive of this kind of leave for personal "vacation" activities.

If it's not approved and you leave, it could mean losing your job. Are you willing to proceed if that's the case?

Chapter 7
The Thief

WHEN SHO AND I FIRST DECIDED TO MAKE THIS TRIP, I KNEW I might get fired, but I chewed my thumbnail nervously as I realized that this theoretical risk suddenly had become likely. I began typing my response with purpose, ignoring the growing discomfort as I sat precariously on the bathtub's edge, huddled over my laptop:

> Sorry to give you a headache, Lisa. I am going to proceed with the ride, regardless of the president's decision. It will be a real shame if he chooses to fire me, and I will vigorously defend myself.

I went on to summarize the trip, our work with the United Nations, the Intel business unit that was sponsoring us, and the press attention we had received. I read over the note three times before clicking the "Send" button. Finally, I closed the laptop, exhaled nervously and stood up. As I took a step, I realized that my butt had gone numb. It was certainly on the line!

I spent the day touring Sapporo with Eiko and the kids, and we rode a cable car to the top of Mount Miura. We took turns looking through a telescope at Sapporo's urban sprawl, which stretched many miles into the distance. The city streets' grid structure, borrowed from the Americans in the 1870's, was clearly visible. Much of Hokkaidō is mountainous, but the capital city sits on the Ishikari Plain, a large, flat expanse of land. Hundreds of silver and brown buildings of varying sizes crowded together like a concrete sore growing over the plain. A few patches of green dotted the cityscape: a neighborhood park here, a school playground there.

The distraction of touring the city helped me forget the workplace drama. But in the evening when I returned to our hotel room, I hastily opened my laptop to check e-mail. Lisa had responded:

> Thanks. I'll send the summary to the president and see what he says. He probably won't respond, and my next 1:1 with him isn't for another two weeks. I hope we can resolve this before then. We'll see.

The next morning, Eiko, Sho, Saya and I drove five and a half hours from Sapporo to Cape Sōya on the northern tip of Hokkaidō. We passed by lush green rolling hills and sprawling farms. Occasionally we saw a few workers hunched over rows of crops, but cows and horses far outnumbered humans.

"Daddy, are we going to ride over that big mountain?" Sho asked, pointing to a craggy beast looming in the distance.

"No, we're not cycling this way. We'll ride along the coast for the first week before crossing our first mountain. Don't worry, it's not nearly as big as that one. At least, I don't think it is."

Arriving in Cape Sōya, we checked into Minshuku Sōya Misaki, a small, comfortable inn only a few hundred meters from the starting point of our ride.

Sho and Saya turned on the TV in our room and were immediately mesmerized by a kids' show. Eiko and I unpacked a few things, then I settled cross-legged on the floor and opened my laptop. It took a few minutes to establish a virtual private network connection and download my e-mails.

Finally, there it was: a new message from the president with "Personal LOA Approval Request" in the title.

I glanced up at Eiko, who came over to join me. She crossed her fingers. "Good luck!"

I clicked on the message and relief coursed through me as I read the single word:

Approved.

Eiko gave me a kiss and then a high five. "You knew all along he was going to approve the leave, right?"

"Honestly, I didn't know," I said, shaking my head. "I'm sure he would have preferred that I stayed around making money for Intel."

"Well, I'm glad you'll have a job to return to. I am intrigued and honestly a bit concerned that you were willing to risk getting fired. Do you want to leave your job at Intel? Were you secretly hoping you'd get fired?"

"No, of course not. I'm not ready to leave Intel, but I was willing to get fired rather than back down. This is a test of my priorities. Am I really serious about asserting more control over my life? Or am I going to let my employer tell me how to live? I imagined myself as an old man looking back on this period of my life, and he advised me to go for it."

"Well, tell the old man that I'm not interested in being the sole bread winner right now."

"Yes, ma'am," I said with a laugh. But Eiko wasn't joking.

I awoke early the next morning, the day of our departure, hopeful and apprehensive. It had been nearly a year and a half since Sho and I had come up with the idea for this trip. And now, finally, we would begin to ride! My footsteps made gentle squeaking sounds on the tatami mats as I walked quietly past Eiko and the kids, who were sprawled out asleep on thick futons. Sliding my shoes on, I gently closed the door behind me and slipped out of the *minshuku* inn.

A few minutes' walk in the early morning light and I stood before Cape Sōya's Monument of the Northernmost Point in Japan. A thick circular stone slab with five inlaid steps leading to a dramatic pyramidal sculpture rising into the sky sat on a rise looking over the confluence of the Sea of Japan to the west and the Sea of Okhotsk to the east. Just out of vision to the north lay the island of Sakhalin, which the Soviet Union captured from Japan at the end of World War II and remains part of Russia today. It was not yet 6 a.m., but the sun already sat well above the horizon, its rays glistening off the undulating ocean expanse. The sky promised a glorious day ahead.

No one seemed to be awake in this sleepy outpost; the tourists would arrive later. Immediately in front of the monument, a large parking lot stood empty next to shops offering food and souvenirs with a northernmost theme. Not far away stood Japan's northernmost lighthouse, the northernmost elementary school and the northernmost gasoline station. I realized that I was now the northernmost human in all of Japan.

Three hours later, Sho and I posed with our fully loaded bikes in front of Cape Sōya's monument as Eiko took our picture. The sun shone high above in a nearly cloudless blue sky. And despite a strong ocean wind that buffeted us with occasional gusts, I was comfortable in the warm air wearing only bike shorts and a short-sleeved jersey. Saya bounded barefoot back and forth between us, and it was only later that I noticed her contribution to the official photograph of the start of the ride: her tiny gold and pink shoes near my bike's front wheel.

After Eiko took our picture, I glanced down at Sho. "Are you ready to ride?"

"Sure Daddy," he said nonchalantly, strapping on his helmet.

"Good luck!" Eiko said, giving us both big hugs.

I kneeled down and gave Saya a kiss and a hug. "It's time for us to go. I love you, Sweet Pumpkin Punch." As I started to release the hug, Saya held on to my neck. "You need to let Daddy go, okay?"

"No!" she said, squeezing tighter.

"It's time to stay with Mommy. You're going to get in the car with her, and we'll see you again a little later today." I pulled Saya's hands off my neck and handed her to Eiko. Saya reached out for me and started crying. I gave her one final kiss on the forehead and turned away.

"It's okay, Saya," Sho said in a soothing voice as he mounted his trailer cycle. I pushed the bikes a few yards before hopping onto the saddle. The handlebar bag was loaded with my wallet, camera, iPhone, some snacks, my journal, and a map of Hokkaidō. The two fully loaded saddlebags were attached to the bike's front fork. Because of the weight, I had to grip the handlebars tightly to keep the front wheel under control. But as we gained speed, momentum took over, and the bikes settled into a stable line.

We rode a lap around the parking lot, then Sho and I merged onto the main road, Highway 238, and began riding east along the coast. Few cars were out, and the buildings and homes of Cape Sōya disappeared quickly behind us. As we cycled on the remote coastal road, I felt a giddy sense of liberation. Like school had just let out. Like I was getting away with something. A middle-aged businessman wasn't supposed to live this free. I yelled out, "We're doing this baby!"

To our left beyond a broad gray beach lay a glistening expanse of water stretching to the vast horizon. Sea gulls prowled for food overhead, coasting lazily on the wind currents. Occasionally we saw the distinctive long white neck, elongated sharp bill and stick-thin legs of a Japanese Great Egret stepping carefully through shallow water in search of a meal.

I glanced up toward the top of a nearby hill and muttered, "Uh-oh."

"What's wrong, Daddy?"

"Look up there," I answered, pointing to a collection of towering gray poles standing sentry on the distant hilltop, each with three massive rotating blades. "Those are turbines that use wind to generate electricity."

"That's cool! Why did you say 'Uh-oh'?"

"Because where there are lots of big wind turbines, there must be lots of strong winds. And strong winds means you and I have to work a lot harder."

"That's okay, Dad. I feel great. Look! An eagle on the beach!"

I glanced over and pulled the bikes to a stop when I saw the bald eagle. It seemed to strike a pose, head turned in profile so that we could see its sharp, curved beak as it perched majestically on a piece of driftwood in the middle of the empty beach, like a king surveying his lands. I quickly retrieved a camera from the handlebar bag and snapped a picture. The bald eagle remained motionless, as if meditating on the surrounding natural glory.

When we resumed cycling, I heard a car approaching from behind, then shouts of encouragement as it pulled alongside. Eiko and Saya smiled out at us from the open windows of the rental van.

"You're looking great!" said Eiko.

"Hi Daddy. I take off shoes!" Saya added from her car seat in the back while wiggling her bare feet over her head and giggling. She seemed to have completely forgotten her earlier tears.

We pulled to a stop to chat for a moment. "Did you see the eagle back there?" Sho asked. "And the sea gulls and egrets?"

"We missed the eagle," Eiko replied. "But we've been enjoying this incredible view."

I said, "You know, we're making good progress. It gets windy at times, but I think we should be able to average around fifteen miles per hour."

"Let me know where that will put you at the end of the day. I'll find a place for all of us to stay."

I looked at the map. "Hmm. I'm thinking that we'll ride for around seven hours. So, we should make it to about here on the map before it gets dark." I pointed to the coastal town of Esashi.

Eiko looked at the spot I indicated and said, "Sounds good. I'll find a place to stay there and call you."

The next few hours along the gentle rolling hills of the coastal highway were a cycling fantasy come true. The scenery was gorgeous, the temperature ideal. The bright sun warmed my muscles, and the ocean breeze kept me from overheating. With Sho humming happily behind me as we pedaled, I thought, "There's no place I'd rather be."

Sho and I finally came to a small town and decided to stop at a convenience store to pick up some snacks. The cacophonous caws of the crows, a common backdrop in Japan, echoed off the buildings and side streets. We leaned the bikes against the store front and spent a few minutes inside, picking out goodies: beef jerky, Aquarius sports drink, *onigiri* rice balls with salmon, and a pack of six rolls filled with sweet bean paste.

As we returned to our bikes, I set the sack on the ground and began to unzip the handlebar bag, where I would store the food. In that instant, I detected a flash of movement at my feet and heard a harsh crinkling sound. Looking down startled, I watched in disbelief as a large black crow leapt away with the six-pack of rolls. The crow bounded into the air, holding the package in its beak, rapidly beat its wings several times and alighted on the roof of a house across the street. As if to taunt us, the bold thief settled on the edge of the roof in full view and began tearing open the plastic. Sho and I watched in stunned silence as the crow nonchalantly ate our rolls.

Chapter 8
Temper Tantrums and Hospitality

AFTER LUNCH, WE CYCLED ALONG THE PICTURESQUE OCEAN-front. We took occasional short breaks to stretch our legs or snap pictures of the dramatic view. The wide ocean to our left reflected a bright blue sky and pounded out a soothing rhythm as its waves lapped back and forth over the empty shore. Eagles, egrets and sea gulls prowled the beach and shallows for food. On our right, we passed sprawling farms, deep green forests, hawks, horses, and lounging cows.

"Ugh, what's that smell?" Sho asked, as we passed by a farm with a dozen cows huddled together chewing grass behind a fence.

"That, son, is manure. You're gonna smell it plenty more over the next few weeks as we ride through Hokkaidō's countryside. Don't worry; it grows on you."

"It's awful! What's their problem?" He pointed an accusing finger at the cows, called out an exaggerated "Moo!" and was greeted by bovine stares of disdain and boredom.

"I actually love the smell of cow manure. It reminds me of visiting your great granddad Scott, who lived in a small town in Oklahoma that had lots of farms."

"Was he a farmer?"

"No. He owned a local grocery store and was full of country wisdom. He sprinkled his stories with the funniest sayings that used to crack me up as a boy."

"Like what?"

"Well, one of his favorites was, 'I had about as much chance as a one-legged man in an ass-kicking contest.'"

Sho laughed, "That's great! What's another?"

"Hmm, let me think. I remember one time he was complaining about a worker in his store who was incompetent. Granddad said, 'He couldn't find his own butt with two hands and a search warrant.'"

Sho nearly fell off his bike laughing at that one. "Did he make those up?"

"Oh, I doubt it. I think a lot of them were sayings he heard growing up."

"When did he grow up?"

"In the early 1900's. In fact, he was born almost one hundred years ago."

A powerful wind gust slammed suddenly in my face, and I gripped the handlebars tightly to maintain control over the bikes. "Holy crap, that's strong!"

"Is that another of your granddad's sayings?"

I tucked low over the handlebars to become more aerodynamic and immediately shifted down to the gear I used for climbing steep inclines. We slowed to perhaps five miles per hour, and the muscles in my legs started to burn. I yelled back to Sho, "Get in aero position and pedal!"

The wind didn't let up all afternoon. Sometimes it slammed directly in our faces so that we struggled to maintain little more than a pitiful crawl. At other times, it surprised us with sudden gusts from the side, threatening to knock our bikes off the road.

By 5:30 p.m., I realized that we would not make it before nightfall to the town where Eiko and Saya were waiting. My earlier assumption that we would average fifteen miles per hour throughout the day had been completely unrealistic. We were still about forty miles away from an inn where Eiko had booked a room, and I was exhausted. We had cycled for seven hours throughout the day, and my back ached and my quadriceps moaned. My right knee was tender, no doubt from pushing so much weight hour after hour into the wind. I glanced back at Sho to see how he was doing. He was pedaling lethargically and wore a stoic expression. It was time to stop riding for the day.

I pulled the bikes to the side of the road across from a small collection of farmhouses and called Eiko. "Hey, I'm sorry to do this, but I was completely off on the pace I thought we could maintain. We're not going to make it to Esashi tonight. I know you've already checked in, so just stay where you are. Sho and I will free camp tonight. We can meet up tomorrow."

"Shoot," Eiko replied, disappointment obvious in her voice. "We've only got a few more days together before Saya and I fly back to the U.S. It's a shame we can't spend the night together. I could just eat the cost of the room we got and drive back to you. Are there any towns with inns near you?"

"No. We're in the middle of farm country. The sun is gonna set in the next hour, and there aren't any towns I can get to in that time."

"That's too bad. You sure you'll be okay?"

"Definitely. We've got camping gear and are fully self-sufficient. Don't worry."

As I hung up, Sho gave me an exhausted and unhappy look. "We're not going to see Mommy tonight?" he asked accusingly.

"I'm sorry, buddy. The winds slowed us down too much. That's okay though. We'll just ask one of the farmers over there to let us set up our tent on their property. It'll be fine."

"No it won't!" Sho said, slamming his fist on his bike's handlebars and starting to cry. I was surprised by his sudden emotional reaction. All day, he had been in a wonderful, playful mood, singing songs and making up silly word games. I watched helplessly as he melted down and demanded repeatedly to spend the night with Eiko and Saya.

"It's not gonna happen, Sho. I'm sorry."

"I want to see Mommy!"

"You'll see her tomorrow. Right now, we need to figure out where we're going to sleep tonight."

"No!" he screamed.

For the next few minutes, Sho stomped his feet, kicked dirt at the ocean, clenched his fists and cried. He looked so small and overwhelmed. I fought hard to maintain composure. Exhausted and disappointed in myself, I felt like yelling back.

I realized the anxiety he must feel anticipating a two-month separation from his mother, and I began to question the wisdom of attempting such an ambitious trip with him. Maybe it was too much to ask of an eight-year-old, after all.

I closed my eyes for a moment, took a deep breath, and focused my attention on the crashing surf behind us. I imagined the churning water telling me, "You sought out discomfort and challenge. You knew this trip wouldn't be easy. Relax and deal with it." I felt my tension and frustration start to abate.

"I want Mommy!" Sho repeated over and over.

I said firmly, "I know you're upset. It's okay. Breathe. Relax. When you've settled down, we'll find a place to sleep."

Finally, Sho had cried himself out, and I said with as much compassion as I could muster, "I know you're disappointed. I am too. But sometimes you just have to change plans, and that's what we're going to do."

He climbed onto his trailer cycle, shoulders slumped in resignation, tear stains on his cheeks. We crossed the coastal highway and rode down a narrow road into the small farming village. There were perhaps twenty modest houses spread along the road. Behind them, green fields and pastures merged into a dense forest that stretched as far as I could see. We rode to the nearest home, a single story ranch house. Pulling the bikes into the driveway, I walked to the entrance and knocked. After a minute, an elderly, bent woman with short silver hair slowly opened the door. Seeing a mixture of suspicion and concern in her eyes, I moved aside slightly so that Sho was clearly visible behind me.

"I'm very sorry to bother you," I said in polite Japanese. "My son and I are cycling the length of Japan and need a place to sleep. Would you mind if we set up our tent on your property?"

Her look softened as she glanced at Sho, but she clearly did not want to be burdened with us. Pointing to a two-story house down the lane, she said, "Go to that house. They will take care of you."

We rode to the home she had indicated.

The man who answered the door was obviously drunk, his face red, the smell of sake on his breath. Perhaps in his sixties, he wore a blue, checkered short-sleeved button-down shirt and jeans. His thick silver hair sat in a wavy bunch on his head. He looked utterly surprised to see a foreigner and a young boy standing on his doorstep.

I repeated the same polite request to use his property. He glanced at Sho, and a broad grin spread across his face. "Well, I don't see why not." He yelled back over his shoulders in slightly slurred Japanese, "Honey, we've got two extra visitors staying the night!"

His wife, wearing a brown apron, stepped into view behind him, and I gave her a polite bow.

"Why don't you come in? We'll find a place for you to sleep." She had kind eyes and an easy smile that reminded me of Eiko's mother.

"No, no. That's too much trouble," I said. "We have a tent and everything we need. It's going to get dark soon, so I would like to set it up now, if that's alright."

"Okay," the man said. "Follow me." Slipping on shoes, he pushed past me a little unsteadily and led us along a dirt drive behind his house. A field of tall wild grass spread around us, and a large blue backhoe sat beside the drive. The grass was too high to set up a tent, and I wanted a place to prop up the bikes. I leaned the bikes against the backhoe's large black tires, which stood taller than Sho, and pointed to the ground beside it. "This spot will work perfectly. Thank you for letting us sleep here. We appreciate it."

"No problem," he said, pausing a moment to watch us unload the tent from our saddlebags before returning to his house.

"What a dramatic first day we've had, huh?" I said to Sho, as we kicked away a few rocks, rolled out a blue tarp and began to assemble the tent on top of it.

"Uh-huh," Sho said, distracted. Eyeing the backhoe, he added, "Can I drive the tractor?"

"That's probably asking a bit much of our hosts. Let's just get the tent set up and eat. I've got some rice balls, seaweed strips and energy bars. It's not gourmet cooking, but should give us enough calories at least."

I threw a rain cover over the bikes and tossed sleeping bags into the tent for Sho to unroll, then crawled inside to join him. As we took out our food, I heard approaching footsteps.

"Excuse me," our host said as I popped my head out of the tent. "We've got more crab than we can eat for dinner and would be honored if you would join us." As if we needed any more enticement, he added, "You won't taste crab like this in Sapporo."

I glanced at Sho, who gave an enthusiastic nod. "The honor would be all ours. Thank you!"

As we entered their home, I saw that we were not the couple's only out of town guests. A genial silver haired man who was just as inebriated as our host sat on a cushion at a low table, which had been set for five. We spent the next hour feasting on sautéed mountain vegetables, various seafood dishes and finally an entire crab. I was famished from cycling and relished the delicious food.

"This is the best crab I've ever had," Sho announced in his accented Japanese.

"His wife makes great food, doesn't she!" the guest said, smiling at Sho and re-filling my glass from a large bottle of Asahi beer. Accustomed to drinking manners in Japan, I held my glass while he poured, then took the bottle from him and, holding it with two hands, filled his glass. Our host's wife smiled shyly, excused herself from the table and returned with another dish from the kitchen.

"I'm the local teacher," our host said. Although he was clearly drunk, he remained remarkably coherent. "And this old guy drinking all our beer is my childhood friend visiting from Hakodate. He's drunk, so don't pay attention to anything he says."

His friend let out a belly laugh and nodded, "It's true. Don't believe a word I say . . . Including what I just said!"

Our host chuckled and continued, "There are six elementary students in our village, and they take classes in my house. But two are going to graduate this year and move on to middle school in the next village up. I need more students. There aren't enough people around here."

"You have lots of cows!" Sho observed. Everybody laughed.

After we finished off the food, we continued to drink and talk. But Sho seemed bored by the adult conversation. Although exhausted and eager to return to the tent, I thought it would be rude to rush out immediately after eating. I handed Sho his journal and asked him to write a summary of the day. While I chatted with the others, he drew a picture of the thieving crow and wrote, "A crow stoll my bread. I was mad!! He is a total thief!"

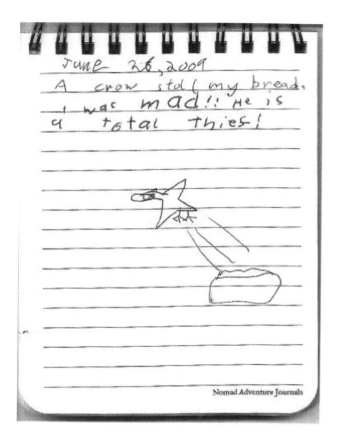

Finally, Sho yawned loudly. I said, "I'm sorry to be rude, but we should get back to our tent and go to sleep. It's been a long day. The food was delicious, and we enjoyed meeting you." I took out a pen and magnet with United Nations logos on them. "*Tsumaranai mono desu ga . . .* Please accept these gifts. They are nothing special, but we hope you like them. Thank you again for the excellent hospitality."

"Don't mention it! I'll see you out," our host said, staggering to his feet and losing his balance. His friend stood at the same time. They bumped shoulders and nearly fell over one another, causing both men to laugh uproariously.

"Sorry about them," the wife whispered to me as we left.

When we crawled into our tent and snuggled next to one another in separate sleeping bags, Sho said, "Those guys were really silly."

"Yes they were, and they were also very generous," I said, my arm draped over his shoulders. "I hope we meet more people like them on this trip." A few minutes later, just after 8:30 p.m., we were both in a deep sleep.

Chapter 9

Tempest

THE NEXT MORNING, I AWOKE TO THE OBSTREPEROUS CALLS of a rooster. I fished out my watch from a mesh pocket in the tent ceiling: 4:45 a.m. The morning light already filled our tent with a bright glow. Sho snored lightly beside me as I sat up with a yawn and stretched my stiff back. My right thigh stung, and I glanced down to see a broad rectangle of sunburned skin painted from the base of my bike shorts to the top of my knee. Should've worn sun block.

The cool morning air turned my breath to steam, and I kept the sleeping bag wrapped around me as I pulled out my journal. "What a first day!" I began, and spent the next hour recounting our adventures. I was exhilarated, filled with a sense of adventure and nervous excitement. The empty pages of the journal teased me. What would the next two months bring?

I looked over at Sho. He was wrapped against the morning chill in a blue sleeping bag, and his chest moved gently with each breath, the soft features of his face partially covered in shadow. I tried to imagine this trip from his perspective. He enjoyed cycling, loved Japan and seemed to treasure sharing time with me. I felt his need for my approval and assurance. But was I setting him up for failure by expecting him to complete this ambitious trek? Like most eight-year-olds, much of his life fell outside his control. And although the two of us had come up with the idea for this ride together, Sho certainly had no practical understanding of the scale of the challenge that awaited him. His temper tantrums seemed like desperate expressions of this sense of powerlessness and were reminders that even though I wanted to challenge him to improve himself, I also needed to protect him with reasonable boundaries.

Sho finally began to stir. "Hey Daddy," he said groggily, sitting up and rubbing his eyes, disoriented. "Where are we again?"

"On a farm on the northern coast of Hokkaidō. Let's eat a little bit, then break down the tent."

We huddled close to one another, sleeping bags draped over our shoulders, as we divided up sections of a *mikan* orange and nibbled on rolls filled with *anko*, a sweet bean paste. Once we had enough calories to stop our stomachs from grumbling, I unzipped the tent's front flap and scooted my legs out without touching the ground. I stuck my feet into shoes I had left outside under an awning to keep from getting dirt inside the tent. The shoes were damp with morning dew and squeaked as I wiggled into them.

Thirty minutes later, we had reduced our gear to four tightly packed saddlebags. We pushed our laden bikes around to the front of the farmhouse and knocked on the door. The wife emerged, wearing a checkered brown apron over a flower printed short-sleeved shirt. Her husband followed, hung over no doubt, a slightly dazed look in his eyes.

"*Ohayo Gozaimasu. Kino no oishii yoru gohan arigatou gozaimasu.* Good morning, and thanks for the delicious meal yesterday," I said. "We appreciated your hospitality, and thanks again for letting us sleep on your property. We'll leave in a few minutes."

"It was our pleasure," she responded, giving Sho a smile. "Wait here one minute. I'll be right back."

As she disappeared into her house, her husband stepped outside and took a closer look at our bikes.

Bending over to examine Sho's trailer cycle, he asked, "So, he rides behind you and pedals too?"

"That's right," I said.

He stood up straight, paused a moment, and gave me a curious look. "It's a long way to Cape Sata. Are you sure it isn't too much for an eight-year-old?"

I thought about Sho's temper tantrum the night before and the months of riding that lay ahead of us. Who knows, I thought. But it wasn't helpful to express any doubts in front of Sho, who was watching our exchange closely.

"He can do it," I answered confidently, mussing Sho's hair and giving him a nod. "His legs are crazy strong."

Just then, the wife hopped down the steps of her house, door clanging shut behind her, and extended a bag to Sho. "I thought you might want something for the road." Inside were Ritz crackers, a bottle of Pocari Sweat sports drink, and a salmon *onigiri* rice ball. Sho beamed at her.

The couple waved as we cycled away from their farm. Half a mile later, we merged onto the coastal highway. Although it was still early, the sun hung in the sky well above the vast sparkling blue water. In the direction we were headed, a broad line of clouds hung low. A cool wind rose off the ocean, and I was glad to be wearing a long-sleeved fleece.

We rode in silence for a few minutes before Sho asked, "Daddy, this trip isn't too hard for me, is it?"

"Don't worry about what other people think," I answered over my shoulder, pedaling steadily. "If your great granddad Scott were here, he'd say that worryin' gives little things big shadows."

"So, my shadow is gonna get bigger?"

"He meant that worrying you can't do something only makes it harder. So don't stress out when you meet someone who thinks you're too young to ride across Japan. Tell them you'll send them a post card from Cape Sata!"

"Yeah!" Sho answered with enthusiasm. "I'll send them a picture of me sticking out my tongue and saying, 'Told ya!'"

"That's the spirit."

We cycled for several hours beside the peaceful coast, passed occasionally by the stubby, pale green mini trucks ubiquitous in Japan's countryside. Utilitarian in design, the vehicles boasted a two-person front cab and a flat bed about the size of a twin mattress. There was usually an elderly man in overalls behind the wheel and farm equipment or long stalks of dried kelp strapped down and hanging off the back, the seaweed's bouncing tips only inches from the road.

I attached my iPod to a small speaker nestled beneath my bike saddle and, at Sho's request, played the soundtrack from *Billy Elliot*. Sho sang along unselfconsciously, his passion matching the lyrics to the song "Electricity," which described the joy Billy felt when he danced, as if he had sparks inside.

Ahead, the coastal highway disappeared into a protruding cliff jutting out to the water's edge.

"Look at that," I said over my shoulder, turning down the volume on the speaker.

"What is it, Daddy?"

"Our first tunnel. Let's see how long it is." The tunnel's entrance was a broad semicircle cut into the jagged cliff wall that seemed to swallow the road. Above the tunnel, the steep wall of the cliff was strewn with large boulders.

"Those big rocks look like knuckles, Daddy. It's like a giant's hand trying to scratch the ocean. I hope the giant doesn't try to grab us when we go through!"

As we entered the tunnel, I could see that it was about half a mile long. Large openings were cut into the left wall, allowing in light and even an occasional spray from the ocean surf. Sho yelled out "Hello hello hello! Here I am!" and laughed at the cacophonous echoes that bounced all around us before dissipating into the darkness.

I felt a peculiar melancholy intrude on the lovely scene. Perhaps it was the sudden transition from the big open sky to the tunnel's gloomy constriction. Or the strange play of light sifting through the thick stone windows, clawing at the darkness. The tunnel seemed like a metaphor; the giant's hand began to squeeze. I felt a sense of foreboding and picked up the pace, but Sho kept shouting out, making echoes. As we emerged out the other side, I noticed that the air was cooler.

Sho complained, "Aww. That was it? The echoes were cool."

"Don't worry. Japan has a lot of mountains. We're gonna go through plenty more tunnels."

My cell phone rang, and I pulled the bikes to the side of the road. Unzipping the handlebar bag, I took out the phone.

"Hey," Eiko said. "How was your stay on the farm?"

"Kinda like a party, actually. We slept next to a tractor and ate outrageously delicious crab with a nice family. I'll tell you all about it when we meet up. How was your evening?"

"Not as exciting as yours sounds. It was pretty much what you'd expect when traveling with a two-year-old. We ate dinner and then did the nighttime routine of bath, books, and songs before bedtime. I fell asleep singing to her." Eiko sounded tired, and I thought about the effort she was putting into helping me on this trip. This was clearly a father-son adventure, with Eiko taking time off from her demanding job at the United Nations to play the role of supportive wife and mother.

"Yeah, sorry. I know spending a week tracking us in a car isn't the ideal use of your vacation days."

She gave a surprised laugh, "You think?" Then her tone grew softer, all sarcasm gone. "Well, thanks for appreciating my effort. That helps. How far will you ride today?"

"I learned my lesson from yesterday and will be conservative in my estimate this time. Let's spend the night in the town of Omu. It's about seventy kilometers from our starting point at the farm. We should be able to make that before sunset, even if the winds get crazy."

"Okay. I'll find us a place to stay there. Also, I discovered something that should help on your trip. There appears to be an entire network of rest stops throughout Japan called '*michi no eki.*' Literally translated, that means 'street station.' They often have campsites, playgrounds, food, and other stuff. I got a map for you that shows their locations."

"Thanks. You're my star researcher! What am I going to do when you go back to New York in a couple days?"

"Suffer and realize how much better your life is with me in it."

"Ah yes. So true . . ."

"Um, Dad," Sho said.

"Hold on a second. You're interrupting my conversation with Mommy," I said, glancing back over my shoulder. Sho was straddling the frame of his trailer cycle and pointing out to sea with a concerned look. I followed his gaze and saw a boiling wall of black clouds obscuring the horizon. I could see white caps churning below the storm.

"It looks like a cloud army or something," Sho said. "And it's coming this way fast."

"Sweetheart, I've got to go," I said to Eiko. "I'll see you in Omu. Looks like we're gonna get wet."

I hung up and started digging through my rear saddlebag. I had buried the rain gear at the bottom and had to remove a pile of clothes to get to it. The first raindrops were already hitting us by the time I had re-packed the saddlebag. I handed Sho a jacket, rain pants and booties, and pulled on the same. When I was finished dressing, I looked back to see Sho taking off his rain pants.

"What are you doing?" I asked.

"These aren't comfortable."

"Sho, we're about to get hammered by a major storm. Put on your rain pants."

"But they don't feel good."

Fat raindrops thumped into my helmet, making a thwomp thwomp sound as they hit.

"Sho, you're gonna get soaked, and it's cooling down. You really need to wear those pants. When you tried them on back in New York, you said they felt fine."

"Well, they don't now. And the booties make me look stupid."

"Sho, you don't look stupid in the booties," I said, exasperated. "And you need them to keep your feet dry, which will keep you from getting chilled." He didn't respond, so I added, "Look, I think they make you look like a knight or a king elf or something."

"No they don't. And I don't like elves."

"Sho, we are in the MIDDLE OF NOWHERE. Even if they did look stupid, no one is around to laugh at you. Just put on the friggin' rain pants and booties."

Sho stuck out his lower lip in a pout, slumped his shoulders and lethargically pushed one leg into the black rain pants. He moved frustratingly slowly, and I stood by, steadily getting wetter. I bit my lip, closed my eyes, breathed deeply, and willed myself not to yell at him.

We finally began riding again. Sho sulked, barely pedaling and not speaking. I wouldn't have been able to hear him anyway, as the storm intensified. Heavy rain pounded us, and I held the handlebars tightly against strong gusts from the ocean side. A stream of water cascaded off the front of my helmet, dripping to my lips and down my cheeks. The tires splashed over the wet road surface, sending spray against the front fork and all over the saddlebags.

A quote from a book I'd read ten years earlier came to mind. Jim Whittaker, a renowned mountaineer, wrote in his autobiography, "I believe the key to a life well lived . . . is discomfort." I had highlighted that passage when I first read it and thought about it many times since. Whittaker saw discomfort as the secret to personal growth and character development, a way to stretch "yourself beyond what you already know or know how to do." When I was uncomfortable or suffering, I often thought of Whittaker and looked for the value in the experience. It was precisely in a moment like this, when Sho and I were drenched and struggling against the unrelenting wind, that I most deeply appreciated the simple joys of life: a meal shared with people I love, soaking in hot water, snuggling up to read to my kids at night. The suffering made the pleasure, when I finally experienced it, so much better!

And to Whittaker's point, handling the discomfort was really a lesson in perseverance for Sho and me. While my instincts as a father were to protect my kids, I thought that a parent shouldn't make a child's life too easy. I wanted Sho to internalize one of the most satisfying experiences in life: overcoming hardship through effort and focus.

After a while, I heard Sho yelling, but could not make out the words in the storm. Bracing myself for a continuation of his rain pants temper tantrum, I glanced back. But instead of tears, I saw he was belting out a song. He paused, gave me a smile and screamed, "Isn't this awesome? We're totally soaked!"

We rode through the mess for a few hours before reaching the town of Omu, population 5,000. Eiko and Saya were waiting for us at a *minshuku* inn, a plain, single-story motel beside the two-lane coastal highway. We rolled our bikes to the side of the building, parking them out of the rain beneath an overhang.

"Daddy and Sho are willy wet," Saya exclaimed excitedly and ran over to me.

"I'd pick you up and give you a hug, sweetheart, but I'm worried you'd drown."

Sho stood dripping beside the trailer cycle, arms stretched out to either side. His rain pants and booties had long since soaked through. Eiko rushed over with a towel, fussing over him and hustling him inside. "Let's get you out of those wet clothes." Saya followed them, while I stayed out in the parking lot, unloading the dripping saddlebags. Sheets of rain sprayed across the pavement, pounding out a violent rhythm.

Chapter 10

Mr. Saito

EARLY THE NEXT MORNING, THE FOUR OF US AMBLED GROG-gily from our room down a long hallway to the *minshuku's* dining area. I cradled Saya against my chest as she snuggled her head on my shoulder. Eiko and Sho held hands, walking a few steps in front. We entered a modest room, our footsteps scraping over the worn hard wood floor. A few guests ate quietly at small tables, whispering to one another. A large rice cooker and a dozen serving plates filled with food sat on a table pressed against the far wall.

"Do we take the food ourselves?" Sho asked, his voice filling the quiet room. I noticed the other guests glance our way.

"Not so loud," Eiko whispered. "Yes, it's a buffet. Let's see what they have."

As I set Saya onto a chair, a middle-aged woman wearing an apron emerged from a side room and hustled over to us holding a booster seat.

"*Doozo, tsukatte kudasai.* Here, please use this," she said, placing the booster seat on the chair and smiling at Saya. "*Nan sai desu ka?* How old are you?"

"*Ni sai!* I'm two!" Saya answered enthusiastically.

"*Kawaii ne.* You're cute," the woman cooed at Saya.

"*Arigatou gozaimasu.* Thank you," I said, lifting Saya into the seat.

Sho came back to the table carrying a plate containing grilled mackerel, pickles, scrambled eggs, and a bowl of *miso* soup. Eiko followed behind with four bowls of rice, setting them before each of us.

"I want fish!" Saya demanded loudly, pointing at Sho's plate.

"Shh!" Eiko and I said simultaneously.

I caressed Saya's head and said, "Not so loud, sweat heart. Be patient. I'll get you a plate with fish and whatever else you'd like."

"I'll share with her," Sho said, picking off a piece of fish with his chopsticks and dropping it into Saya's mouth like a mother bird.

"Umm, good!" she said, rubbing her tummy.

"What's the deal with all the shushing?" Sho complained.

"In Japan, it's considered rude to be too loud in public," Eiko explained.

I added, "We're trying not to play into the stereotype that Americans are loud."

"But I wasn't being loud," Sho said.

"Well, loud is relative . . ." I answered, and Sho gave me an unsatisfied look.

After eating, we handed our plates to the waitress, and I spread out a map of Hokkaidō on the table.

"Let's go over our planned route," I said, pointing to the top of the island. "We're here in Omu, heading east along the northern coast on Highway 238. Let's eat lunch today in Monbetsu and spend the night around Lake Saroma. After that, we'll ride to Abashiri, then Utoro. That's about fifty miles of cycling each day and will get us to Shiretoko Peninsula in three days."

"Do they have a game room in Shiretoko?" Sho asked.

"I'm not sure, but I think you'll have fun regardless. It's a nature preserve by the ocean filled with deer, brown bears, and beautiful lakes. It's so rugged and wild the Ainu called it the 'end of the earth.'"

"Who are the Ainu again?" Sho asked.

"The indigenous people in Hokkaidō," Eiko answered. "They lived here before modern Japanese moved in. Their language and culture are closely linked with nature. And they were good at hunting and wood carving."

"Most of the Ainu were killed off in the past century," I added. "But some still remain. In fact, we're going to cycle through a village called Nibutani that still has a large Ainu population." I pointed to it on the map.

Eiko raised her eyebrows. "What route are you planning to take to get there?"

"After Shiretoko, we'll cycle through the interior and head south."

"You're going right into a mountain chain that way, you know," Eiko said with a worried glance at Sho.

"I know. But I want to see the village, and we should be able to . . ."

Sho interrupted, "Wait, who killed the Ainu?"

"It's complicated," I said. "The Ainu lived in this area for probably a thousand years, trading with the Japanese and Russians. They spoke a different language and had a different religion and customs from the Japanese. But in the late 1800's, the Japanese government took away the Ainu's land and gave it to settlers who moved in to set up modern farms. The Ainu were forced to assimilate, and many who resisted were killed."

"What does assimilate mean?" Sho asked.

"It means that the Ainu had to give up their language and way of life, and learn to speak Japanese. It was only last year that the Japanese government finally recognized the Ainu as a separate ethnic minority group. By the way, a similar thing happened to Native Americans in the United States. In human history, when one culture expands into another's territory, it usually doesn't turn out so well for the ones who were there first."

"Why didn't they just share the land?" Sho asked.

"Not everyone has learned to share as well as you."

It took nearly an hour after breakfast to prepare the bikes and re-pack our saddlebags. I had emptied out the contents the evening before in an attempt to dry out the gear. Most of our items were in waterproof bags, but the saddlebags had soaked through, and some of our stuff had sat in an inch of water for hours during yesterday's ride. Thankfully, the small computer I was using to post blog updates had remained dry. The black saddlebags were still damp as I clamped them onto the bike rack, but I knew they would dry off quickly as we rode. The forecast called for sun and sixty-five degrees Fahrenheit.

Eiko and Saya drove ahead in the rental van, promising to meet us for lunch at a *michi no eki* rest stop in Monbetsu. Sho and I began cycling at 9:30 and made it through the town of Omu in minutes. We were soon pedaling beside a vast brilliant ocean, no humans in sight. The bike wheels rolled over the pavement with a satisfying whir, and a light wind danced through my helmet.

Striking, sharp-winged birds prowled the waterfront, adding their song to the idyllic scene. Their white wings, tipped with black, flashed overhead as they performed fluid acrobatics in the air.

After a while, Sho asked, "Daddy, can I have some dried squid?"

"Sure. Here you go," I said. Without stopping the bikes, I pulled some of the dry white strips from my handlebar bag and handed them back to Sho.

He gnawed on the tough squid for a while. Then he said, "You said there isn't a game room in Shiretoko. And I haven't seen any so far on our ride. I need to find the greatest game room in Japan! I know it's out there, but when are we going to find it?"

I chuckled. "I don't know, but I promise that you will be able to play in plenty of game rooms on this trip. We're way in the north of Japan, where there aren't a lot of people. But in the next couple months, we're going to ride through lots of towns with game rooms."

"Okay, Daddy. Because I want one that has Pokemon Battorio, Dinosaur King and . . ."

Sho stopped talking abruptly as the pleasant morning's quiet was broken by a loud "gwah gwah gwah!" The eerie croaking sound sent shivers up my back.

"Daddy, what was that?" Sho asked, clearly spooked.

"I'm not sure. That was freaky."

We rolled to a stop and scanned in the direction of the sound, an inlet surrounded by tall reeds and grass. And there it was: a large, elegant bird wading carefully through knee-deep water. At least three feet tall, its long narrow bill and intense eyes were yellow, a beautiful contrast to its grey, slightly frayed powder down feathers. It peered down into the water, head cocked to the side atop an elongated neck. Perched on bony legs, it suddenly froze in mid-stride.

It was a great grey heron, common in rice paddies and along the oceanfront. The large bird often wades through shallow water, catching fish and frogs, and sometimes even drops worms into the surface as bait for unsuspecting fish. Herons often appear in old Japanese tales, their strange calls used to set a spooky scene.

"He looks cool, but sounds really freaky," Sho said, warily eyeing the bird. The heron remained motionless, his unblinking yellow eyes gazing hard at the water near its feet.

"Why isn't he moving?"

"He's concentrating on catching a fish. Let's wait and see what happens."

Sho and I straddled our bikes by the roadside and watched silently. Then the moment came. A fish swam within range, and with a sudden powerful jab of its deadly yellow bill, the hunter snatched its prey. The heron raised its head high, neck undulating several times until he fully swallowed the fish. Then the glorious bird spread out broad wings and jumped into a soaring glide over the calm water, letting out another round of eerie calls. "Gwah gwah gwah!" The guttural noise echoed on the wind as the heron disappeared into tall grass at the water's edge.

Sho's eyes shone. "Whoa! That was amazing. The fish never had a chance . . ."

A few hours later, we cycled around a curve and saw a towering stone sculpture of a crab claw. "That's the *michi no eki* rest stop near Monbetsu where we'll eat lunch with Mommy and Saya," I announced to Sho over my shoulder.

"Yay!"

As we pulled into the half-filled parking lot, we saw Saya chasing Eiko around a broad field next to a restaurant and shop.

"I get you Mommy!" Saya yelled, squealing with joy as she latched onto Eiko's shirt. They both fell giggling to the ground. Sho jumped off his trailer cycle before I had brought the bikes to a stop, nearly tipping me over.

"Hey, watch it!" I complained.

"Sorry!" he yelled over his shoulder as he bounded into the thick green grass to join the fun.

Swinging my leg over the saddle and leaning the bikes against a wall, I let out a loud roar and ran into the field, arms out and hands extended like claws. Both kids screamed in delighted fear, tumbling over one another as they scrambled away. Instead of chasing them, I dropped into the grass beside Eiko, who was lying down and looking up at the sky. White wisps of clouds slowly crawled over the peaceful blue.

"Hey you," I said, kissing her cheek and lying down on the grass next to her.

"Hey," Eiko answered with a smile, propping up on one elbow and turning toward me. Sho and Saya were now bounding after one another. "You'd think Sho would be tired after cycling all morning, but apparently not."

I said, "I, on the other hand, could use a ninety-minute deep-tissue massage."

"Don't look at me!" Eiko teased. Then, brushing some grass out of my hair, she asked, "But seriously, how are you holding up?"

"My legs and lower back are pretty sore, but it's nothing debilitating. Actually, my hands bother me more than anything else. I have to grip the handlebars tightly because of the heavy load, and after a while my fingers go numb."

"Well, take care of yourself. You've got a lot ahead of you."

Saya suddenly ran past us, looking back over her shoulder and screaming with delight. Sho was close behind and bounded over my legs in an impressive leap, reaching out to tag Saya, then tucking into a roll.

"Nice jump!" I said, as Sho regained his footing and bounded off.

"By the way, I called a couple of inns in Lake Saroma," Eiko said. "But everything is booked up for tonight. Apparently, a lot of people are in town for some big race tomorrow. I'll keep looking and let you know when I find something."

"Okay. I saw on the map that there's a campsite next to Lake Saroma. If we can't find a place for all of us, Sho and I will set up a tent there. The next town is too far for us to reach before sunset, but you and Saya can drive there and get a room."

"That's fine. I'll keep checking, and we can decide what to do at the end of the day."

I called Sho over and told him that we might sleep apart from Eiko again. "Okay," he said distractedly and ran after Saya again.

I said to Eiko, "Hopefully that registered, and he won't have another monster break-down like two nights ago."

After letting the kids burn off a little more energy, we left the field and entered the restaurant. Large windows looked out over the ocean, sunlight streaming through.

"We place the food order at that counter, then carry our food to the table," Eiko instructed as we moved inside.

"I'm not hungry," Sho said, as I asked him what he wanted to eat. "I got full on the squid."

"Well, I'll eat for you then," I said. "After riding all morning, I'm famished."

A young woman behind the counter gave me a friendly smile as I started to order. "*Ikura don to miso shiro kudasai.* A rice bowl with salmon roe and miso soup, please."

"*Kashikomarimashita.* I understand," she said in polite Japanese. Then leaning forward and glancing down at Sho, she added excitedly, "You are the ones on the bikes! I passed you on the way in to work this morning. I live in Hamatonbetsu, back in the direction you came. Where are you going?"

I looked at Sho, and he answered, "Cape Sata."

The girl let out a loud "*Sugoiii!* Incredible. Just the two of you?"

"Yep," I said. "We are raising money for an environmental charity. Here's our card." I handed her a small business card with English on one side and Japanese on the other. It included a United Nations logo and read, "UNite to Combat Climate Change—Ride Japan. Father-son bike ride across Japan, Sho (age 8) and Charles Scott." A small map to the side showed our starting point at the top of the country and ending point at the bottom.

"*Shinjirarenai!* Unbelievable," she gushed. Then after a pause, her face turned serious, and she said, "You sure that isn't too hard for an eight-year-old?"

After lunch, Sho and I followed Eiko and Saya out to the parking lot toward the rental van parked near the looming crab claw. As Eiko climbed behind the wheel, I strapped Saya into a car seat in the back.

"I'll try to find us a place to sleep around Lake Saroma and give you a call with directions," Eiko said over her shoulder.

"Sounds good," I said with a nasally voice, Saya's fingers clamped around my nose. "Watch it, you trouble maker!" I joked, tickling her until she began squealing with laughter and let go.

Sho climbed into the front passenger seat and put on a seat belt.

"Um, buddy?" I asked, giving him a puzzled look.

"What?" he said with a mischievous grin.

"No cheating. We're cycling across Japan, not driving. You're coming with me, rascal."

"Oh man," Sho whined.

"Give your mommy a kiss, then let's get rolling."

Sho leaned over, gave Eiko a kiss, and dragged himself out of the van lethargically.

We waved goodbye to Eiko and Saya as they pulled away. Walking toward our bikes, I patted his back encouragingly, pulled him close and said, "You can do it."

An hour into the ride, we rounded a bend and saw a lone cyclist ahead beside the road. His bicycle had fenders and was packed with a large handlebar bag, two fully loaded saddle-bags, and a tent roll strapped to the rear rack. He was one of us—a cyclist out for a multi-week journey. He was leaning over the side of his bike, examining something, and I wondered if he might have a mechanical problem.

"*Daijoubu desu ka?* Is everything all right?" I asked as we rolled to a stop beside him. He wore a white helmet with a cap underneath, orange tinted sunglasses, cycling gloves, a blue short-sleeved technical shirt, and blue shorts. He looked to be in his 50's, with the powerful calves of a much younger athlete.

He stood up straight and turned to us, taking off his glasses to reveal kind eyes with a lively spark. "*Hai, zenzen daijoubu desu.* Yes, everything is absolutely fine," he answered with an appreciative smile. "I'm just taking a break and reviewing some pictures I took."

He spoke Japanese with a regional accent that I found appealing. In contrast to the crisp formal staccato I often heard when talking with businessmen in Tokyo, his voice was earthy and warm, the words tumbling out with a pleasing rhythm. I could see now that he had been crouched over his camera's digital screen, creating a shadow to block the bright light. He held out a sturdy Nikon camera with a telephoto lens and showed us a gorgeous close up of the great grey heron.

"Hey, that's the bird we saw!" Sho said excitedly.

"Yes, isn't he magnificent. I took a few other pictures you might like," he said and began scrolling through his roll. Sho and I huddled close to get a good view, and he held the camera low so that Sho could see easily. He was a gifted photographer and I felt a stab of inadequacy. I had brought along a compact digital camera that until now had produced what I thought were perfectly acceptable shots. But as we marveled at dramatic close-ups of animals and flowers and sweeping high-resolution shots of the ocean and mountains, I realized what a difference good equipment and talent make.

I pointed at his gear and said, "It looks like you're going a long way."

"Yep. I left my house in Yamagata over two weeks ago, and plan to ride along the coast around the entire country. It should take me about five months. I'm sixty-one years old and just finished working. I thought this would be a great way to start off my retirement. How about you two?"

"Wow! We're only riding from Cape Sōya to Cape Sata, about 4,000 kilometers. I'm thinking it will take us just under seventy days." I told him our names and handed him the card for our ride with two hands, Japanese side up, and bowed slightly. He bowed in return and took the small white card with two hands, examining it politely for a moment before putting it into his handlebar bag.

"What a great thing to do with your son." He looked at Sho. "You look nice and strong. I bet you'll have no trouble making it all the way to Cape Sata."

Sho blushed and gave him a smile.

"My name is Akira Saito. It's very nice to meet you. Here, take my card. Maybe I'll see you again on the road."

Chapter 11

Lake Saroma Ultra

AFTER RIDING FOR A FEW HOURS, INCLUDING A BRIEF LUNCH break by the road, we spotted another *michi no eki* rest stop, this one a collection of large buildings and walking paths beside the ocean. Parking our bikes near the main entrance, Sho and I ambled inside. I spotted a restaurant and a small grocery store.

"Let's get some snacks in the store," I said. Sho wasn't paying attention. Across the lobby was a boy his age, wearing tan cargo pants and a light blue T-shirt that hung over his slightly chubby belly. He was seated on a bench hunched over a dozen Pokemon battorio playing coins.

"Daddy, can I play with him?" Sho asked. "I've got my Pokemon coins right here. I keep them in my pocket just in case."

"Sure. I'll run into the store. Anything special you'd like?"

"Dried squid and beef jerky please. And Aquarius sports drink. Oh, and *mochi* if they have it."

"You got it. Protein, electrolytes and simple carbs. Sounds like a good combination for someone cycling all day. See you in a sec." I estimated that, while cycling through Japan, I needed to double the number of calories I normally consumed in a day to about 5000. I assumed that Sho needed more calories, too, and did not think twice about giving him sports drinks and sweets on this trip.

The store had all the items except for beef jerky. I bought two packets of *mochi*, dense chewy sweet glutinous rice cakes that are a delicious and underappreciated contribution from Japan to the world. I took a bite of one as I left the store, enjoying an instant carbohydrate rush, and returned to the lobby. Sho and the boy were fully engaged. They had organized their Pokemon coins in neat rows across from one another and were haggling good naturedly.

My phone rang. "Hey," I said to Eiko, "Where are you?"

"Next to Lake Saroma. I just found out that the camp site where you wanted to sleep here has been closed due to brown bear activity."

"Hmm, I guess we shouldn't spend the night there then."

"Not if you want to stay married to me!" she said with more seriousness than I think she intended. Then she continued in a calmer voice, "Remember the race I told you about? Well it's pretty big apparently, and all the hotels and inns are booked. But I was able to find a place that might work for you guys. It's an abandoned train where they are putting up some of the runners. Doesn't look too comfy, but it will probably be cheap at least."

"A train?"

"If you don't want to do it, you can load your bikes in the rental van, and I'll drive you to our hotel in Abashiri."

I thought for a moment and said, "No, that feels like cheating. We'll sleep in the abandoned train."

"Okay. Also, I found a small amusement park Sho might like. It's just a couple kilometers from the train. The only problem is that it closes at 5 p.m. Do you think you can get here in time?"

I looked at my watch: 1:50 p.m. "Possibly."

"Good luck. Give me a call when you're getting close."

I hung up and walked over to Sho and the boy.

"*Kore wa sugoi!* This one is great," Sho said. "Dialga is the strongest." Sho held up a coin with an image of a powerful dark blue horse-like creature. Two horns stuck out of its head, making it look like a ceratopsian dinosaur. It wore a silver armored chest plate with a diamond in the center and shiny armor on its back with five prongs sticking out. The Pokemon stood regally, an impressive pointed crest resting like a crown on its head.

"*Chigau yo!* No way!" the other boy said, shaking his head and waving another coin that showed an orange monkey-like creature with protruding ears and flames gushing out of its head and hands. "Infernape is more powerful than Dialga. It has the flame thrower attack."

"*Infernape wa tsuyoi kedo . . .* Infernape is strong," Sho conceded. "But Dialga can stop time."

I interrupted, "Speaking of time, we should hit the road." I spoke in English, and Sho's new friend looked up at me with a puzzled expression.

"Let me stay a little longer, Dad."

"Mommy found an amusement park, but we've got to pedal hard if we're going to get there before it closes."

Sho's demeanor changed immediately. "An amusement park? Cool!" He quickly gathered up his Pokemon coins and said to his friend, "Sorry, but I gotta go." The boy waved good-bye and returned to organizing his coins.

Walking back to our bikes, Sho said, "I traded five of my weak Pokemon coins for two of his awesome ones. It was totally worth it."

The next two and a half hours were exhausting. I tucked my head against a powerful wind that blew steadily off the ocean and pedaled as if I were in a race. My quadriceps burned, my shoulders ached, and my hands went numb. I sipped water every so often, a quick grab of the bottle from its holder on the bike frame, a turn of my head to swallow the liquid, and a return of the water bottle to its cage without changing the cadence of my spinning legs. Sho pedaled hard too, head down and focused. Every so often, he asked whether we would make it to the amusement park on time, raising his voice over the loud wind. I was impressed by the amount of work he was willing to do in order to play.

At 4:35 p.m., out of breath but triumphant, we pulled into the amusement park's nearly empty parking lot. A large, brightly lit Ferris wheel loomed overhead just inside the park, but it held no passengers and was not moving. Eiko stood outside the rental van, waving to us. We rolled to a stop beside her, and straddling my bike, I flopped my arms over the handlebars and threw my head face down with a whimper.

"I'm getting too old for this," I wheezed.

Sho was already off the bike and tugging on Eiko's hand. "Hurry up, Mommy! We've only got twenty-five minutes before it closes!"

"Saya's asleep in the van. Do you mind watching her?" Eiko asked as Sho pulled her away toward the park entrance.

"No prob. I'm just gonna curl up in the fetal position over here for a little while. Maybe get an IV drip."

Eiko flashed me a smile, then took off running with Sho. I rested the bikes on the ground beside the van. After recovering my breath, I poked my head inside the open window and gave Saya a gentle kiss on her forehead. She was strapped in a child seat, breathing deeply, her head bent to one side in a way that looked uncomfortable. I gently pulled up her head to rest against the side of her car seat at a more natural angle. As I moved her head, she stirred briefly, making soft sucking sounds on her fingers for a few seconds before settling back into a peaceful sleep. I felt a wave of sadness that Sho and I would be apart from her for two months.

I looked back toward the modest amusement park, noticing its name for the first time: Family Island Yuu. The place seemed deserted except for a single attendant, a middle-aged man wearing a park uniform, who followed Eiko and Sho from ride to ride. I could make out Sho's small form passing in and out of view as he sprinted from the hanging swings to the bumper cars to a shooting game. Eiko ran after him, trying to keep up.

Their voices and laughter floated up from the park, dissipating into the bright blue sky. The cool air dried off my sweat as the summer sun threw my shadow across the bikes that lay on the ground beside the van. I tried to hold onto the blissful sound of my wife and son's enthusiastic laughter and the sonorous calm of Saya's gentle breathing. But like a leaf disappearing down a flowing river, I knew the moment would soon drift away into memory.

At 5:01, Eiko and Sho returned hand in hand, talking excitedly to one another, radiating happiness.

"Daddy, there was nobody there except us. We never had to wait for a single ride. It was great!"

"I'm glad you had fun. And tonight you get another adventure sleeping in a train."

"A train?"

Saya was still asleep as Eiko pulled out of the parking lot. Sho and I rode behind on our bikes, tracking the edge of Lake Saroma, Hokkaidō's largest lake.

"Sho, I read that this lake's name comes from an Ainu term meaning 'place of many Miscanthus reeds.' Maybe we can see some of them as we ride."

"What do the reeds look like?"

"I have no idea."

After fifteen minutes, we followed Eiko into a parking lot. Immediately in front of us, a series of connected black train cars sat in the middle of a large grass field. The train looked like it had not moved in decades, a fading relic of an earlier time. Through the windows I saw silhouetted forms moving. Our soon-to-be bunk mates, no doubt.

Eiko parked the van while I leaned the bikes against a small building. Saya had awakened, but was groggy, and Eiko cradled her as they walked from the car. Saya peeked at me through squinting eyes, sucking her two fingers and curling up in her mother's arms.

The four of us followed a path into a small office near the train. A man who looked to be in his sixties sat behind a desk. He wore a red T-shirt and glasses and had bushy eye brows and silver hair peeking out beneath a blue hat with the word "rabbit" across the front.

"*Sumimasen.* Excuse me," I said. "I'm sorry to bother you. My son and I are looking for a place to sleep tonight. Would you possibly have space for us?"

Looking down at a piece of paper and tapping his pen against a list of names, he shook his head slowly and inhaled with an audible hiss. In Japan, this sound usually means your request is about to be denied. Glancing at Eiko, he said, "Yeah, your wife told me earlier. I may have something, but I'm juggling a lot of people . . ."

His voice trailed off and I interjected, "My son and I are cycling from the top of Japan to the bottom to raise money for a United Nations environmental charity. We planned to sleep in the campsite, but it was closed because of brown bear activity. Here's our card."

The man sat up straight, looked at me with raised eyebrows and examined the card. "*Shinjirarenai*. That's unbelievable. Your son is cycling the whole way?"

"Yes," I said. "On connected bikes. Want to see them?"

"As a matter of fact, I do," he said, standing up. He followed me back out to the parking lot, where he appraised our bikes with approval.

"So, you ride on the back, right?" he asked Sho.

"*Hai, so desu*. Yes, that's right." Sho answered.

"You must do most of the work," he said with a smile. He turned to me and said, "I've got a bunch of runners who need a place to sleep, but I should be able to fit you in somewhere. Just you and your son, right? Your wife and daughter have another place to stay?"

"Yes, that's right,"

"Sounds good. My name is Ishiwata. Follow me, and I'll show you the train." He led us onto the grass and up some rusting metal stairs leading into one of the train cars. Dozens of ridiculously fit-looking men were lounging on cots shoved against the walls, reading books or laying out their gear. No spare body fat here to hide their rippling abs and protruding leg muscles. A few people spoke in whispers, and I could sense the anxious tension of competitors preparing for the following day's race. Although it wasn't a particularly hot day, the train car was stuffy and humid. Only a few windows were open, and I speculated that the others were stuck closed.

"It's hot in here, Daddy," Sho said.

Mr. Ishiwata thought for a moment, patted Sho on the head with a sympathetic look and said, "I may have another option for you, if you don't mind sharing a room with one or two of the runners. Follow me."

He led us out of the train, past his office to an adjoining building. Inside there was a large common area kitchen, a few public showers and an empty side room about twenty feet long and ten feet wide. Stepping into the side room, he said, "You can sleep here, if you like this better than the train."

Sho gave me a nod, looked at Mr. Ishiwata and said, "We'll take it!"

He smiled and said, "Expect a few others to show up before bed time."

I unloaded the saddlebags from our bikes and brought them inside the room, while Eiko supervised Sho and Saya playing in a field behind the train. Unsure of how many people would join us in the room, I tried to take up as little space as possible. I consolidated our gear into a corner, unrolled our sleeping pads, pushed them close to one another by a wall and laid our sleeping bags on top. After taking a shower and changing out of cycling clothes, I joined Eiko and the kids outside. Sho and Saya were running in circles after one another, giggling.

We bought *una-juu* rice bowls with cooked eel on top at a store next door and ate them at a picnic table as dusk fell around us. Then Eiko and Saya drove away, and Sho and I returned to our room. Inside was a slender man with a muscular build, his black hair cut short. He wore blue shorts over powerful legs, a large silver sports watch, and a white T-shirt with a logo from the Tokyo Marathon. He was laying out gear in a neat row: a pair of running shoes, socks, running shorts, and a short-sleeved shirt.

"Hi!" Sho said to him, smiling as we walked in.

"Well hello," he said, turning around and standing up.

"*Hajimemashite.* Nice to meet you," I said and introduced ourselves. "We're going to be roommates tonight."

"*Hajimemashite,*" he responded. "I'm Sato. Mr. Ishiwata told me that one more guy was supposed to sleep here, but found another place to stay. So I think we've got the room to ourselves."

"That's great!" I said. "We'll have lots of space to stretch out. Tell me, what exactly is the race tomorrow?"

"It's the Lake Saroma Ultra Marathon. It's a one hundred-kilometer (sixty-two-mile) race and quite prestigious in Japan. There should be something like 4,000 runners."

"Have you run that far before?" Sho asked.

"Your Japanese is good," Mr. Sato said. "This will be my fourth ultra. I'm sixty-two years old, which is the retirement age in Japan. Now that I have lots of free time, I've taken up Ironman triathlons and ultra marathons."

I stared in disbelief. I would have guessed he was forty-five years old. I told him that I had raced in five Ironman triathlons and many marathons, including the Boston Marathon earlier in the year.

"That's great. You're one of us!"

"Well, I've never run one hundred kilometers and I'm not sure I could. That's intimidating."

"Oh, it's not that big a deal. If you train for it, you can do it. What brings you to Lake Saroma, if you're not here for the race?"

When I told him about our plans to cycle the length of Japan, he grew animated. "That is the coolest thing to do with your son. You know, no father in Japan could get away with taking off so much time from work, and no Japanese mother would allow her son to do something that insane."

"Well, I was worried that I might get fired for doing this, and his mom is Japanese by the way."

"She's special then," Mr. Sato said with a chuckle. "Do you have plans to ride through Niigata? Do you know where that is?"

"Yes, it's on our route. We should get there in about a month."

"Here's my card. Give me a call when you come through. I'll introduce you to the local Ironman club."

"Sounds great. Here's my card. I promise to get in touch."

"Sorry to be rude, but I've got to get up extremely early tomorrow and should go to bed," he said. "The race starts at

5 a.m., and the leaders should pass this spot at about 7:30 a.m. Make sure to cheer on the runners, if you're still here."

"No problem. We're going to bed soon, too. If we're asleep when you leave, good luck! We'll look for you out on the course."

Chapter 12
New Cycling Buddy

EARLY THE NEXT MORNING, WE ROLLED OUR CONNECTED bikes past the old train toward the main road. Sho wore a long-sleeved Under Armor shirt, a striped Adidas sweatshirt and black sweat pants. I wore long black cycling tights and a brightly colored jacket designed to make it easier for motorists to see me.

Ultra marathoners jogged by, grabbing cups of water from a handful of volunteers who stood by the roadside. Mr. Ishiwata, the man who'd let us sleep in a comfortable room instead of the train, was among them. When he spotted us, he ran over, holding a race volunteer's jacket. "*Ohayou gozaimasu!* Good morning! I'm glad I caught you before you left. Here, take this," he said, holding out the jacket. "It's quite cool this morning, and I don't want you to be uncomfortable."

"You don't need to do that. I'll be fine."

"I insist," he said, handing me the jacket with a look that told me I should not continue to protest. I thanked him and packed it into an already over-stuffed saddlebag.

"You're headed toward Shiretoko Peninsula, right?" he asked. When I nodded, he said, "Then you'll be riding alongside the runners for a couple hours and can cheer them on."

"That sounds like fun," Sho said.

Mr. Ishiwata turned to him and said, "Please be careful on your long journey. You should come back to Lake Saroma again. Maybe some day, you'll run the race!" He then gave both of us hugs.

This was remarkable. When I lived in Tokyo for two years in my early twenties, I created several awkward moments by hugging Japanese people as a form of greeting. It is simply not part of the culture to hug another person, even a family member, in public, except when people are drunk, their rowdy behavior generally tolerated as an acceptable release in a society that is otherwise highly restrained.

Having grown up in a touchy-feely family in hug-happy Nashville, I often embraced old friends and new alike. In Japan, this was simply weird and made people uncomfortable: an unexpected and mildly shocking invasion of personal space. People usually responded with a grunt of surprise and a limp noncommittal flap of the arms. I quickly learned to keep my distance and bow or, at most, shake hands if offered.

I returned Mr. Ishiwata's hug appreciatively and thanked him again for his hospitality.

"I hope you have a wonderful time in Japan," he said with a wave as Sho and I pulled away on the road and merged next to the line of runners.

The air was cool as we cycled along the southern rim of Lake Saroma, its quiet waters shrouded by lightly churning morning mist. The steady footfalls from the line of lycra-clad runners tapped out a pleasing rhythm that complemented the misty morning peace. A few spectators stood by the road, their backs to the expansive water, clapping and encouraging the runners with shouts of "*Gambatte! Gambatte!* Keep it up!"

This was an elite group, the front phalanx of over 4,000 participants in the one hundred-kilometer event. All the participants I saw were Japanese, and there were a few women in the mix. The runners shared similar lean body types and moved with extreme efficiency. Backs straight, their bodies leaned ever so slightly forward to gain a slim advantage from gravity. Eyes looking out ahead, heads barely moving up and down, their relaxed arms slid back and forth in a tightly controlled arc that helped maintain momentum. Although we were cycling about ten miles per hour, Sho and I were only slightly faster than the efficient runners.

"Daddy, do you think we'll see Sato-san?" Sho asked, scanning the athletes for our roommate from the previous evening.

"Let's keep our eyes out for him."

As we cycled by a group of cheering spectators, they pointed excitedly at our connected bikes. One of them exclaimed, "Hey look at that!" and the group pumped their arms in the air, shouting, "*Gambatte!*" as we rode past.

"We're not in the race!" Sho yelled out, and one of them responded with a laugh, "We know!"

After about two hours, we split off from the runners. Sho said in a disappointed voice, "We never saw Sato-san."

"Don't worry. We'll see him again in Niigata in another month."

At lunch time, we met Eiko and Saya for sushi in the town of Tokoro. Famished after cycling all morning, I relished the delicious raw fish and returned to the road reinvigorated. Our destination was Abashiri, population 40,000, the largest town we had cycled through so far. Eiko and Saya drove ahead to find the four of us a place to stay.

We discovered a narrow, tree-lined cycling road that hugged the coast. The route was deserted, and I appreciated the luxury of riding on a protected, paved path free of automobile traffic.

After riding in silence for a while, surrounded by the sounds of bird song and tree branches swaying with the intermittent breeze, Sho asked, "Daddy, would you rather be eaten by sharks while in the water or by lions while on land?"

"Neither one."

"No, you have to choose one."

"I don't want to choose."

"You have to."

"No, I don't."

"Just choose!"

"Sheesh. OK, um, well, I guess, sharks, because I think I would be killed faster."

"Lions could kill you faster than sharks."

"Maybe. I don't really know. Whatever, I'm just choosing sharks."

"Is that your final answer?"

"What is this, a quiz show?"

"No, it's not, but you have to . . ." Sho interrupted himself. "Hey, I see somebody." Up ahead, a cyclist was standing by the road taking pictures. He wore a black sleeveless jacket over a long-sleeved yellow shirt, and his bike was packed with two rear saddlebags and a tent roll strapped to the rear rack.

As we got closer, Sho yelled out, "Saito-saaaaan!" It was Mr. Saito, the sixty-one-year-old cyclist we had met two days earlier, who was riding the circumference of Japan. He looked up with a smile as we stopped beside him.

"*Konnichi wa.* Good afternoon," he said with a slight bow. "We meet again! You're looking strong," he said to Sho.

"I'm full of sushi energy!"

"Well no wonder then. You know, you're the first people I've seen on this path since I started riding on it over an hour ago."

"It's great to be away from the traffic, isn't it?" I said. "And it goes all the way to the outskirts of Abashiri."

"That's where I'm headed. I was just taking a short break to get some shots of these stunning lupins." There were hundreds of the thin, long-stemmed flowering spikes lining the road, waving in the gentle breeze. They stood like colorful towers of pink and purple and light blue growing out of a base of deep green multi-pronged leaves.

"Sho, you know who would love to see a picture of you with these flowers?" I asked.

"Nona!" he said enthusiastically, jumping off his trailer cycle and posing in front of the gorgeous display.

I took several pictures, and Mr. Saito snapped a few as well, no doubt higher quality than mine. "Nona is Sho's grandmother," I explained.

"Wonderful! She's lucky to have a grandson like you," he said to Sho.

I said, "Since we're headed to the same place, want to ride together?"

"Absolutely," said Mr. Saito. We set off, enjoying the opportunity to ride and talk side-by-side, something we would not do on a street with traffic.

"Where are you staying tonight?" I asked.

"I made a reservation at a bed and breakfast in Abashiri. Usually I camp, but I decided to sleep with a roof over my head tonight. You're welcome to stay in the same place, if you want."

I thought that was a great idea and called Eiko to let her know that, for once, she did not have to arrange our lodgings for the night.

As we entered the outskirts of Abashiri, Sho said, "This town looks pretty big. Do you think it has a game room?"

Mr. Saito nodded, "Oh, I'd think so. Let's ask at the bed and breakfast."

"Yes!" Sho shouted with a fist pump, which elicited a surprised laugh from Mr. Saito.

"Sho is *really* into game rooms," I said with a grin.

"I'm trying to find the greatest game room in all of Japan!"

The bike path ended, and we began cycling on city roads with stoplights and traffic. We rode single file, Mr. Saito leading the way, and stayed to the left, moving in the same direction as the cars that rushed by a few feet to our right. Rolling to a stop at a traffic light, I pressed down and twisted my right foot to release my bike shoe from the Shimano clip pedals. It was a move I had done thousands of times. Riding "clipped in" with bike shoes made it easier to pedal in full circles, allowing me to pull up with my feet as well as push down. It's an efficient pedal stroke, but has one major downside: when you come to a stop, if you don't unclip quickly enough, you find yourself precariously balancing on an unmoving bicycle, heading for a fall.

Which is where I was when my shoe stayed clipped into the pedal despite my effort to release it. A minivan was idling three feet to my right, waiting for the light to change. As I lost balance, both feet still stuck to the pedals, I fell over, reached out, and slapped the minivan driver's side window hard with both hands and the side of my face. The driver, a young man wearing overalls, jerked his head toward me in surprise, our eyes only a few inches from one another. I imagined how ridiculous I must look with my cheek squished across the glass. I quickly pressed myself away from his car in a kind of vertical push-up and finally managed to unclip my shoe and regain my balance.

I bowed and apologized to the driver. He returned my bow with a gracious nod of the head, politely ignoring the cheek stain on his window. We both glanced back at the stoplight, hoping that it would turn green quickly and end the awkward moment.

Mr. Saito was straddling his bicycle in front of me, facing away and looking down at a map. To my relief, he didn't seem to have noticed what had happened. Sho, however, saw the whole thing. "Why did you do that?"

"I was just showing you what not to do."

Eiko, Sho, Saya and I shared dinner that night with Mr. Saito in the bed and breakfast's dining room. We nibbled on a tasty collection of scallops, crab, tofu, rice, and a variety of vegetables.

"The food here is really good!" Sho said between bites.

"I would guess that most of what we are eating was harvested locally," Mr. Saito responded. "Much of the economy along the northern coast of Hokkaidō is based on dairy farming and fishing."

"I want to go fishing," Sho said.

"Me too!" Saya added loudly.

"You don't even know how to fish," said Sho.

"Yes I do!"

Sho rolled his eyes.

"Relax guys," I said, patting them both gently on their backs. "We can't go fishing tomorrow, but I read that Abashiri has a prison museum that might be interesting to see."

Eiko raised her eyebrows and said, "It housed political prisoners during the Meiji Era. I'm not sure how interesting that will be for the kids."

"What about the game room?" Sho asked.

Chapter 13
Tantrum

THE NEXT MORNING, SHO GOT HIS WISH TO VISIT PALO GAME Station, an entire building in downtown Abashiri dedicated to deafening electronic distractions. It was like being in a Las Vegas casino for kids.

We stood in front of two stubby cylindrical *taiko* drums that stuck out at waist height from a large game console and pounded the platter-sized drums with two scarred wooden drumsticks, attempting to follow the rhythm of a fast-paced Japanese pop song. Small red and blue circles streamed across the console screen at a ridiculously quick rate. When a red circle reached a vertical line at the edge of the screen, we were supposed to beat the middle of the *taiko* drum, which emitted a satisfying solid thwump. A blue circle meant that we should hit the edge of the drum, which produced a short staccato clacking sound. Every so often a larger red circle would appear, requiring us to bang the center of the drum harder than usual. And a long, uninterrupted stretched-out circle meant that we should beat the drum as many times as possible in a few seconds. We frantically tried to keep up with the overwhelming rush of colored circles, as the background music helped us follow the rhythm. But the speed and volume of the expected drumbeats was simply unmanageable.

"Daddy, you're totally off!" Sho admonished, just as he missed the rhythm for three red circles that rushed past.

"You're not doing much better," I said in a raised voice, so he could hear me over the din of the game room.

When our song finally ended, the screen showed an animated chubby red *taiko* drum with a disappointed face. It hovered over the words, "Level failed."

"That was painful," I said and turned to Eiko, who had been watching us play. Handing her the drumsticks, I said, "Here, you try. Good luck. It's harder than it looks. I've already got a blister on my hand."

"Mommy, stand here," Sho said, indicating a spot beside him. "Daddy sucked at that game. I bet you'll do a lot better."

"Because I know not to start off at expert level," she said with a smile. "Would you watch Saya? She's over there." Eiko pointed beyond a line of Super Mario race car games to a nearly life-size plastic blue truck. It resembled the squat mini trucks so popular in rural Japan. Saya sat inside, one hand on the steering wheel, the other pressing buttons on the brightly colored plastic dashboard and honking the squeaky horn. Her favorite stuffed animal sat in the back seat, a soft beige lamb whose four legs were splayed out, its head flopped to one side.

"I'm driving Lamby to the liberry," Saya said excitedly, as I approached. "I'm a taxi driver! Wanna get in?"

"Yes, thank you. May I go to the library too?" I said, squeezing into the cramped back seat next to Lamby, bending my neck at an uncomfortable angle with the side of my head pressed against the ceiling.

"Sure! Buckle up!"

Eiko, Sho, Saya and I spent the next hour and a half amidst the loud beeps and clangs and crashes in Palo Game Station. I felt like I had returned to an earlier phase of my life. When I was a boy around Sho's age, arcades started to pop up in my hometown of Nashville, Tennessee. They were simple places, usually just large rooms filled with rows of pinball machines and various hulking stand-alone game consoles. A manager sat behind a counter next to the bathrooms and a change machine for quarters. Arcades quickly became a favorite hang out for my friends and me. I would ride my bike there and spend whatever pocket money I had, a quarter at a time, on Space Invaders, Asteroids, Galaga, PacMan, Centipede, Donkey Kong, etc. And when I ran out of money, I watched others play and traded tips with my friends on how to beat various levels in the games.

Despite the rapid emergence of personal computer games and home consoles, the arcade concept survived, especially in Japan, where Space Invaders was released by Taito Corporation in 1978 and where electronic fun in a variety of forms permeates the culture. Although the first "cathode ray tube amusement device" was patented in the U.S. in 1948, and American companies and universities were responsible for much of the early innovation in computer games, it was the success of Space Invaders that ushered in what is often called the "golden age" of the arcade game industry. At its peak in 1982, this industry brought in more than twice the revenues generated by Hollywood movies that year.

Most towns in Japan still have numerous "game centers." These are often multi-story complexes filled with an overwhelming variety of electronic fun. Some have entire floors of curtained off *puri kura* photo booths that produce mini stickers with pictures of you and your friends animated with silly characters drawn around your faces. There are games that allow you to box against opponents, play a fake guitar, or try to follow a series of complex dance steps. There are claw games, dinosaur battling games, martial arts fighting games, racing games, dress up games. All designed to get as many one hundred yen (one dollar) coins out of you as possible. In the end, Eiko and I spent fifty dollars for an hour of flashing, beeping fun at the Palo Game Station in Abashiri.

As I watched Sho and Saya run breathlessly from one machine to the next, I remembered the excitement I used to experience when exploring those first arcades. As an adult, I seldom felt such excitement anymore, but cycling through Japan with my eight-year-old son had rekindled a similar sense of play and wonder.

While Eiko was playing with Saya, Sho ran up to me, holding out a Pokemon coin he had received from one of the games. On it was an image of a red dragon rearing up on its hind legs, its claws extended and broad wings flared out to either side. Its gaping mouth showed off four sharp fangs, and roaring flames licked up from the tip of its tail. "Daddy, I got Charizard! He has the Pearl of Thunder attack! It's awesome!"

"That's great."

"And you should see this kid back at the *taiko* game. Remember the expert level we failed? He's totally doing it."

We walked over to the *taiko* game and settled in a few feet behind a boy who looked no older than twelve. He stood with his feet shoulder-width apart, holding the drumsticks comfortably, as if they were extensions of his arms. He focused intently on the screen as a rush of red and blue circles poured across, bunched up on one another and moving so quickly that they were nearly a blur. And this kid was hitting every beat without a mistake. While one hand was beating the middle of the drum in syncopation with a red circle, his other hand was tapping the outside of the drum in time with a blue circle that was squeezed just behind. His movements, timed perfectly with the song's rhythm, were too fast for me to follow. I watched in amazement and enjoyed the show. He had utterly mastered this game. When the song ended, the animated *taiko* drum jumped up and down on the screen and squealed out, "Perfect score!" The kid nonchalantly pulled a cell phone from his pocket, snapped a picture of the screen and sidled away. I suspected that a dozen middle school students had just received an instant message with the image of his perfect score, boosting his social status among the game room geek set.

Sho and I finally left Abashiri in the late morning with plans to cycle about fifty miles, which would take about five and a half hours. Eiko and Saya drove ahead to find accommodations in Utoro. The only town on the western coast of Shiretoko Peninsula, Utoro has a number of inns and hotels with natural hot spring baths. I eagerly anticipated the soothing warmth of soaking in one of those deep tubs at the end of the day. The town also serves as a jumping off point to explore the rugged peninsula. We planned to spend the following day doing just that and enjoying a break from cycling.

In 2005, the United Nations designated Shiretoko Peninsula a World Heritage Site: "it provides an outstanding example of the interaction of marine and terrestrial ecosystems . . . largely influenced by the formation of seasonal sea ice at the lowest latitude in the northern hemisphere."

The seventy-kilometer strip of pristine forest jutting out into the Sea of Okhotsk is a haven for threatened migrating birds and home to brown bears, Blackiston's fish owls, sea lions, and many other animals. The Ainu named the peninsula "the end of the earth" and revered many of the animals that lived there. They considered the Blakiston's fish owl a divine being, calling it *"kotan koru kamuy,"* "God that protects the village."

As we cycled past large, black, volcanic rocks strewn along the coast, the misty, snow-lined mountains of Shiretoko Peninsula loomed ahead, and I felt we were approaching a place of mystery and danger.

A few hours into our ride, we caught up with Mr. Saito, pedaling his heavily laden bike steadily along the gorgeous coast.

As we pulled close behind him, Sho yelled out, "Saito-saaaaaan!"

He jerked his head back with a smile and said, *"Hayai neh!* Hey, you're fast!"

There was no traffic, so we pulled alongside him, pedaling at an easy pace. "We were trying to catch up with you," Sho said. "The game center in Abashiri was incredible, so we stayed for a while."

"I'm sorry I missed the fun. I left early to get a head start on you guys. So, do you think you already found the greatest game room in Japan?"

Sho thought for a moment and said, "That was a really good one. But I need to see more before I decide."

We rode together for a few hours, much of the route on a coastal highway with beautiful ocean views. As we neared Utoro, Mr. Saito pointed to a sign by the road. "Oshinkoshin Falls are just up ahead. It's one of Japan's best one hundred waterfalls and is supposed to be spectacular."

I eagerly anticipated seeing the falls and soon followed Mr. Saito into a parking lot next to a souvenir shop and toilets. Several cars and large tour buses sat in the lot. A group of elderly Japanese slowly spilled out of one of the buses, trailing behind a uniformed guide carrying a long stick with a red flag. As she walked, she yelled out to the group, "This way, please. Follow me, but please be careful."

As we walked past the souvenir shop, I could hear the satisfying roar of the falling water and saw a long wooden staircase leading up a steep hill into a forest. I overheard one of the members of the tour group complain, "How many stairs do we have to climb?"

After a few minutes, we reached a spot across from the falls designed for a photo op. Glistening white water streamed down a towering cliff bounded on either side by flourishing green foliage. The sound of the rushing water was soothing. We asked a friendly young man to take our picture. As Mr. Saito, Sho and I squeezed together with the waterfall at our backs, the young man held up the camera and yelled out, "*Hai, cheesu!* Say cheese!" Mr. Saito raised his left hand in a peace sign, while I draped an arm over Sho, who was still wearing his helmet.

We left the waterfall and thirty minutes later rolled into the heart of Utoro. Eiko and Saya were waiting for us outside of Shiretoko Prince Hotel, a large building at the top of a short, steep hill. Sho and I stood as we pedaled, swaying the bikes back and forth to generate momentum up the climb.

"Where's Saito-san?" Eiko asked, as we pulled to a stop in front of the hotel's ornate entrance.

I caught my breath for a moment, then said, "We just split up at the bottom of the hill. He's sleeping in his tent at a campsite tonight." Looking up at the luxurious hotel, I added, "I'm almost embarrassed to show him where we're staying."

"Well, after cycling for five days, I thought you both deserved a treat. This place is supposed to have a good *onsen* hot spring bath."

Dinner was an all-you-can-eat buffet in the hotel's monstrous dining hall. Sho filled his tray with five pieces of sushi, crab legs, tuna and salmon sashimi, sautéed broccoli, corn, white rice, *mikan* oranges, a bowl of *miso* soup and two scoops of ice cream.

I asked, "You sure you have enough there, buddy?"

"I'm a growing boy," he answered with a grin, stuffing a piece of tuna sashimi into his mouth.

As I was about to eat a bite of tofu precariously squeezed between my chopsticks, my cell phone rang. "*Moshi moshi?* Hello?"

"*Moshi moshi. Ishiwata desu.* Hey, it's Ishiwata. The guy from the place with a train in Lake Saroma where you slept two nights ago."

"Yes, of course, I remember you! How are you? How was the race?"

"Volunteering for the race was a lot of fun. Thank you for asking. I'm just calling to make sure you and Sho made it safely to Shiretoko Peninsula."

Mr. Ishiwata didn't need to hear about the cheek-on-window incident in Abashiri. "Yes, we made it here no problem, and we're enjoying a good meal."

"Oh, sorry to interrupt dinner. I just wanted to check on you. Please be careful on the rest of your journey."

"We will, I promise. Thanks for checking on us."

I hung up and explained who it was. Eiko grinned, "I can tell that you guys are going to make friends all over Japan."

After dinner, Eiko, Sho, Saya and I hiked from the hotel to a nearby overlook to watch the sun set. We arrived just in time to see the glowing orange orb dip into the Sea of Okhotsk's deep blue waters. The sun seemed to melt into the horizon, throwing off streams of colors as if being devoured by the shimmering sea. The speed with which it sank almost made me feel the earth's movement, and I swayed with a strange sense of vertigo and nervous urgency. I wrapped my arm around Sho's shoulders and felt his head cradled in my side.

After watching the sun disappear, we returned to our hotel room and donned slippers and colorful *yukata* robes. They were covered in a bright floral pattern, the robes for males blue and white, those for females red and white. Wearing only underwear underneath, I folded the front of the robe across my chest, right over left, and tied the colorful cotton sash around my waist to keep the front from falling open.

I looked at myself in a wall mirror as Eiko was helping Saya tie the sash on her tiny robe, which fit surprisingly well on her two-year-old frame.

Staring at my reflection, I said, "I can never remember— do men fold the robe right over left, or left over right?"

Eiko said, "I'm not sure actually. You'd think I'd know, having grown up in Japan. Why don't you wear it right over left, and I'll wear it left over right."

"Okay. It must not be that important."

We took an elevator to the first floor and shuffled through the lobby then down a broad corridor toward the hotel's indoor hot springs area. Our loose slippers made a funny flap flap sound as we walked, and Saya's bare feet slipped out of hers several times. We passed souvenir shops, restaurants and lounges while dodging meandering hotel guests, many of whom also wore the comfortable robes and slippers.

"There's the sign for the *onsen*!" Sho announced, pointing to a red cloth hanging over an entrance. On the cloth was the large white Japanese character 湯, pronounced "yu"and meaning "hot water." On the wall to the side was the character 女.

"That's the women's entrance." Eiko pointed to the sign on the wall, which meant 'woman.' "You and Daddy go in through the door with the blue cloth over there."

"Excuse me," interrupted a middle-aged woman wearing a *yukata* robe who had approached Eiko from the side. "Women are supposed to wear the robe right over left."

"Oh, excuse me. Thanks," Eiko said with a polite bow, fumbling with the robe. As the woman walked away, Eiko rolled her eyes. "I didn't want to contradict her, but honestly I am not sure she's correct. We should look this up when we get back to our room."

Sho and I entered the men's bath, took off our robes and folded them into baskets on a shelf. Sitting naked on plastic buckets set in front of low mirrors and sinks, we washed our hair and body with soap and shampoo supplied by the inn. After thoroughly rinsing off the suds, we sank carefully into a deep, hot pool, perhaps ten square feet. It would have been a faux pas to enter the water without cleaning off first or worse, to soap up in the tub. Another blunder in etiquette would have been to place our heads under the water. The same water would be used by numerous guests, and it was to be kept absolutely clean. Having bathed many times in Japanese *onsen* baths, Sho and I had internalized these strict rules and did not even think to violate them.

We returned to our hotel room relaxed and drowsy and were soon fast asleep. The next morning, we invited Mr. Saito to join us for some sight seeing and met him in front of our hotel. I sat behind the steering wheel, while Eiko, Sho and Saya sat in the back seat of our rental van, leaving the front seat for Mr. Saito. He locked up his bicycle beside the hotel and hopped in.

"*Ohayou gozaimasu!* Good morning! It feels strange to get into a car," he said, settling into the front seat and buckling his seatbelt.

"Yeah, my butt isn't used to so much cushioning!" Sho said with a grin.

We drove from the hotel along the coast. The road soon began to climb until we had a gorgeous view back down on Utoro and the sea. We pulled into a turnout to enjoy the sight. Several huge rocks jutted out of the hills along the shoreline.

"That one is known as Oronko Rock," said Mr. Saito, pointing to the largest and most impressive rock, which stood nearly 180 feet high.

We began driving again. The road left the coast and began to meander through deep forests. A light mist hung low, sifting through the glistening green all around us.

"Look Daddy! Deer!" Sho shouted excitedly.

"Where? Where?" Saya asked frantically.

Several brown deer lounged languidly beside the road and paused from nibbling grass to stare at us as we slowly drove past. Sho and Saya's faces and hands were plastered against the glass staring back. A few minutes later, I saw a fox dart from the road and disappear into the forest as we rounded a bend.

We finally reached the visitor center for Shiretoko Five Lakes, piled out of the van and entered the building. Mr. Saito, Eiko and Saya walked over to a counter manned by a park ranger, while Sho and I paused in front of a warning notice in Japanese on the wall with a picture of three brown bears lumbering across a road.

"Daddy, what does the sign say?" Sho asked.

"It says 'Lots of brown bears live in Shiretoko. Recently some bears seem not to be afraid of humans.'"

"That doesn't sound good," Sho said. He found another sign written in English and Japanese, entitled "To Help Save

Both You and Brown Bears." It included a collection of tips on avoiding a bear encounter, which I read out loud to Sho:

"Usually brown bears would not attack humans. They would rather avoid it," I read.

Sho interrupted, "Except for the ones who don't seem to be afraid of humans anymore."

"Hmm, maybe," I said and continued reading. "To avoid a brown bear encounter, let them know where you are in advance by talking, singing, having a bell to avoid a close surprise encounter. No dogs in bear country. Dogs would bark at brown bears, which excite them."

"That's fine. We don't have any dogs," Sho said. Then he added with a concerned look on his face, "But we do have Saya, which may be worse."

I continued reading, "What if you came across brown bears? Do not panic freak out! Stay calm. Do not run away or brown bears might follow you. What if you were attacked by brown bears? Spray 'bear spray' and/or lie on your stomach with your hands on the back of your neck. Remember, this should only be done as a last resort."

As I finished reading, Eiko came over to me and said, "I just spoke with a park ranger. He said that three of the five lakes are closed to tourists because too many bears are out."

"I'm fine with only visiting two lakes," Sho said quickly.

I threw Saya onto my shoulders as we left the information center and began hiking along a marked trail and wooden boardwalk toward one of the Shiretoko Five Lakes that was open to humans. Eiko and Mr. Saito walked beside one another chatting, while Sho ran back and forth, announcing his discoveries as he went.

The lakes, fed by underground springs, are said to resemble the fingerprints of a god and were created centuries ago when a local volcano, Mount Io, erupted. We hiked beneath a thickset green canopy, occasionally passing ancient, gnarled trees whose knotted roots formed intricate designs. As we emerged from the woods and came to a stop at the edge of the first lake, I gasped at the beautiful scene. In the distance a rolling mountain chain was dusted with snow, its reflection in the placid lake water yielding a beautiful symmetry. Saya let out an appreciative "Wow" at the sight. I lifted her off my shoulders and kneeled down to take a picture. Sho suddenly barreled into me from behind, knocking me over and nearly hitting Saya too.

"Ow, Sho. That hurt. Be careful," I said, pulling myself back up. I gave him an unhappy look, and he sulked away. I took a few pictures, then returned Saya to my shoulders. As I started walking again, Sho ran up to me and in an annoyingly whiny voice said, "Daddy, I want to ride on your shoulders."

Saya immediately said, "No!"

"Calm down, guys," I said. "Sho, I'll let you ride on my shoulders in a minute. Right now, it's Saya's turn."

"You never let me do anything!" Sho screamed and ran off.

Eiko left Mr. Saito and came over to me. "What was that all about?"

"I have no idea. I just told him to wait his turn to ride on my shoulders, and he overreacted."

As we hiked around the lake, we looked for Sho but could not find him. We followed the trail, which finally looped back toward the parking lot. I became increasingly anxious, as twenty minutes passed without any sign of him. Finally, I caught a glimpse of his scowling face peeking out from behind a tree.

"Come here, buddy," I said.

"No!" he yelled and sprinted ahead. I handed Saya to Eiko and said, "I'm gonna get him. I don't like him disappearing from sight, especially when there might be bears around."

I ran ahead until I finally reached the parking lot. I saw Sho duck behind the bathrooms, a small concrete structure about fifteen feet across. He peeked around the edge of the building, and when he saw me approach, he sprinted away. "Come back here, Sho. Right now!"

He tried to cut around the back of the building, but I had anticipated his move and he ran into me as I came around the other side. He tried to sprint past me, but I grabbed his arm and stopped him. "Sho, calm down. What is going on?" I noticed several Japanese tourists staring at us and immediately felt my face flush with embarrassment.

"No! Let go!" he yelled.

"I'm not letting go," I said angrily. "You shouldn't disappear like that when we are out hiking."

"Let go!" he yelled again.

"I'm taking you back to the van right now," I said and threw him over my shoulder.

He kicked his legs and flailed his arms, screaming, "No! Stop!"

I ignored the stares and marched toward the van, struggling to dig out my keys while maintaining a firm grip on Sho. As I got to the van and pushed him inside, Sho looked at me with wild eyes, tears flowing, and screamed, "I hate you!"

Chapter 14

Shiretoko Pass

SHO SULKED IN THE BACK SEAT OF OUR RENTAL VAN THROUGH-out the ride back to the Shiretoko Prince Hotel in Utoro. Head turned to the side and pressed against the window, he managed to pull his sweatshirt hood so far forward that it served as a cowl, partially covering his tear-stained face.

"Mommy, what wong with Sho?" Saya asked from her car seat by the opposite window. Eiko sat between the kids.

"He's just upset," Eiko said. "Let's leave him alone for a while."

"Sorry about the scene back there," I said to Mr. Saito, who sat in the front seat as I drove.

"*Kinishinaide*. Don't worry about it. My kids did the same when they were young. It's part of growing up, right?"

"Thank you for being so understanding."

When we reached the hotel, I parked the van near the entrance. Mr. Saito retrieved his bicycle and met us in front of the hotel. Strapping on his helmet, he said, "Well, I should head off now, if I'm going to make it to Rausu before nightfall. I enjoyed spending time with you all and hope the rest of your journey goes well."

He bowed to Eiko and me and waved to the kids.

Saya, who was cradled in Eiko's arms, waved back enthusiastically. Sho shuffled his feet, hiding behind Eiko and staring at the ground. As we watched Mr. Saito disappear down the steep hill leading away from the hotel, Eiko said, "Let's get some lunch into the kids. Hopefully that will help Sho out of his funk."

We found a cozy seaside restaurant perched atop a bluff and settled at a table by a window. Looking out, I could see a few people walking along a broad beach strewn with driftwood. In the distance, the hulking form of Oronko Rock stood sentry before the deep expanse of water.

Sho went to the bathroom, and I turned to Eiko, "What's your take on what happened with him on the hike?"

She thought for a moment, then said, "Well, he's probably a bit overwhelmed by this trip. It's been an intense first week, and he's figuring out how to cope with all the challenges—the weather, cycling all day, sleeping in a different place each night. He may be anxious about the prospect of spending two months apart from his mom and sister and dreading our departure in two days. And he is likely worried that he may not meet your high expectations. That's a lot for an eight-year-old."

I nodded, appreciating her wise counsel, and decided to bring this up with Sho when the time was right.

Eiko and I ate rice bowls topped with fresh crab and sea urchin, while Sho ate seafood curry on rice. Saya sat in her mom's lap, eating bits Eiko fed her with chopsticks, reminding me of a baby bird being fed. After swallowing a mouthful of curry, Sho looked at me as if he had just experienced an epiphany and said, "You know, some things look bad and smell bad. But they taste good. Like squid."

"And sea urchin," I added, holding up a piece of the brown, oozy goo between my chopsticks. "The first time I tried sea urchin, I thought I wouldn't be able to keep it down. The texture was so unappetizing. But I soon grew to love the taste."

Sho nodded, "Yep, that's the way I was with squid."

"You seem like you're in a better mood," Eiko said to Sho. "Can you tell me why you got so upset when we were out hiking?"

Sho blushed and looked down while stirring his curry. He mumbled, "I don't know."

"Well, don't worry about it," I said, leaning over and kissing him on the head. "Just try to use words to explain how you feel, instead of throwing a tantrum." I added, "You know who has every right to throw a tantrum? Saito-san. He's in the middle of a monster climb right now up to the Shiretoko Pass."

"Wouldn't it be funny if he jumped off his bike and started stomping his feet up and down?" Sho said, looking up with a sparkle in his eye.

"Yeah, and started wailing like a baby!" I said, laughing. "Boo hoo! This hill is too hard. No fair. Wah wah!"

Saya looked at us excitedly and joined in with a loud squeal.

Eiko glanced around at the handful of people in the restaurant, embarrassed, and shushed us. "Guys, quit being so . . ."

"American?" Sho asked sarcastically.

" . . . loud, I was going to say." Eiko said to me, "Thanks for getting the kids riled up."

"Well, it was funny," I said, bowing apologetically to the waitress who had glanced at our table. "But you kids keep it down, okay?" I said with mock seriousness.

"Daddy, actually do you think Saito-san is alright?" Sho asked.

"That's a good question. You know what? Let's find out. I wouldn't mind seeing Shiretoko Pass. It's the highest point on the only road that cuts across the peninsula and is supposed to have excellent views of Mt. Rausu and Kunashiri Island. And now that you mention it, I want to make sure that Saito-san isn't in trouble."

We finished our meal, apologized again to the waitress for being boisterous, and began to drive along Route 334 across Shiretoko Peninsula. The early afternoon was cloudy and pleasantly cool, and I kept my window rolled down to enjoy the fresh clean air. The flourishing forest seemed to breathe all around us, and I inhaled the crisp oxygen appreciatively. As we climbed further toward Shiretoko Pass, droplets of water began to form on the windshield, and the air cooled noticeably. A fine mist hung over the road and surrounding forest and grew steadily thicker as we climbed.

We drove slowly in the worsening conditions, the van's engine revving with the effort to maintain speed up the steep incline. As we rounded a corner, Sho shouted out, "There he is!"

Mr. Saito's head was down, his torso swaying back and forth to generate momentum as he slowly turned the pedals on his heavily laden bike. "It looks like he's barely moving," Sho observed.

"Well, it's a steep climb, and he's carrying a lot of gear."

We pulled alongside Mr. Saito, and I leaned out the window. He was panting hard and staring down at this front wheel as he pedaled, several beads of water hanging precariously across the front of his helmet. When I called his name, he looked over with a surprised smile and came to a stop.

"We decided to check on you," I said, putting on the flashers and stopping the van. "How are you doing?"

He caught his breath, then smiled at Sho and Saya in the back seat. "Hi kids!" He turned back to me and said, "I'll survive, but man, this is challenging. It's not only steep, but the winds are gusting from the front and side. It's slow going."

"You're making good progress," Eiko said from the front passenger seat. "We've been tracking the mileage, and you're about half way up."

"That means I've gone less than five miles in an hour and a half." He shook his head. "Looks like it's going to take me three hours to make it to the top."

"Do you need anything?" I asked.

"No, I'm good. But I appreciate that you all checked on me."

"We're headed to the pass. We'll come back and let you know about the conditions."

"Thanks. That's nice of you."

"You got it. Hang in there," I said and pulled away. Sho and Saya waved out the window and yelled, "Go Saito-san!"

We drove up and up, around winding turns, and soon the road and surrounding forest were shrouded in a thick mist. I squinted into the soupy mess and mumbled, "Well . . ." letting my voice trail off.

Eiko knew what I was thinking and said, "Oh, this is not good."

"I was trying to think of an optimistic thing to say, but frankly, this is going to be a tough climb for Saito-san. It just doesn't stop."

"We're inside a cloud," Sho said, staring out the window. "This rocks!"

When we finally reached the pass and pulled into a parking lot by an overlook, Eiko said, "You can't see a thing. Saito-san won't even get the reward of a good view after cycling all the way to the top."

"And it's going to be treacherous riding down the other side of the mountain with such poor visibility. The road is wet, and there will certainly be a lot of sharp curves on the steep grade. He'll need to be extremely cautious."

I stepped out of the car and was met with a strong blast of cold, wet air. My glasses immediately fogged up, and I pulled my jacket closer around my neck. "Want to walk around a little?" I asked, but Eiko, Sho and Saya were content to stay inside the comfort of our van.

"Okay. I'll be back in a sec." I shut the door and walked over to a large stone monument at the edge of a steep, tree-covered incline. Wisps of mist streamed around the white characters that were engraved in the monument's side, "Shiretoko Pass."

I turned on my video camera and narrated the scene, wind gusts threatening to drown out my words. "This probably would have been a nice view," I said, panning the camera from the monument across the white nothingness. Although I could not see more than a few dozen feet, I could feel the expansiveness of the surrounding wilderness like a powerful silent presence and sensed the danger I would be in if I chose to wander into the shrouded forest.

When we returned to Mr. Saito, I explained, "You have about four miles to go before you reach the top. It gets really foggy about two miles out, so be careful of drivers who may not be able to see you until the last minute." He had already turned on a blinking red light that made the surrounding mist glow faintly with each pulse.

"Please promise to call us when you get to Rausu," Eiko added. "And take it very slowly on the descent."

"Yes ma'am," Mr. Saito said with a smile and pushed off. We waited inside the van for a few moments, watching him lean into the gusting wind and struggle his way up the mountain road.

That night, Sho and I sat next to one another in a steaming *onsen*, nude and submerged up to our necks in the hot pool. Small white towels rested on our heads, mine folded neatly, Sho's precariously leaning to one side in a haphazard bunch. Five other men shared our tub, each one sitting quietly. As one got up to leave, he moved slowly so that he would not create a splash and modestly covered himself with a small towel as he stood up.

I leaned my head back against the side of the large stone tub, stretched out my legs and breathed deeply. Sho copied my movements and seemed, like me, to be deeply relaxed.

"Tomorrow's forecast calls for a big thunderstorm, you know," I said.

"Are we gonna ride?"

"Yep, nearly sixty miles to a town called Bihoro. Expect to get wet. The weather is cool, so you have to wear a rain jacket, your rain pants and booties over your shoes. Understand?"

"Yes."

"You're not going to throw a tantrum like you did during that storm a couple days ago, right?"

"No."

"Good." I turned to look him in the eyes. "Sho, I want you to understand that we are a team on this ride. When Mommy and Saya leave the day after tomorrow, it will be up to the two of us to figure out our route, where to get food, where to sleep, and deal with any mechanical problems."

Sho nodded, and I continued, "Think of yourself as a team member, not as a little kid. You don't need to throw a temper tantrum to get my attention for what you need. Just use your words. I'd welcome your advice on any of our decisions. I may not agree with every one of your suggestions, but I promise to listen to you. I can't do this trip without your help. And I know that you can do it."

A smile grew on Sho's face and he stuck out his hand. As I shook it, he looked me in the eye and said, "Deal!"

Chapter 15
Saying Goodbye

I KNEW WE WERE IN FOR IT WHEN I WAS AWAKENED BY A lightning strike that lit up our hotel room with a bright flash. Immediately after, a monstrous thunder clap rattled the water glasses that sat on a wooden side table. I struggled unsuccessfully to fall back to sleep while the heavy downpour raged outside. The storm had knocked out phone and Internet service throughout the entire town of Utoro. I knew this because the police announced the fact every few minutes on a booming loud speaker in the center of town, adding helpfully that they had no idea when service would be restored.

I glanced at my watch. 5:00 a.m. As I lay on my back looking up, strange shadows scratched across the ceiling in syncopation with the lightning dancing outside our window. Another thunder clap boomed overhead, rousing Sho, who had been asleep next to me. He rolled over with an annoyed groan and, eyes still closed, asked groggily, "Daddy, do we really have to ride today?"

"Yeah, sorry. If we only ride when the weather is pleasant, we'll never cover the 2,500 miles to Cape Sata before it's time to return to the U.S." In fact, one week into the trip, we were already a day behind schedule. I had overestimated our average speed and underestimated the head and cross winds. "It's not yet time to get up, though. Try to go back to sleep if you can."

He gave me a baleful look, then pulled his pillow from beneath his head and draped it over his eyes.

A few hours later, Sho and I bundled up in our rain gear and rolled out of the hotel parking lot into the wet, windy, cold day. I expected the nearly sixty-mile trek to the town of Bihoro to take us about seven hours. Eiko honked good-bye as she and Saya drove off, wipers on high and spraying rainwater off the sides of the rental van's windshield. The heavy thumping of thick raindrops echoed inside my helmet and made it difficult to hear Sho as we pedaled through the storm. He wasn't saying much anyway, head down and hunched over his handlebars attempting to keep the rain out of his eyes.

Although I wore several layers of clothing beneath my rain jacket and pants, I was soon chilled. As we wound our way along the windswept coast, I actually looked forward to the uphill climbs, when the exertion would warm me up. After riding for two and a half hours through the driving rain, we met Eiko and Saya in the parking lot of a 7-11. We left the bikes beneath the convenience store's awning and crammed inside the rental van. Eiko had laid towels on the seats, and although the van's engine was off, the air was still warm.

"It f-f-f-feels nice in here," Sho said, squeezing into the back seat, while I plopped into the front passenger seat, my soggy rain pants making a squishing sound.

"You're so wet!" Saya said, perched in her car seat and pointing at Sho's head. "Everywhere!" she added, looking at his soaked clothes.

"You're shivering, Sho!" Eiko said, admonishing me with a quick look. "Let's get you out of those wet clothes." She turned around in the driver's seat and reached back to rub his head with a towel. Helping Sho to pull off his dripping jacket and shirts, she asked me, "Do you have some dry clothes for him?"

"Yeah, back on the bike," I said, not relishing the thought of leaving the comfort of the van. I sprinted through puddles across the parking lot and took refuge from the steady rain under the store awning. As I dug out a change of Sho's clothes from a saddlebag, a speaker overhead played the catchy Japanese theme song for 7-11. "*Sebum Erebum . . . Ee kibun!* 7-11 . . . Good feeling." In a nearby parking spot, a man sat in his idling car, smoking a cigarette with the windows up.

I ran back to the van and jumped into the front seat, slamming the door behind me. Rain pounded rhythmically on the roof, and water streamed down the fogged up windows. Eiko had moved to the back seat next to Sho, who now had one of her sweatshirts wrapped around his body and a towel around his head. He looked up at me with a contented smile, snuggling into her. I felt a pang of inadequacy. No matter how nurturing I tried to be, I knew I could not match the comfort Sho felt in his mother's arms.

After Sho and I were dry, the four of us huddled in the van, nibbling on salmon rice balls wrapped in seaweed and listening to the rain.

"I decided to start the ride in Hokkaidō because it's not supposed to have a rainy season, unlike the rest of Japan this time of year," I complained.

"Yeah, it's as if the rainy season has moved north," Eiko added. "Strange. Hopefully it will clear up for you guys later in the day."

After we finished eating, I said, "We should get under way, so we make it to Bihoro before nightfall. It doesn't look like the rain is going to let up any time soon. You ready Sho?"

Warm and dry with a full belly, he looked at me with renewed vigor and said, "Let's teach this rain a lesson!"

"That's the spirit." Turning to Eiko, I said, "We'll see you around six."

Sho and I gave Saya a kiss goodbye and returned to our bikes. The man was still sitting in his car, which had been idling for at least thirty minutes. He was now talking on his cell phone, reclining in the driver's seat. I made a face and shook my head.

"What's wrong, Daddy?" Sho asked.

"I'm just annoyed at that guy for idling his car for so long. I can taste the exhaust hovering all around our bikes."

"I like the smell," Sho said, taking a few whiffs.

"Well, it's terrible for you."

"Why?" Sho asked, looking suspiciously at the exhaust pipe of the man's car.

"Exposure to soot and fumes increases the chance of heart disease, lung disease and asthma. Exhaust is particularly bad for kids, whose lungs are not fully developed. And the carbon dioxide collects in the atmosphere, contributing to global warming."

"Okay. I'll hold my breath!"

Sho and I pedaled our connected bikes onto the black, shiny, wet road and soon encountered a series of rolling hills that slowed our pace and made my knees ache as I pushed our heavy load up the long climbs. We passed farms and verdant forests that glistened with drops of water steadily pattering off shivering green leaves. The rain finally let up near the end of the afternoon, although it remained cloudy and cool. We had been soaked, but the steady breeze from cycling dried our clothes quickly.

A small shop on the left side of the road appeared ahead, several vending machines lined in front. It was the first shop we had seen for a while.

As we came to a stop, a woman in her fifties, presumably the manager, stepped out of the small store. Farmland stretched around us in all directions, and I saw no other customers.

"Hello," she said with a smile. "I like your bikes!"

"Thanks. I just relax up front while he does all the work," I said pointing back at Sho.

She laughed at my joke and said, "Well, you picked a miserable day to ride. I'm sorry the weather isn't better for you. It's rained a lot more than usual this summer." Then glancing at our saddlebags, she added, "How far are you going?"

When I told her our plans to cycle the length of Japan, she said, "*Sugoi!* That's incredible! Just the two of you?"

"Yes, it's a charity ride for a tree planting campaign."

"Hold on," she said and rushed back into her shop. She returned with two rice balls and a 1,000 yen bill (about ten dollars). "Here, you must be hungry from all that riding. Take these, no charge. And here's a donation."

"That's very generous of you. Thanks," I said. Sho immediately started eating one of the rice balls and let out a satisfying "mmm good."

"Where will you sleep tonight?" the store manager asked.

"We'll stay at a *minshuku* inn in Bihoro."

"That's where I'm from. It's about fifteen miles down the road." Turning to Sho, she asked, "Do you know what 'Bihoro' means?"

Sho thought for a moment then guessed, "Place with a game room?"

The woman laughed, "Hmm, I don't think so. It's mainly a farming town. The name comes from the Ainu word 'piporo', which means, "place with a lot of water." Probably because there are some impressive lakes around here. Lake Abashiri is back the way you came. And if you ride over Bihoro Pass, you'll get a good view of Lake Kussharo. But it's a tough climb over the pass even for a car. I can't imagine trying it on a bicycle."

"We're headed inland over to Highway 274, then south on Highway 237 until the coast," I said.

"Wow, you're ambitious. You'll go over several mountain passes and through some long tunnels on that route."

"Well, we may have to walk the bikes up some of the steep sections, but we'll give it a go." I could tell by her look that she did not like the idea, but she held her tongue.

That night, I lay in bed reading to Sho and Saya, who were snuggled close on either side of me. We had taken long, hot baths in the inn and were wrapped in comfortable cotton *yukata* robes. Eiko lounged at the base of the bed, giving Sho a foot massage. His eyes were dreamy and his look said, "Life is good." Riding much of the day in cold rain intensified a sense of luxurious comfort. And knowing that Eiko and Saya would return to the U.S. the following day magnified the joy I felt from their presence.

The next day, Sho and I rode thirty-five miles to the town of Rikubetsu. After the previous day's long ride through cold rain and wind, we were relieved to encounter cloudy and cool weather. My legs felt heavy, and we rode at an easy pace, paused for a tasty lunch of soba noodles in a town called Tsubetsu, and visited a wooden craft museum with Eiko and Saya.

We arrived in Rikubetsu, population 2,800, in the late afternoon and checked into a room at the visitor center, a simple concrete structure with small guest rooms next to a Seico Mart convenience store. Eiko and Saya had an early flight out of Sapporo the following morning and planned to drive four and a half hours to Chitose Airport in the evening.

The four of us stood beside our rental van in the convenience store parking lot. It was time to say goodbye. I knelt down beside Saya and gave her a hug, then another and another. "Daddy is silly!" she said, finally pushing me away.

"Well, this is it," I said, turning to Eiko. I hugged her tenderly and said, "Thanks for everything. I'll miss you."

She gave me a kiss. "I was happy to be a small part of this crazy trip. Just be careful and promise me that you will use good judgment."

"I will."

She turned to Sho and gave him a long hug. "You keep your daddy out of trouble, okay?" He nodded. "I love you."

Sho and I stood in the parking lot and waved goodbye as they drove off. After they disappeared, he looked up at me and said, "It's just you and me now."

Chapter 16

Unexpected Treats

THE NEXT MORNING, SHO AND I ENTERED THE HOTEL'S SIMple breakfast room and lined up by a small buffet to fill our plates. We sat at a long table that already held about a dozen men wearing work clothes or business suits.

A man in a suit sitting across from us nodded his head in a friendly greeting. "Good morning."

"Good morning," I responded.

"You speak good Japanese," he said politely. "Are you and your son here on vacation?"

I explained our plans, and he nodded his head slowly. "I did not expect that answer. Wow. I don't know anyone who has tried to do such a thing, let alone with a kid. I'm Okuda by the way. Nice to meet you."

We introduced ourselves, and I asked, "Are you here on a business trip?"

"Yeah, an extended one. I manage Nissan's Hokkaidō Proving Ground Vehicle Test Department. My wife and children live in Tokyo, but I spend six months out of each year up here testing cars for all-weather driving. Rikubetsu is the coldest town in Japan. If a car can handle this place, it will do fine anywhere in the country. In the winter, the temperature regularly drops to below zero degrees Fahrenheit and often gets much colder than that, although not as much recently."

"Doing *tanshin-funin* must be hard," I said sympathetically.

He nodded, acknowledging the sacrifice stoically.

I had used the Japanese term for a business person who lives apart from his family for work. Literally translated, the words mean, "to be deployed alone." It is not uncommon for companies to ship an employee off to another city or even foreign country with only a few weeks' notice. The assumption is that if the employee, typically male, has children, his wife takes care of them back home.

I said to Mr. Okuda, "We decided to start our ride in Hokkaidō because we thought it would be drier than the rest of Japan this time of year. But we're not having great luck."

"Yeah, something weird is going on with the weather. In the past few years, there seems to be more rain and more intense storms, and it's definitely getting warmer around here."

We chatted for a while longer while finishing breakfast. Then Mr. Okuda accompanied us outside to see our bikes. He took several pictures, saying, "My kids will love to see this set-up."

We finally said farewell to him and were loading the saddlebags on our bikes when my phone rang. It was Eiko. She and Saya were getting ready to board their flight. "Did you get my e-mail?" she asked.

"No. I haven't checked yet. What did you say?"

"Last night, I drove on Highway 274 along the route you are planning to ride. It's dangerous, worse than what Saito-san experienced at Shiretoko Pass. There are steep mountain climbs with switchbacks, fog, long tunnels and dangerous descents. It isn't safe for you to ride that way."

I recalled the store manager's knowing, concerned look from two days earlier. And even though I had planned to ride over mountains on this trip, I wasn't sure I was ready to tackle them yet, worried I might injure my knees or back riding with so much weight on our bikes.

Taking out a map, I said, "Well, we could change our route so that we head back toward the coast, which would avoid the mountains. It's longer and will probably add a day or two . . ."

"Yeah, do that," Eiko said with obvious relief in her voice. "I've got to go. They are calling our flight."

I hung up and explained our change of plans to Sho. We spent a few minutes hunched over the map before deciding to cycle sixty-five miles to the town of Urahoro. I estimated we would cover the distance in about eight hours, including stops.

We rode for several hours through the morning before stopping for lunch at a *michi no eki* rest stop in a comfortable small town called Honbetsu. As we parked our bikes beside a restaurant, a slender middle-aged man wearing overalls and boots approached us. His face was deeply tanned and creased, his hands worn and wrinkled.

Leaning over to inspect our bikes, he said, "I've never seen a set-up like this before. Mind if I take a look?"

"Feel free," I said. From his dress and demeanor, I guessed that he was a farmer. And from the close interest he was taking in our bikes, I suspected that he had many years' experience fixing a variety of equipment. Pointing to the sturdy aluminum hitch that was mounted on my bike's rear rack, I explained, "The front of my son's trailer cycle fits into the hitch here and is held in place by these two chrome hex nuts. The hitch has ball-bearing guided pivots so that it moves smoothly. And the trailer cycle has a twist grip shifter with seven speeds, so that my son can spin easily up steep climbs or use a heavy gear on fast flat sections."

I did not know the Japanese words for "hitch", "chrome hex nuts," or "ball-bearing guided pivots," so, using a common trick that sometimes works, I simply inserted the English words with a Japanese pronunciation. "Hitch" became *"he-chu."* "Chrome hex nuts" became *"kuromu hekusu natsu."*

And "ball-bearing guided pivots" became *"bo-ru beyaringu pibotto."* He didn't show any sign of confusion at my creative Japanese.

"*Naruhodo neh.* Hmm, I see," he said, nodding his head. "How far are you riding?"

Sho answered nonchalantly, "All of Japan. We started at the top and are riding to the bottom."

I gave the man our card and explained that it was a charity ride. He said, "Whoa, that's amazing. Hold on." Digging into his pocket, he pulled out 3,000 yen (about thirty dollars) in change and handed it to Sho. "Here, take this. Good luck with your trip. Thanks for letting me look at your bikes."

"Wow, thanks mister!" Sho said gratefully, and the man waved goodbye and walked to his nearby truck.

Sho and I entered the restaurant, sat down at a small table and ordered lunch. As we waited for our food to arrive, I pulled out a pamphlet about Ainu culture. "Sho, check this out," I said. "You know how we keep passing through towns whose names end in '*betsu*'?"

"Like Rikubetsu, where we slept last night?" he said.

"Yeah. We've also gone through Hamatonbetsu and Tsubetsu. We're now in Honbetsu. This pamphlet explains that the word '*betsu*' is derived from the Ainu word '*pet*,' which means river."

"So all those towns must have a river in them!"

"That's a logical conclusion," I said. "I like the way you figure things out."

Sho nodded with pride, then asked, "I've been trying to figure this one out: if a baby farts in his mommy's tummy, does she burp?" I burst out laughing, causing a few guests at neighboring tables to glance at me.

After lunch, to confirm that we were on the correct route to Urahoro, Sho and I approached a silver-haired man with liver spots on his forehead and deep rings under his eyes. He stood behind a candy stand and wore a light blue short-sleeved button-down shirt covered by a yellow apron monogrammed with the words "*Honbestu Michi no Eki*" (Honbetsu Rest Stop) across the front.

"I'm sorry to bother you," I said, taking out my map. "We're cycling to Urahoro, and I just wanted to confirm that we are taking the correct route."

He looked at where I pointed on the map and said, "Yes, you're going the right way. Are you riding too?" he asked, looking down at Sho.

"Yes, sir!"

"What do you like best about riding?" he asked, smiling.

"I like all the farms and horses and cows we've seen so far."

"Well, you might like this too. Follow me," he said, stepping out from behind the small counter. He took us through the rest stop entrance, around a corner and pointed at a large window on a shaded side of the building. "Ever seen one of those?"

About three feet off the ground, a large shiny black beetle clung to the glass, unmoving. Around three inches long and nearly two inches wide, it had a rigid armor-like exoskeleton and small spiny legs that seemed too small to hold its heavy body to the glass. The creature's most distinctive feature was a dramatic curved horn that stuck out from its thorax. Another shorter horn jutted out, reminding me of a rhinoceros tusk. "*Kabuto-mushi!* A Rhinoceros beetle!" Sho exclaimed.

"That's right," the old man said approvingly. "This one is a male. You can tell because it has horns, which are used for digging or to fight other males during mating season. You can touch it if you want. Rhino beetles don't bite or sting. Just be gentle."

Sho demurred, preferring simply to look at it and snap a few pictures.

"Rhino beetles are nocturnal," the man continued. "So it's unusual for one to be hanging out like this in the middle of the day. But I've seen this one several times over the past few weeks. I think he likes the warmth of the glass, but I'm not sure."

We thanked the friendly man and turned toward our bikes.

"One moment, please," the man said, scurrying back into the rest stop. He returned holding out a small, bulging bag. Handing it to Sho, he said, "You'll need plenty of energy on your long journey. Here's some candy."

"Wow, thanks!" Sho said, taking the bag with a polite bow. As we returned to our bikes and started to ride away, Sho looked back at the Honbetsu rest area and said, "This was our best stop ever!"

We rode for several hours along Route 56, a fairly flat, picturesque country road that occasionally took us past sprawling farmland. The early afternoon sun was hidden behind clouds, and I wore a light jacket against the cool air. Dense forests loomed in the distance, framing large fenced-off pastures. As we passed a dozen big-bellied cows lethargically chewing grass behind a roadside fence, Sho greeted them.

"Moo! Yeah, I'm talking to you, third brown cow on the left. Moo! That's right, you, the one with the floppy ears. Moooo!" The cows simultaneously paused mid-chew and looked up.

"Making new friends?" I asked as the cows disappeared behind us.

Sho ignored my question and responded, "Daddy, tomorrow is the fourth of July, right?"

"Yep."

"Can we shoot off fireworks?"

It was a fair request, but I had no idea how to make it happen. Summers in Japan are full of fireworks festivals, but I did not know where to buy fireworks. I said with more confidence than I felt, "Sounds like fun! Let's ask around in the next town. Maybe we can find a store that sells them."

"Shoot!" Sho said in an annoyed tone.

"Relax, buddy. I said we'd look for a store."

"I'm not talking about the fireworks. My chain just fell off."

I glanced back and saw that he was stepping hard on the pedals, but they would not move. I stopped the bikes and investigated. Several links were stuck between the smallest chain ring and the bike frame. I tried to pull them out, but the chain was jammed in.

I worked the gritty links back and forth, but my hands became greasy and started to slip, so I put on gloves and took out a flathead screwdriver. Pulling on the chain with one hand, I slowly wedged the screwdriver back and forth against the frame until the chain finally slipped free. I placed the chain links on the sprocket teeth and spun the pedals several rotations to confirm that it was in position.

"That was a pain," I said. "If it happens again, don't push down hard on the pedals. That just wedges in the chain even more."

After about twenty minutes of cycling, Sho yelled out, "Daddy, the chain's off again."

I stopped the bikes and returned the chain links to the sprocket, just as I had before, but I needed to keep the problem from recurring. While Sho held the rear wheel off the ground, I turned the pedals with my left hand and shifted the gears up and down with my right, watching the rear derailleur move back and forth beside the spinning wheel. After a few shifts, I deduced that the derailleur needed to be adjusted. The chain didn't fall off while I was watching, but I could see how it might with a little extra pressure or jostling. Taking out a multi-tool, I made a few adjustments.

"That should do it," I said, standing up, leaning back into a lower-back stretch, and hoping I had fixed the problem.

As he climbed on, Sho wagged his finger at the trailer cycle and said, "No more trouble now."

My roadside adjustments seemed to have worked, and we had no more mechanical trouble over the next four hours as we covered the rest of the 65-mile ride into Urahoro. Near the end of the afternoon, we rolled onto the quiet town's tree-lined streets, passing suburban homes, community buildings and small shops. As I navigated past a large stone post at the entrance to a bike lane, my front wheel suddenly lurched to the side, and we jerked to a stop.

I slammed my feet to the ground, nearly toppling over. Sho shouted, "Whoa!" as he leapt off his saddle. "What happened, Daddy?" I had miscalculated the extra width of my heavily loaded bike and slammed the front left saddlebag into the post. The front rack was still attached, but the screw was bent, and the saddlebag leaned in precariously close to the wheel spokes.

I pushed the saddlebag back in place, but when I let go, the heavy bag flopped back toward the wheel spokes like a loose tooth. The bag was held in place by only two screws connected to eyelets on the bike's front fork, and now one of them was bent.

Sho rummaged through our gear and pulled out a bungee cord. "Good thinking," I said, mussing his hair. I fastened the cord tightly around the dangling saddlebag and the front rack, then gently tested the strength by pushing the saddlebag from the side. It held firm.

"Did you fix it, Daddy?" Sho asked. I was squatting beside the front wheel, and he leaned over my shoulder to inspect my work.

"Yeah, kinda sorta, thanks to your idea, but it's only a temporary fix," I said. "I need to replace the screw, but I didn't think to bring any spares. If the screw snaps while we're riding, the saddlebag will swing into the front spokes. That could happen if we hit a bump while zooming down a steep hill, which would make for a nasty crash. Let's look for a bike shop in town."

After asking around, we found out the locations of a campsite on the outskirts of town and a public bath. Urahoho did not have a bike shop, however, and I hoped that the saddlebag would stay in place until we found one. We set up at the campsite first, paying fifteen dollars for the privilege, and stowed our gear inside our tent. Our four-pound, two-person

Viperine II tent looked like a midget next to the giants that campers had set up nearby. Everyone else had arrived by cars parked next to their tents like protective sentries. One family had set out a charcoal grill and lounge chairs beside a towering enclosure that could probably hold ten people comfortably.

After stowing our gear in the tent, Sho and I climbed on our bikes and rode out of the campsite in search of food and a bath. Without the four saddlebags, the bikes felt wonderfully unburdened, and the pedals responded to my feet like a horse that wanted to canter.

"When are we getting fireworks?" Sho asked in a plaintive voice. I had completely forgotten.

"We'll look for a place that sells them," I said without much confidence. Where I grew up in Tennessee, fireworks stores advertised on large billboards beside the highways, but I had not seen any so far in Hokkaidō.

I thought I saw suspicion in his eyes, but he did not comment further. It was nearly 7 p.m. and would soon get dark, so I switched on the light attached to my handlebars as we rode toward the public bath.

After cleaning off and soaking for twenty minutes in a deep tub of steaming water at the public bathhouse, we cycled further into town and found a local *izakaya* pub and restaurant. A brightly colored rectangular cloth hung from a bamboo pole draped over the door. Called *noren,* these cloths protect the shop from wind and also indicate to prospective customers that the business is open. The cloth nearly reached the ground and had two long vertical slits.

Pushing aside the colorful *noren,* we entered a cramped, smoky room. Its five tables were already filled, but the friendly proprietor offered us seats at the counter, behind which lay an open kitchen with pots of boiling water and surfaces full of food in the making. We squeezed into two seats at the end of a row next to a young man, perhaps twenty-five years old, who was nursing a beer.

"Here, let me give you some more space," he said, scooting his stool over a bit.

I nodded thanks, then glanced at the hand-written menu on the wall. As Sho and I discussed what to order, an apron-clad elderly man behind the counter approached us holding two heated *oshibori* hand towels on a tray. He used tongs to pick up one of the small, steaming white towels and gingerly placed it into my hands. The heat stung for a brief moment, then quickly dissipated as I fluffed the towel open several times before rubbing my hands clean. The sensation was both relaxing and refreshing. When Sho received his towel, he started bouncing it back and forth between his hands like a game of hot potato and exclaimed, "Hot, hot, hot!"

The young man seated beside us gave Sho a sympathetic smile.

We ordered grilled octopus, edamame, sashimi and chicken skewers. "An Asahi beer for me and an orange juice for my son," I added.

"*Kashikomarimashita.* I understand," the proprietor said, turning back to fill our order.

When our drinks arrived, our young neighbor raised his beer, nodded to us and said, "*Kampai!* Cheers!" His face was flushed from drinking alcohol, but his eyes were alert and engaged. Probably has a good buzz, but isn't totally drunk, I thought to myself. I could tell that he wanted to chat, which was fine with me.

Sho and I raised our glasses and said, "*Kampai!*"

"Do you live around here?" he asked.

"No, we're just passing through. What about you?"

"Born and raised, like most of the people in here," he said with a brief glance around the cozy *izakaya*.

The waiter set a plate of sashimi before us, thin strips of raw tuna, yellowtail, squid, and mackerel. The fish were placed on a bed of long, thin strands of daikon white radish amid a few green parilla leaves. With quick, practiced movements, the apron-clad proprietor rubbed the end of a thick wasabi root on a metal *oroshigane* scraper, creating a mound of fresh wasabi paste that he let fall onto a small side dish.

The young man glanced at the wasabi and said, "It's so much better fresh like that than eating it pre-packaged from a tube." Then he looked at Sho and warned, "The fresh stuff is really spicy, though. Be careful when you eat it!"

"I don't eat wasabi. Too spicy," Sho said, pouring some soy sauce into a small dish and dipping in the edge of a fat piece of tuna.

"You're a smart kid," the young man said with a grin. He finished off his beer and ordered another. "You said you're just passing through. Where are you headed?"

"Hiroo, then around Erimo Misaki. We're on bicycles."

"That's cool. It gets windy along the coast though, so be careful."

"Yeah, it's been windy ever since Cape Sōya," Sho said.

"You rode bikes here from Cape Sōya?" the young man said, looking at us with a mixture of disbelief and concern.

"Actually . . ." I explained our plans, and he shook his head and smiled.

"You guys are cool! I want to buy you both a drink."

"No, that's okay," I said, shaking my head. "We've got plenty already. Thanks though." He looked a little disappointed but did not insist.

I added, "It's been rainier than I expected. It's wetter in Hokkaidō this year than usual, I think."

"Yeah, everybody is blaming it on global warming. Who knows? Whatever. It's too big of a problem for me to do anything about. I'll be happy if I can just find a job."

"That's tough," I said, giving him a sympathetic nod.

"I used to work at a paper mill, but it burned down a few months ago. The owner had insurance for the building, but not for the machines. Or so he said. He decided not to rebuild, and I've been looking for a job ever since. But it's hard in a small town like this with only 6,000 people."

After chatting a while longer, he ordered a third beer and offered once more to buy us food and drink. But I demurred.

After we finished eating and prepared to go, he asked, "Where are you sleeping?"

"In the campsite."

He furrowed his brows in thought then declared, "Bears are active this time of year, but I think you'll probably be safe. Don't leave any food in your tent, though."

Sho gave me a concerned glance as we passed out of the *izakaya* into the quiet, dark night. Urahoro was deserted at 8:30 p.m. We cycled back to the campsite, a ten-minute ride through silent, eerily empty side streets. The faint, orange-tinted glowing orbs of occasional street lamps seemed to float within the gloomy mist. "Daddy, this is really spooky. Where is everyone?"

"Probably getting ready for bed, which we should be doing too," I said calmly, although I couldn't help but feel a little spooked myself. We left behind the final streetlight at the edge of town and pedaled into the murky forest toward our campsite. Darkness enveloped us, and the small light on my front handlebars created strange bouncing shadows that leapt across the road. Sho whimpered, and I pedaled a little faster.

We reached our tent quickly, and as we propped the bikes against a tree, Sho complained, "We never found fireworks!"

"I know. I should have asked that guy at the *izakaya*. Let's check around tomorrow," I said, slightly ashamed that I continued to put off his request. I wanted Sho to have fun, but after cycling sixty-five miles, figuring out how to find fireworks felt like a low priority compared to finding food, a place to sleep and bathe, and worrying about the bikes' mechanical issues.

Sho pouted but was suddenly distracted by a boy about his age who tiptoed by holding a net. The boy glanced at us with a serious demeanor, put a finger to his lips and said, "Shh."

"What are you doing?" Sho asked in a whisper.

"Hunting beetles," he whispered back.

"I saw a Rhinoceros beetle earlier today!" Sho said.

"That's what I'm looking for!" the boy replied. "Want to help me find one?"

Sho looked up at me. "Daddy, can I?"

"Fine with me. Just don't go so far that I can't see you," I said, tossing my helmet onto the bike's handlebars. As Sho moved off with the boy, a man walked up, holding a net identical to the boy's.

"Hello!" he said with a polite bow. "My name's Oomori, and that's my seven-year-old son, Kazuki. We're in the tent over there," he said, pointing to the large tent I had noticed earlier. The charcoal grill was now lit and its coals emitted a satisfying red glow. Mr. Oomori's wife and a younger boy who looked around three were standing nearby carefully studying a tree. "We're all trying to find beetles. And we're going to shoot off fireworks a little later. You and your son are welcome to join us."

We spent the next hour hanging out with the Oomori family. When they handed out sparklers to the kids, Sho danced around like a wild boy, giggling and making crazy faces. When the sparkler finally burned itself out, he gave me a hug. "Daddy, I can't believe that we actually got to shoot off fireworks, even though we're in the middle of nowhere!"

I turned to Mr. Oomori and explained, "He kept asking me for fireworks, but I didn't know where to find any. Then you magically appeared!"

He laughed and said, "You can buy them at pretty much any convenience store. They are easy to find."

Mr. Oomori explained that he loved the outdoors and was introducing his wife and kids to camping. "I've got a blog about fishing, and I'm trying to get my family to spend more time in nature. My boys love sitting in front of the TV or playing video games, but they don't know how much of the real world they are missing. Is there anything better than looking for Rhino beetles on a summer night?"

Sho and I slept in the next morning and hung around the campsite with our new friends until 11 a.m. While Sho explored a nearby stream with Mr. Oomori's two boys, I broke down the tent and loaded our gear onto the bikes. I discovered that my rear tire had a flat, which must have occurred at the end of last night's ride through the dark. I patched the tube and secured the front saddlebag with the bungee cord, adding a second one for good measure.

Sho didn't want to say goodbye to his new friends, but he finally gave them a reluctant farewell. Leaving Urahoro, we quickly reached the end of Route 56, then turned east on Highway 38, joining a steady stream of trucks that roared by us at high speeds. Although we were only on the busy highway for a few miles, I breathed a sigh of relief when we turned onto Highway 336, a lightly trafficked road that rolled through gorgeous countryside. There were no stores and few vending machines along this stretch, but we had plenty of snacks with us. We covered fifty miles in six hours of riding to the seaside town of Hiroo on the eastern coast of Hokkaidō.

Arriving at the end of the afternoon, we stopped by a Seico Mart convenience store to pick up snacks and a packet of fireworks. As we checked out, Sho asked the uniformed cashier, "Are there any game rooms around here?"

"Sure. There is one at the department store a few blocks away from here," he said, pointing us down the road.

"What about a camp site and public bath?" I asked.

"The bath house is not far from the department store, and the campsite is next to the beach a mile away."

Sho looked at me with a gleam in his eye and said, "A game room *and* fireworks? It's my lucky day."

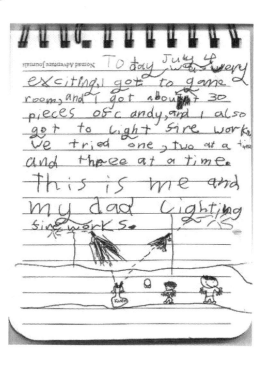

Chapter 17
Crash!

I AWOKE EARLY THE NEXT MORNING TO THE RUMBLING rhythm of powerful waves a few hundred yards from our campsite. There was something deeply soothing in the water's rhythmic roar. On my back inside our tent, eyes closed, meditating with the sound, I began to discern a structure within the crashing waves' complex refrain: the steady build, an overwhelming sense of inevitability leading to a booming crescendo, followed by the struggling fade to silence. And then the process began anew. A metaphor for the circle of life, perhaps, or at least a connection to something ancient, like a hint at the rhythm of the universe itself.

I relished the peaceful moment enveloped in the sounds of nature, but also felt a foreboding sense of vulnerability. The waves seemed to warn against overconfidence on this trip, reminding me of how many variables lay outside my control.

I lost track of time, and soon Sho began stirring. We ate breakfast inside our tent, then crawled out into the early morning sunlight. We had camped amidst a copse of trees set back a quarter mile from the ocean. A gossamer mist clung to the surrounding foliage, but the rising sun hanging just above the glorious water was already beginning to burn it off.

Emerging from the tent in a crouch, I stood up and groaned involuntarily. Sho asked, "What's wrong Daddy?"

"I'm just a little sore from all the cycling we've been doing."

"Really? I'm not."

"Seriously?" I asked, surprised and—truthfully—somewhat annoyed. "Sho, except for our one rest day on the Shiretoko Peninsula, we've cycled on average about six and a half hours a day for the past week and a half. Your butt isn't sore?"

"Nope."

"How about your fingers? Mine keep going numb."

"Nope."

"Sore neck muscles? Stiff lower back? Tight hamstrings? Aching quads?"

"Nope, nope, nope and nope. Can I play on the beach?" He slipped on the pair of shoes that were just outside the tent.

"Sure," I said without much thought. "Just be careful and stay close, okay?"

"I will."

Twenty minutes later, after I had disassembled our tent and loaded the bikes, I strolled down to the beach looking for Sho. From the campsite, my view of the water had been partially obscured, and it was not until I emerged from the tree cover that I realized the danger. I scanned the area, but could not see him anywhere on the broad, sandy beach. Myriad seaweed-covered boulders and massive pylons designed to prevent erosion obscured my view. I suspected that he was playing behind one of the boulders and called out his name, but the heavy surf and wind swatted the words back in my face. Even if he were twenty yards away, Sho would have had difficulty hearing me.

A group of six fishermen clad in waterproof coveralls stood on the top of a stone outcropping that jutted into the sea a few hundred yards away, the taut lines from their long poles stretched within the churning surf. Just then, a powerful wave slammed dramatically against the base of their rocky overlook, and walls of ocean spray careened skyward, engulfing the group of hardy fishermen. They held their ground as foamy water washed over them and poured back into the churning surf.

Under different circumstances, I would have marveled at the sea's beauty and power, but the sight triggered a sudden panic. I looked left and right for Sho and saw only an empty beach stretching into the distance. All along the shore, rushing waves raced out of the deep and tore into the pylons and boulders with diabolical power, sending jets of spray skyward before being sucked back into the depths. A horrifying image sprang to mind of Sho screaming for help as he thrashed his arms, struggling against the unrelenting undertow as it dragged him out to sea.

I needed to find my son.

I detected movement from behind a nearby boulder and sprinted over. But I was disappointed to see a man in overalls carrying a broom and trash can. I ran up to him breathlessly and said, "I'm sorry to bother you. Have you seen an eight-year-old boy around here?"

The man pointed down the beach and said, "Yeah, I saw him playing near those rocks earlier, but I'm not sure where he went."

A massive wave slammed into the rocks he had just indicated, sending spray hurtling into the sky. The man saw the concern in my eyes and offered with a kind voice, "Here, I'll help you look for him." Setting down his cleaning equipment, he led me to the spot where he had last seen Sho. Some of the boulders were wet with spray but just beyond the reach of the rolling surf. As we neared a large boulder, Sho sauntered into view holding some long, dripping green strips. Glancing at me nonchalantly, he said, "Oh, hey Daddy. Want to help me find more seaweed?"

The man nodded to me with a smile and said, "*Yokatta!* That's good."

I bowed to him and said, "Thank you for the help. I'm sorry I bothered you."

"Not a problem," he said over his shoulder, shuffling back toward his trash can and broom.

"Sho, you totally freaked me out," I said, hugging him tightly.

"Why? Did you think I was stupid enough to get near the monster waves? No way, man."

We gathered seaweed for a while, made gooey piles and enjoyed the slimy feeling of squeezing water from the strands, then sat on the rocks, mesmerized by the pounding surf, my arm draped across Sho's shoulders.

The day's destination was Cape Erimo, the southeastern tip of the large island of Hokkaidō, a straight shot about forty-four miles down the coast. We pedaled out of the campsite and into the town of Hiroo, looking for a bike shop that might have a replacement screw for the front saddlebag. But the best we could find, after asking around, was a general store that sold "Mama Chari's," cheap bicycles with front baskets designed for running light errands around town. There were no specialized screws for low rider front racks there.

I did my best to strap down the saddlebag, once again using bungee cords and hoping that they would continue to hold. We rode south out of Hiroo on Highway 336, which hugged the rocky waterfront. The shimmering sea glistened beneath a clear blue sky. It was a gorgeous day for cycling. Immediately after leaving the town, we emerged from a short tunnel and encountered a stunning coastal scene radiant beneath the bright sun. A rippling waterfall churned down sheer cliffs to our right, while in the distance, a shrouded mountainous peninsula stretched into the wild sea. I was overwhelmed by the scene's perfection, and as if I were hyp-notized by the ocean's siren song, I let the bikes drift toward the inviting water.

My reverie was violently interrupted as the vulnerable front left saddlebag rammed into the highway's four-inch curb, breaking the bent screw and jamming the rack into my front wheel. I heard the disconcerting sound of a spoke snapping as the bikes came to an immediate, lurching stop. I crashed to the ground, scraping my elbow, but Sho managed to spring off his bike unharmed.

"Well that's one way to come to a stop," I said, pulling myself off the ground and brushing grit off my tender arm.

"Daddy, did you see my jump? I was like a ninja!" We both started laughing, relieved that the accident had not been worse. Looking at the front wheel, he said, "That's gonna take a long time to fix. Okay if I play on the beach?"

"Sure, knock yourself out. Just make sure I can see you at all times."

Sho hopped a short fence and climbed down a gentle slope toward a collection of pylons at the edge of the water. He stood a safe distance from the waves and began throwing pieces of driftwood into the surf.

I turned my attention to the bike and surveyed the damage: one broken spoke, another bent, and a front left saddlebag rack that needed a new screw to be usable. I removed the front wheel and leaned the bikes against a roadside railing. The road's shoulder was about five feet wide, plenty of room for me to lay out gear and repair the wheel. Thankfully, I had a handful of spare spokes, and I took out two. Digging through my equipment bag, I also pulled out a multi-tool with a spoke wrench and a small book, "Roadside Bicycle Repair." Finding the section on replacing spokes, I began to follow the instructions.

As I worked, cars zoomed by occasionally. The incessant waves pounded out a pleasing background rhythm. And a steady breeze complimented the warm sunny day. I finally replaced both spokes and began truing the wheel.

From the corner of my eye, I detected a shadow approaching and glanced up to see a smiling older man walking purposefully toward me. He was pushing a blue two-wheeled handcart that looked like a dolly you might use to move a refrigerator. Several small duffle bags were strapped to one another on the cart. Unruly gray hair poked out beneath his blue baseball cap. He wore canvas pants and a tan vest with a yellow reflective band draped across his chest.

The man stopped a few feet away from me and leaning on his handcart, said, "Good day."

"Good day," I responded with a nod, remaining seated, spoke tool and wheel in my hands.

"I'm hiking around the entire coast of Japan," he said. "Started seven years ago, exactly seven days after I retired. I've been walking along a different coast for two months every year since then."

"Wow," I replied. Under different circumstances, I would have asked for more details from his journey, but I was singularly focused at the moment. "You don't happen to have a four-inch bike rack screw handy?"

"Can't say I do," he said with a shrug, bending over to get a closer look at the wheel in my lap.

"My son and I hope to ride our bikes the length of Japan, assuming I can repair this wheel," I said.

"Interesting quest. I live in Mie Prefecture, home of Japan's most famous and sacred Shinto shrine. Are you going to visit it?"

"I know the shrine. Isn't that the one every Japanese person is supposed to visit at least once in their lifetime?"

"Yes, exactly!"

"I wish we could go there on this ride, but we are following a route along western Japan, before cutting over to Kyoto. The closest we'll get to Mie is Mt. Kōya."

He furrowed his brow with what looked like irritation and said, "Foreigners all seem to love Mt. Kōya. It's curious." He shrugged, offered me good luck and continued on his way. I got back to work.

All the spokes need to be aligned in order to keep a bike wheel from wobbling. Following my book's guidance, I tightened the new spokes until my bike's front wheel spun with only minor lateral bend. Not bad, I decided, for an emergency roadside repair. The wheel was fixed, but without a new screw, I could not reattach the front left saddlebag rack. I needed a place to put the saddlebag, which held about fifteen pounds of gear. It was too bulky to fit on top of either rear saddlebag, and the rear rack space was taken up by the rotating hitch attached to Sho's trailer cycle. Then I remembered that the saddlebag included shoulder straps to turn it into a backpack. Soon Sho and I were once again rolling down the beautiful coast, my front wheel slightly unbalanced with a fully loaded saddlebag attached on its right side only. The left saddlebag sat heavily on my back, mercilessly digging into my shoulders.

We spent the rest of the afternoon coming up with ever more impressive superlatives to describe the gorgeous scenes we enjoyed: sublime, flawless and breathtaking. The Hidaka Mountains, a folded range uplifted by crashing tectonic plates three million years ago, extend from one hundred miles in the interior of Hokkaidō all the way to the sea. The section of Highway 336 between Hiroo and Cape Erimo was nicknamed the Golden Road because of the amount of money spent by the government to carve the seaside route into the mountainside. I imagined how vulnerable we must have looked from above: tiny, slow-moving creatures precariously making our way along a scratch in the mountain cliffs that loomed over us, presiding over the powerful ocean.

We rode through many well-lit tunnels, the longest of which stretched for nearly two miles. Many of the tunnels had large openings cut into the wall facing the sea, and spray from the crashing waves often soared into the air and drizzled over us as we passed. A few tunnels were long, burrowing enclosures with huge spinning fans hanging from the towering ceiling at regular intervals to suck out exhaust. I thought they looked like Boeing 777 engines. An approaching car or truck made itself known as a low growl emanating out of the darkness far ahead, advancing steadily, ever louder, until reaching a roaring crescendo that drowned out all other sounds as the vehicle passed.

I grew accustomed to riding through the tunnels but was unnerved by the tsunami evacuation signs, plain white rectangles posted on poles every few miles. On each sign was the simplified shape of a person running away from a threatening wave, and a red arrow pointing toward a nearby evacuation route, usually a path carved up the steep mountainside. As we rode, I imagined our options if a tsunami were to strike. Hokkaidō, like the rest of Japan, has regular earthquakes. On September 25, 2003, a magnitude 8.3 earthquake shook the seafloor about fifty miles offshore, generating a tsunami that tore into the coastline we were cycling along. I glanced up at the unending cliffs of the Hidaka mountain range to our right and realized with a sense of dread that, unless we happened to be very close to an evacuation route when a tsunami approached, we would have no chance to escape the onslaught.

As we paused in front of a house by the road to take a picture of a tsunami evacuation sign, we met Shimpei Sato, who was playing outside with his five-year old daughter. We spent the next twenty minutes meeting his extended family, accepting several cans of juice, and brainstorming ways to fix my bike's front rack. Mr. Sato had ridden a motorcycle from Sapporo in central Hokkaidō to Cape Sata, the southern tip of Japan, when he was in college, and he loved the idea of our adventure along a similar route. Although he didn't have the type of screw we needed, he gave us some extra reflectors and told me where to find a bike shop in the next major town, two days' ride away.

We thanked the family for their kindness, then pushed hard over the next two hours to make it to Cape Erimo before dark. As we neared the cape, we caught up with a cyclist in his early twenties who was attempting to ride the circumference of Japan. His heavily laden bike weaved as he rode, and I wondered if he was not used to carrying so much gear. He had started four months earlier from his home in central Japan, he explained, stopping along the way to earn money through part-time work. He had just finished a five-week stint milking cows on a farm that ended, unfortunately, with him in the hospital for a day with a bacterial infection.

"I couldn't eat or drink anything until yesterday, and I still feel weak," he said. "I feel like I can barely keep the bike upright." We parted company at the entrance to Cape Erimo's campground, where Sho and I planned to spend the night and clean up at the public bath. I invited our cyclist friend to join us, but he chose to continue on his own a few more miles to the tip of the cape, where he planned to save the $3 camping fee and sleep in a bus terminal.

After a wonderful bath, Sho and I set up the only tent on Cape Erimo's lonely, windswept campgrounds. We shot off

bottle rockets, watching the wind catch the screaming jets just as they cleared the treetops and send them off at a ninety-degree angle to disappear into the night.

The bright morning sun climbed over the sea and had me up the next day at 4:45 a.m. I spent two pleasant hours writing in my journal in the tent, while Sho slept soundly beside me. When he awoke, we finished off the rest of our provisions: dried squid, sweet bread and cheese. Not the most impressive of breakfasts, but enough calories to hold us until we reached the shops at the tip of the cape, a twenty-five minute bike ride away.

We chugged up a steep climb to reach the official point of Cape Erimo, and although I generally don't enjoy the juxtaposition of souvenir shops with a place of natural beauty, I was relieved to re-stock our snack bag and to linger over a meal of sea urchin on rice. Cape Erimo has a romantic image in Japan thanks to a famous *enka* song, a traditional Japanese sentimental ballad named after the gusty cape: "In the northern towns, they seem to have already started to temper their grief over the fireplace . . . Let us warm ourselves by recollecting our silent incommunicable past." And each year, over 400,000 tourists flock to the destination. The strip of stores beside a large parking lot sat at the top of a jagged promontory overlooking a series of dark rocky islands stretching into the sea. A staircase, perhaps a mile's worth of switchbacks cut into the cliff face, descended from the shops to the rock-strewn beach below.

As Sho and I stood at the top of the stairs, enjoying the scene, an older couple approached us. The woman glanced down at Sho and asked, "Do you see the Kurile harbor seals over there?"

"Where?" Sho asked, "I can't see them."

"Look closely at those rocks," she said, pointing to the edge of a dark peninsula jutting out into the sea far below. Large numbers of sea gulls were collected on the rocks, squawking loudly and jostling one another.

When what looked like a small black boulder suddenly moved, Sho said excitedly, "Oh, I see one!" Then more boulders moved, and we realized that there was a large family of seals bunched together by the water.

"Have you tried out the wind museum yet?" the woman asked. Sho and I shook our heads. Seeing that we weren't familiar with the museum, she pointed to a stone structure beside the parking lot. "It's in that building over there. Erimo is famous for its strong winds. In fact, the Erimo Elementary School gets all of its electricity from its own wind turbine."

After sharing the view for a while longer, we nodded thanks to the couple and entered the wind museum. Inside, we discovered a man-made wind tunnel that simulated the

power of a raging storm. A large fan roared away at the front of a long, rectangular room with support bars placed every few feet. At the back of the room, a placard on the wall explained that the wind gusted in our faces at ten meters per second. We trudged our way to the front of the room, leaning into the wind and steadying ourselves with the support bars. It became increasingly difficult to move forward until we came level with another placard showing the wind speed buffeting our bodies at twenty-five meters per second. It was all I could do simply to remain standing. Sho loved the exhibit, running back and forth, with and against the current, before crashing into me full of mischievous laughter.

We left Cape Erimo and struggled for an hour and a half against an unrelenting wind. The saddlebag-turned-backpack bit into my shoulders painfully. Finally, I took a break in front of a small Bridgestone car repair center. Catching my breath and tenderly removing the saddlebag from my burning shoulders, I had an epiphany. All this time, I had been searching for a bike shop, but I only needed a screw to re-attach the front rack. The Bridgestone mechanic dug through a drawer full of random screws until he found one that fit the eyelet on my front fork. The rack was back on, and the saddlebag was off my back.

We resumed cycling and passed beaches covered with long strips of kelp being placed into neat rows by teams of workers. Known as Hidaka *konbu*, the edible kelp from this region of Hokkaidō is well known throughout Japan and widely used in Japanese cooking. Most of the locals participate in the summer kelp harvesting, and I saw many young children alongside their mothers, who were laying out the long strips across the sand to dry before tying them together in bunches and loading them into mini trucks.

A minivan pulled up from behind and slowed to match our speed. I glanced over to see the friendly older couple who had pointed out the seals at Cape Erimo. They gestured for us to pull over.

"We got you something," the wife said, as she stepped out of the car and handed Sho a bag. Inside were some sweets and a can of lemonade. "We didn't realize you were on bicycles until we saw you ride out of the parking lot at Cape Erimo. We thought you could use some extra snacks."

Sho and I thanked the couple and took pictures with them. As they drove off, Sho said, "I've been trying to remember how many people have helped us so far on this trip, but I've lost count."

I had planned to sleep in the town of Urakawa, but when we came across the playground and beach in Samani, six miles before our destination, Sho and I were smitten. We set up our tent in the grass next to a sandy beach and proceeded to beat the crap out of each other with driftwood that magically turned into Samurai swords. The two local restaurants were closed. "Because it's Monday," one proprietor said, as if that were an obvious explanation. But we were able to buy dinner at a nearby grocery store run by Hitoshi Kudo. As we checked out, we told him about our plans to ride across Japan. He reached beneath his counter and handed us a large homemade octopus *kamaboko* fish cake. "Here, take this as a gift. I made it from octopus caught just over there," he noted, pointing across the road to a glistening inlet.

The light of a full moon shimmered off the gentle sea that night. As we settled down to sleep, the glowing orange orb hung in front of our tent, draping us with moonbeams.

Chapter 18
New Friends in Nibutani

WE WERE UP EARLY THE NEXT MORNING AND EMERGED FROM our tent onto the beach. A calm sea spread out before us, glistening and inviting. With the lapping waves as soundtrack and the clear sky as backdrop, we immediately resumed our Samurai battle. A few passing motorists applied their brakes suddenly, perhaps surprised to see a motley foreigner with the scraggly beginnings of a beard sounding a battle cry and racing across the sand with a piece of driftwood held high, chasing an eight-year-old.

When Sho and I had enough of battling, we broke down our tent and began loading gear onto the bikes. As we were working, a young couple in a sports car pulled into the adjacent parking lot and sat at a nearby table, presumably to enjoy the ocean view. After a moment, they approached me. Holding out a steaming paper cup, the man said, "We thought you might enjoy this coffee."

"Thanks," I said, taking the cup. "That's very thoughtful of you."

He and his wife nodded with shy smiles, returned to their car and drove off.

A short while later, the campsite manager approached, a middle-aged woman we had met briefly the evening before when we paid to set up our tent. She handed me a sack with five hard-boiled eggs and three bottles of frozen water. "I thought you two could use a snack. Eggs are the best when you're exercising. And the ice will melt slowly, so you'll have chilled water all day!" She gave Sho a wink and said, "It's a trick I learned as a girl."

Sho and I began riding in mid-morning, full of optimism from the sunny weather and support from strangers. "I think Hokkaidō has the friendliest people in the world," Sho said. I speculated that the generosity may have been linked to a Japanese cultural emphasis on politeness to guests, but was also specific to the rugged communities of Hokkaidō. Concern for others might be a particular communal advantage among people struggling to survive in a place where nature still held sway. Sho said, "No, dad. It's just because I'm so cute!"

We cycled for the next seven hours with occasional breaks to rest and eat and pushed the pace as much as my tiring legs would allow on the rolling roads. Sho let his mind wander unselfconsciously, sometimes singing out loud or conducting imaginary conversations. Often, he asked me random questions like, "How is water created?" or "Why are bugs attracted to light if it kills them?" At one point, he dragged me into a series of 'Would You Rather' questions, demanding that I choose between two equally unappetizing choices.

I was growing weary of the game, having answered a dozen of these already, but Sho seemed determined to continue. "Daddy, would you rather wear twenty jackets on the hottest day of summer for five minutes, or go naked outside on the coldest day of winter for five minutes?"

"Ugh! Enough of these ridiculous questions. Who knows and who cares?" Sho seemed offended and didn't speak for a few minutes. I felt bad about my outburst. Usually I enjoyed his ramblings, but I began to notice a pattern. Whenever his questions and observations started to annoy me, it was a sign that I needed to take a break from riding. I had a flashback to my seventh grade science teacher explaining that irritability is one of the early signs of dehydration and exhaustion.

I pulled over the bikes, took a long drink of water and sat down in the grass by the road. Taking out some strips of dried squid, I started chewing one and held out another to Sho. "Have some squid, buddy. Sorry I got pissy. It happens when I need to take a breather." He accepted the snack and my apology, and we spent the next fifteen minutes digging for worms in the grass before getting underway again.

After nearly seventy miles of riding, the bottoms of my feet ached with each pedal stroke, as if I had bruised my metatarsal bones. And Sho was becoming increasingly irritable himself, complaining that he was ready to stop for the day. We were within an hour of our destination.

"Just hang in there a little longer. We're getting close to Nibutani, where we'll sleep tonight," I said.

"But I'm tired."

"I know. Me too. Sometimes an adventurer just suffers for a while. We'll get there soon."

"Where are we going to sleep?"

"We'll ask around once we arrive. Hopefully they have a campsite."

At 6:30, Sho and I came to a stop at a traffic light in Nibutani, a village known for its large population of Ainu, and paused to catch our breath. I stepped off the pedals and gingerly shook out my aching feet. Across the street I noticed a restaurant named BEE House that advertised "Ainu Food."

A bright-eyed woman wearing an apron suddenly emerged from the restaurant and ran across the street to us. "*Konbanwa!* Good evening," she said with a big smile. "Your connected bikes are neat. Where did you come from?"

"We rode from Samani," I said, and told her about our plans to cycle the length of Japan.

"Oh, you have to meet my family and friends and tell them all about your trip!" she said excitedly. "Come over to my restaurant. You must be starving."

Sho nodded vigorously, and she led him by the hand, while I pushed the bikes alongside. She looked down with a smile and said, "My daughter is about your age. I'll introduce you. My name is Maki Sekine."

"I'm Sho," he said, adding, "My name means 'to fly' in Japanese."

"Yes, I know what it means," she said with a laugh.

Maki led us to a long wooden table in the restaurant's covered outdoor courtyard and seated us next to a group of four men drinking beer. Sho and I sat at the end of the table, nodding to the inquisitive faces.

"Meet our new friends," Maki said to the men. "They are riding bikes across Japan."

The men raised their beers in toast to us and introduced themselves by turn. A man in a tan jacket who looked to be in his fifties said, "Yeah, I passed you guys on the road when

I was driving my truck up here about an hour ago. You were both peeing behind some bushes!" The other men laughed.

"Sorry about that," I said, blushing. "We try to use the bathrooms at rest stops, but when you gotta go, you gotta go."

"Don't worry about it," said a young man seated with the group. He had a gentle face framed by short black hair and a goatee. He wore a tank top that showed off powerful arms. They were not defined with rippling muscles like a body builder's honed in a gym, but were thick and solid. My grand-father from Oklahoma would have called him country strong.

"I'm Kouki," he said. "I think what you're trying to do is cool. But it won't be easy, especially with a kid."

The man seated across from him gave me a serious look and said, "Kouki is famous, you know. He is the number two arm wrestler in all of Hokkaidō!"

Sho whispered to me, "I'm not surprised. His arms are bigger than my legs."

Kouki smiled and said modestly, "Well, I don't think I could ever ride a bike all the way across Japan, like you're doing."

Maki intervened and, speaking to the group, said, "These guys just rode 110 kilometers from Samani and must be starv-ing." Turning to me, she continued, "You have to try some Ainu dishes while you're here."

"Sounds great!" I said. "What do you recommend?"

"I'd suggest starting off with deer meat *miso* soup, then try an Ainu variation of pork on rice *katsudon*. And for des-ert, sweet *dango*. They are made from potato flour and sweet boiled beans, different from typical *dango* made from rice flour."

Sho and I happily accepted her recommendations. As she shuffled inside to the kitchen, a trim man with an ath-letic build approached the table and sat down across from me. "Hi, I'm Kenji, Maki's husband. I want to introduce you to someone," he said, motioning a young girl who had been standing near the kitchen to join us. "This is my nine-year-old daughter, Maya." The girl bowed politely to me and gave Sho a smile. Her fine black hair was pulled back in a ponytail, and she wore a red t-shirt with words printed across the front in English, "Child like a pleasant breeze PAPPSTYLE."

"Cool shirt," Sho said. "What does it mean?"

"Thanks," she said, glancing down at the words. "I don't know. I just thought it looked stylish."

Kenji said, "When she was seven years old, Maya and I took a three-day bicycle trip from Hiroo around Cape Erimo."

"We were just there!" Sho exclaimed.

"It was a beautiful ride, but hilly and windy," I said. Looking at Maya, I added, "You must be really strong to do a trip like that." She nodded proudly.

Kenji asked me about our planned route across Japan, the bike set-up and other details, and I enjoyed the chance to speak at length about our adventures. He was soft spoken and, unlike the other men at our table, sipped on tea instead of beer.

Maki returned with the food and rejoined us at the table. Sho and I ate ravenously, relishing the unusual, delicious flavors. Sho broke out some of his Pokemon cards and began discussing them excitedly with Maya. A few other kids his age materialized and Maya said, "Come with us. My friends and I are going to find cool night bugs. There's a great spot with lots of them over there on the other side of the road."

"Okay if I go, Daddy?"

I nodded, and he ran off toward the main road with the group of kids. Trucks had been zooming by regularly on the two-lane highway next to the restaurant, and Maki yelled out to her daughter to wait for the pedestrian light to turn green before crossing.

Over the next hour, more people arrived and, in the end, I met perhaps twenty of Maki's extended family and friends.

"From the route you described, Nibutani seems out of the way," Kenji commented at one point.

"Yes, it is a detour from the coast, but I wanted to learn more about Ainu culture. I heard there's a large Ainu population here and a good culture museum."

Maki perked up. "I work part time at the museum! My family and many of the people sitting with us are descended from Ainu." She explained that Sapporo, the capital of Hokkaidō, means "dry, large river." And that Ainu means "human being".

Maki, Kenji and I spent the next hour talking about the history and culture of Hokkaidō's indigenous people. Living between the Japanese to the south and the Russians to the north, the Ainu lost their independence in the late 1800's as the Japanese government sought to establish firm control over the country's northern boundaries. The Ainu were forced to assimilate, and their language was outlawed. The territory known as Ainu Mosir or "Land of Human Beings" in the Ainu language became Hokkaidō or "North Sea Road" in Japanese. Those who resisted were killed, and many Ainu hid deep within the mountains while the land was divvied up among Japanese settlers.

Maki and Kenji told me about the Nibutani Dam, which had been built nearby in the 1990's, despite objections from locals that it would flood land considered sacred by the Ainu. It was only in 2008, a few weeks before an international conference of indigenous peoples hosted by Japan in Hokkaidō, that the government officially recognized the Ainu as a separate people with a "distinct language, religion and culture." Very few Ainu remain, however—a 2006 government study estimated their number at 24,000—as the assimilation program was successful in erasing almost all of their traditional way of life, which centered around hunting, fishing and a reverence for nature. To me, their existence rebuked the simplistic notion held by some that Japan is ethnically homogeneous.

One culture subjugating another's is an old story that has been repeated many times through history. I thought of my own distant relative on my father's side, a Native American in the Choctaw Tribe who, as a young girl, walked the Trail of Tears from Florida to Indian Territory (which later became Oklahoma) as part of the first wave of expulsions in 1831. President Andrew Jackson had ordered the southeastern United States to be cleared of most Native Americans, which took place as a series of forced marches that lasted nearly a decade.

Kenji stood up and said, "Come with me. I want to show you something." I followed him into a one-room shack with a green exterior near the restaurant. Six tatami mats, each one three feet by six feet, covered the floor. I slipped off my shoes and left them in the entrance area before stepping onto the tightly woven rice straw. Walking on tatami mats in shoes would have been a significant cultural faux pas. Two colorful couches were placed beneath curtained windows. In one corner sat a low table beside a long wooden cabinet with dishes stored behind smoky glass. And in the far corner, long sinewy white and brown strips of something I did not recognize hung from a pole that stretched horizontally between the walls like a curtain rod.

"This is my mother-in-law's work studio. It doubles as a guest room," Kenji explained. Pointing to the hanging strips, he continued, "I go to the nearby forest to harvest bark from Lobed Elm trees—known as 'atni' in Ainu—and bring it here where she uses a traditional Ainu loom to weave the bark strips into rolls of material. These can be used to make bags, child carriers, even kimonos. Cloth made from the bark is called '*attoshi*.' Here's a picture of an exhibit in Kyoto of a kimono she made from Elm bark cloth."

He pointed to a picture hanging on the wall of the exhibit and another showing the matriarch at work. The silver-haired elderly woman was seated comfortably on the floor in front of a sleek wooden loom. Wearing a white flower-printed dress over a black shirt, her legs were folded beneath her in a pose that would have made my knees ache after only a few minutes. She was interweaving the thin threads, which looked more like yarn than tree bark, under tension on the loom.

A laminated poster hanging next to the photo explained how to identify the particular elm tree to harvest. They grow in mountainous areas, up to twenty-five meters high, have light yellow flowers that bloom in the spring, irregular zig zag leaves with a fuzzy exterior, and the bark is tough but peels off easily in vertical strips.

When I returned to the table with Kenji, Maki was waiting. I said, "Thanks! That was very interesting."

Maki replied, "I'm glad you enjoyed it. By the way, where will you sleep tonight?"

"Not sure. We have a tent. Do you know of a campsite nearby?"

She patted my shoulder and said, "Rain is coming tonight. You and Sho will be our guests. You can use the room Kenji just showed you. There are two couches, and I bet Sho will like the hanging tree bark strips."

"That sounds great. I really appreciate your generosity. Speaking of Sho, he's been gone for a while . . ."

As if on cue, I heard Maya and Sho's excited voices emerging from the darkness a few dozen yards away. I took a step toward the sound and began to make out their small shadows moving quickly across a field. As the children ran toward the two-lane highway that separated us, I saw that they were holding out cups no doubt filled with various insects they had collected, ready to show them off to the waiting adults.

The scene tipped into slow motion as I saw the lights of a semi truck barreling down the highway. It was going too fast along the dark road, and I suspected that the driver was only paying attention to the green stoplight that gave him permission to race through the intersection beside our restaurant. The pedestrian crosswalk light glowed red, but the children seemed distracted by the prospect of sharing their exciting discoveries. They were racing toward the road too fast to safely check for traffic.

Maki also saw the truck, and we began to sprint toward the intersection, screaming out simultaneously, "Stop, stop, stop!" Sho was only two steps away from reaching the road when he seemed to realize the danger. But his momentum carried him into the street as he tried unsuccessfully, arms flailing back, to come to a stop. The driver saw Sho and, at the last moment, hammered his brakes, bringing the truck to a skidding stop that seemed to violate Newton's laws of motion. Sho jumped back off the road, tumbling into Maya. The two of them froze in place staring at the large wheels of the semi only a few feet away.

Maki and I exchanged a relieved look, and the truck lumbered off, slowly regaining its momentum and disappearing on the dark highway.

"You almost got yourself killed there, buddy!" I scolded as Sho and Maya approached us.

"I know, I know," he said apologetically.

"Yesterday it was the beach. Today it's a truck. You're scaring the crap out of me."

"Yeah, I'm sorry." Then he looked up with a playful smile and said, "You *will not* believe the bugs we caught!"

Chapter 19
The Sounds of Nature

THE NEXT MORNING, HEAVY RAIN PELTED US AS WE LOADED gear on our bikes in front of the guest house. Sho didn't want to put on his rain pants ("they don't feel good") or his rain booties to keep his shoes dry ("they make me look stupid"), but I insisted, not wanting his clothes to get soaked. I was ready to go, but as a form of protest, he refused to get on his bike.

"Climb on, Sho. It's time to go," I said sternly.

He crossed his arms, rain dripping off the front of his helmet, and stood his ground with a defiant look, ready to engage in a power struggle. I took a step forward, rising up to my full height to tower over him. As I was about to ratchet up our conflict, I had an image of a comic book villain shouting, "You dare to defy me?" and suddenly felt shamefully immature.

I took a breath, closed my eyes for a moment, and remembered a piece of parenting advice from my mother: "When you don't want a battle, find a distraction."

"Tell me again about the bugs you found last night," I suggested. Sho stared at me suspiciously.

"You got pictures of them, right?" I continued. "If you keep it up, by the end of this trip, you are going to have the world's best picture collection of bugs. When we get back to New York, you could put on a museum exhibit: Freaky Bugs of Japan by Sho Scott."

He started laughing, and I said in a gentle voice, "I'm sorry the rain gear is uncomfortable, and I'm glad that you put it on anyway. Climb on your bike. While we're riding, we can come up with ways to make your exhibit the grossest, most frightening bug show ever."

He nodded, and we rolled out into the pounding downpour. Before leaving Nibutani, we stopped by the BEE House Restaurant. Maki gave Sho a goodbye hug and handed me a piece of paper with a name on it. "When you get to the town of Shiraoi, go to Porotokotan. It's a large Ainu museum complex. Ask for this man."

Sho and I rode out of the inland forests and returned to the coastal highway, cycling toward the town of Mukawa. For the past week, I had planned our food rations carefully because of the long stretches of sparsely populated countryside. Suddenly, we were in the midst of urban sprawl, passing convenience stores every few minutes and being passed by an unending stream of cars and trucks. I was surprised at my reaction to the change—I felt tense and mildly disoriented. Above all, I felt a curious sense of loss.

The sounds I had become accustomed to over the previous two weeks—lapping ocean waves, animal calls echoing in the distance, the gentle rustling of wind-blown tree branches—had been replaced by the roar of engines zooming by. And instead of the saline smell of the sea and fresh earthy aromas from the deep forest, I was sucking in exhaust fumes.

Simply hearing nature's sounds *does* something to you, perhaps because they are ancient, unchanged over billions of years. We literally evolved in their midst and are attuned to them. They are part of our symbiotic relationship with the earth. I felt jarred by the sensory overload of roaring traffic and was surprised by how much I immediately missed the countryside and wilderness. As Sho and I rode into the increasingly dense urban sprawl, I longed to return to nature.

We set up our tent in a grassy field at a rest stop in Mukawa beside a large parking lot filled with motorcycles and RVs. We were up before 5 a.m. the next morning, unable to sleep because of the bright sun and yapping crows. We lounged in our tent for a while, then entered the rest stop to clean up. Despite the early hour, the place was already bustling. A Japanese woman with dark curly hair who looked to be in her fifties approached us.

She introduced herself as Betty and, pointing to Sho, asked, "*Hafu desu ka?* Is he a half?" In Japanese, the English word "half" is used to refer to people who are of mixed race. The term sounded pejorative when I first heard it, but as far as I could tell, it is not considered offensive. When I pressed some of my Japanese friends about the word, they asked me to explain this curiosity of American culture—why is President Obama called black if he is half white? In Japan, he would be called a half.

"Yes," I replied to Betty. "He's a half. I'm American, and my wife is Japanese."

"He's such a beautiful combination of the two," she said, giggling at him. We chatted for a while, and she told us that she grew up in Kobe. After the devastating earthquake in 1995, which killed over 6,400 people in and around Kobe and left over 300,000 homeless, she and her husband started traveling around Japan. "Our home was destroyed, and we didn't have insurance. We decided to just travel."

"Constantly?" I asked.

"Yes, we have an RV. That's our home now."

I knew that Betty wasn't her real name, but when I asked her Japanese name, she said simply, "I changed my name to Betty after the earthquake."

When I told her our plans to cycle the length of Japan, she released a string of exclamations. "Just the two of you?" When

I nodded, she said, "Wait here," and ran to an RV in the parking lot. She returned with a small banjo-playing figurine with a head in the shape of an apple. She handed me the figurine and said, "Please give this gift to your wife. It must be very hard to be separated from her husband and eight-year-old son for two months."

It was a curious gift, not one I thought Eiko would like, but I appreciated the sentiment. We thanked Betty and, after loading our gear onto the bikes, pulled out of the parking lot to return to Route 235 along the coast. It was exactly 7 o'clock. I knew this because Mukawa, like many small towns in Japan, tells its citizens when to get out of bed. At precisely 7 every weekday morning, a blaring thirty-second melody is blasted from loud speakers on a centrally located rooftop. The tune reminded me of elevator Musak and was, I thought, devastatingly effective. I empathized with the poor people who had stayed out too late the previous night and must have been cursing with their heads shoved under pillows.

Sho and I left behind the town alarm clock and cycled for a few hours. We were headed to Tomakomai, population 173,000, by far the largest city we had visited so far on the ride. The amount of traffic increased, as did the debris on the road. Sho saw something and shouted out, "Daddy, stop the bikes for a second." I pulled over, and he ran back a few yards, careful to keep out of the way of the steady flow of automobiles. He picked up a shiny pull tab on the shoulder, found several more and said excitedly, "This is a goldmine!"

"Why are you collecting pull tabs?" I asked.

"They look cool. I thought I'd give them as presents to my cousins when we get back to the U.S."

Sho stored his treasures in his handlebar bag, and we began cycling again. With the heavy saddlebags weighing down the bike's thin tires and the plentiful roadside detritus, I wasn't surprised when I heard the hiss of air escaping a puncture from my rear tube. I pulled the bikes to the side of the road, disconnected Sho's trailer cycle, and removed the four saddlebags and handlebar bag.

"Want to learn how to fix a flat?" I asked, putting on gloves.

"Sure," Sho said hovering over me.

"The secret to fixing a flat tire is having the right equipment. You need tire levers, a pump, and either a spare tube or a patch kit." I laid out the gear and explained that, as long as the hole wasn't too big, I planned to patch the tire, instead of replacing the tube. "You start by opening the brake's quick release so that you can remove the wheel from the bike frame." Sho held the bike as I pulled off the wheel.

"Next, you wedge a tire lever under the bead of the rim on the side opposite the valve hole, then add a second lever a few inches away from the first. Push the second lever all the way around under the bead so that the edge of the tire comes loose over the rim." I let Sho do this part.

"Now, just pull out the tube. It's easy, right?"

Sho nodded, tube in hand. "Next, we want to figure out where the hole is. So we use this hand pump to fill up the tube enough to be able to hear where air is hissing out." Sho heard the sound and pinched the tube by the hole. "Good work! Now, we need to find out if the object that punctured the tube is still embedded in the tire. If it is and we don't remove it, we'll get another flat as soon as we start riding again.

"Line up the valve stem of the tube with the valve hole on the wheel like this," I said. "Then hold the tube against the tire to find out where the flat occurred. Remember where the air was hissing out of the tube?"

Sho nodded, his hand still pinching the spot.

"Now, let's feel inside the tire at that location." I slid my gloved fingers against the inside of the tire and found a small piece of glass stuck in the rubber. "Here's the culprit!" I said, holding up the shard for Sho to inspect. I put a patch over the hole, returned the tube around the rim, and tucked the tire back inside the bead. Because I only had a small hand-held pump, it took a few minutes to get the air pressure in the tire to an acceptable level.

"And that's how you fix a flat," I proclaimed. "What do you think?"

Sho said, "It's not too hard to do, but it's a pain in the butt."

We navigated our way into the center of Tomakomai through many stoplights and alongside the organized chaos of urban traffic until we reached a large shopping complex in front of the main train station. Although I love that many people in Japan run errands and commute by bicycle, I was annoyed to discover that there was not a single free space to park in the rows and rows of bike racks that sat out front. There were probably one hundred parking spots for bicycles, and every one was filled.

After wandering down several streets in an unsuccessful search for an available bike rack, I locked our bicycles to a street sign and hoped the police would not remove them.

The outdoor gear store Mont Bell was on the fifth floor of the shopping complex. I bought some saddlebag rain covers and got directions to a bike shop, while Sho eyed fishing rods.

"Dad, can I catch a fish in the ocean, and then we eat it?"

"Sure, son, as long as you skin it and cook it first."

He began inspecting a six-feet-long pole. "Can I get this one?" he asked, completely serious.

"And where do you plan to put it while we're riding?"

"Oh yeah, that wouldn't work, would it?"

We got another flat tire as we rode out of Tomakomai. I was annoyed, but told Sho, "Well, at least you get a chance to review what I taught you earlier."

We arrived in the town of Shiraoi later in the afternoon and went immediately to the Ainu museum Porotokotan. As we neared the entrance, a deep growl pierced the air. Sho and I froze in place, and he looked up at me startled.

"What was that, Daddy?"

"If I'm not mistaken, I'd say that was a bear."

Chapter 20

The Kindness of Strangers

POROTOKOTAN WAS LAID OUT LIKE A LAKESIDE SETTLEMENT between Lake Poroto and the Kotan Forest. A huge black statue of a regal, bearded Ainu chief towered nearly fifty feet above us. He was clad in an ornate robe and held a staff in one hand and a sheathed dagger in the other like a sentinel guarding both his village and the flourishing forest that stretched into the distance behind him.

Sho and I locked our bikes and walked to the visitor entrance, crossing a short wooden bridge that spanned a creek. A young woman seated behind a window greeted us. Referring to the person Maki Sekine had mentioned two days earlier, I said, "Hi. We are here to see Masahiro Nomoto."

The woman bowed politely. "Yes, of course. He is the museum director. I will call him for you right away."

As we waited, another low growl echoed through the settlement. Sho's eyes widened, and he clutched my hand. A slender man wearing glasses, tan khaki pants and a blue button-down shirt approached us with a smile. His hair, mustache and long side burns were speckled with gray.

"Welcome! Sekine-san told me about you two and your grand adventure. It sounds like you had a good time with her in Nibutani. I'm glad you stopped by. Let me show you around Porotokotan."

Sho stayed put and raised his hand. "Excuse me. Is it safe? I think I heard a bear."

Mr. Nomoto gave him a reassuring look and said, "Yes, you did. We have three Hokkaidō brown bears here. Want to meet them?" He added, "Don't worry. They are in cages."

We followed our host into the grounds of the compact village sprinkled with meandering tourists. The waters of Lake Poroto sparkled off to our left, and the dense trees of Kotan Forest formed a natural barrier a hundred yards to our right. "This settlement was created in 1965 as an outdoor museum to preserve Ainu culture," he explained. "We have five traditional thatched dwellings. They are called *cise* in the Ainu language. There is also a botanical garden with plants that Ainu used for medicine and food, and a museum with cultural artifacts. But first let's see the bears."

The three large animals sat languidly in separate cramped and barren metal cages. Had they risen up on their powerful hind legs, each bear would have stood perhaps eight feet tall. Thick brown fur covered bulging muscles that were no doubt atrophying in the confined space. The bears' bushy ears pricked up, and as we approached, they sniffed the air with black tipped snouts. Their faces reminded me of a stuffed animal I had grown up with, and I had the irrational urge to pet them.

A long narrow chute protruded from each cage. Mr. Nomoto handed Sho a bag of inch-long pellets and said, "Here, drop one into the chute." Sho placed one into the opening, and the pellet zipped out of sight, plopping out the other end into one of the cages. The bear turned his head at the sound and slowly pulled himself to his feet. He nibbled the food from the ground, then placed his mouth expectantly at the opening.

Mr. Nomoto said, "The Ainu thought that gods visited the human world in the form of various animals. Their flesh was considered not only a disguise but a gift for humans, so it was okay to eat them. The most important deity visited in the form of a bear. In fact the Ainu word for bear is 'kamui,' which means god. After killing a bear, the hunter made sure to send the spirit back to its world in a special ritual called 'omante.' Would you like to continue feeding the god?"

Sho nodded and sent a few more pellets down the chute into the bear's waiting muzzle. The animal's latent strength and hunting instinct were useless in the tiny cage. As he ate one pellet at a time, I saw in his eyes boredom and defeat.

After Sho finished feeding the bears, Masahiro walked us over to one of the thatched dwellings. The inside was dark and musty, and a domed ceiling arched a dozen meters overhead. Tourists filled up a few rows of wooden benches that were laid out in front of a low stage. "You're just in time to see an Ainu dance and music performance," Mr. Nomoto said, ushering us to a bench. A group of women dressed in colorful robes with scarves tied around their heads performed a series of coordinated movements to a tune played by a woman using a small wooden instrument held tightly between her lips. It was perhaps five inches long, shaped like an elongated spoon, and it produced a twanging vibrating sound. The performer held the narrow end tightly between her lips while yanking a string to the side to make each note and was able to produce a surprisingly complex tune.

After the performance, Mr. Nomoto called over the musician, a middle-aged woman with long black hair wrapped beneath a wide blue scarf. She bowed politely to us, and Mr. Nomoto said, "Please show our guests how to play the *mukkuri.*"

The woman reached into her pocket and handed each of us an instrument identical to her own. The *mukkuri* was remarkably light, perhaps the weight of a pencil, and had a small string looped through a hole in one end. A single string tied to a small stick was attached to the other end. "Hold the instrument in your mouth like this, and keep it tight between your lips," she explained. "Now wrap the looped thread around your left hand and hold tightly, while with your right hand you quickly and firmly jerk the stick at the end of the other thread. That vibrates the inside, which produces a sound."

Sho and I tried several times, but our instruments made no noise. "The secret is to pull the string out to the side exactly in line with the instrument. A little too high or too low, and the vibration can't hold." She demonstrated, playing a quick melody that reminded me of the beginning of the song "Dueling Banjo's."

Sho and I practiced a little longer and succeeded in producing a few pitiful notes. Soon my finger and lips were sore. "It's harder than it looks," Sho said, rubbing his mouth.

Mr. Nomoto said, "Let's stop for now. Please keep the instruments as souvenirs." We thanked the musician and followed our host to the main museum building. "I'll leave you here to explore on your own," he said. "When you return to New York City, make sure to visit the Ainu exhibit at the American Museum of Natural History."

We thanked him for the tour, then wandered through the museum, which included exhibits of Ainu clothing and tools and descriptions of their hunting techniques and history. We marveled at salmon-skin shoes and water containers made from animal bladders, but Sho's favorite was the decorated skull of a bear, which was part of the *omante* ritual Mr. Nomoto had described to us.

While looking at several Ainu-made long spears on display, Sho declared with bravado, "I could kill a brown bear using that spear."

"You didn't seem so sure of yourself when you heard the bear growl," I teased.

"Well, I didn't have an Ainu spear with me."

I was interested to learn about Shigeru Kayano. The first and so far only Ainu to serve in the Japanese parliament, he was born in Nibutani and wrote perhaps one hundred books about Ainu culture and history. He was one of a dwindling

number of native speakers of the language, and over his many years in the parliament he often asked questions in his native tongue. I imagined the annoyed looks of his fellow politicians as they listened without comprehension to the Ainu words that disrupted the formalized proceedings of the government body and reminded everyone of the sins of their fathers.

Nicknamed the "Ainu Mandela" because of his efforts to highlight the plight of his people, Kayano led the protest movement against the Nibutani Dam. And although he was not able to stop the project from flooding land sacred to his ancestors, as a result of his efforts, a court acknowledged for the first time in 1997 that the Ainu were the indigenous people of Hokkaidō. Kayano died in 2006 at age seventy-nine.

We continued through the exhibit, stopping before a large map showing the names and locations of "The Minorities of the Northern Regions." The area stretched from Hokkaido over the North Pole and down into Canada and the U.S. I was fascinated by the rugged culture that had emerged around a life of hunting, gathering and fishing in such a harsh landscape. Although I did not wish to live that way, I felt a connection to ancestors who, many centuries before, had struggled to survive in the wild. My life in New York City felt so *soft* in comparison and so disconnected from nature's rhythms. It seemed absurd that after hundreds of generations clawing and fighting to cling to life dictated by the harsh rules of the wild, I lived such a comfortable existence that I felt compelled to seek out struggle and discomfort. This trip with my son, riding for hours through forests and beside the ocean, seemed to revive some ancient memory. The human body was designed to hunt and survive in the wild, and as I pushed against my physical limits, surrounded by nature, I felt as if something primal was awakening within me.

After the museum closed, Sho and I cycled on an empty road into a forest on the other side of the lake until we reached a campsite tucked away deep in the woods. The only other campers were an elderly couple who had set up a tent next to their RV. As Sho and I assembled our tent, the friendly pair approached us.

Holding out two containers, the husband said, "We have some extra *miso* soup and tomatoes we thought you might like. I'm Mutsuo and this is my wife Taeko. We are spending a few months driving and camping all over Japan." Sho and I accepted their generosity and chatted for a while before returning to our respective tents. Daylight faded and the campsite was enveloped in darkness.

I was awakened at 2 a.m. by the sound of heavy rain pounding our tent. I had been dreaming of a dog from my childhood, and the final scene from the dream stayed with me. His black hair was flowing in the breeze, and his playful snout was uplifted. I wrestled his head against my chest and laughed as we fell together into the grass. As I lay on my back, feeling his fur under my chin, I looked up into the sky. The bright blue expanse was broad, serene and dotted with puffy clouds. Suddenly the daytime shifted into black night. A canopy of stars immediately filled my view, but their light was too feeble for me to see my dog. I could feel his fur under my chin and held onto his head tightly, afraid to let him go.

I puzzled over the dream, then drifted back into a fitful sleep. Rain was coming down hard when I woke up in the morning. Sho and I huddled inside our tent and whiled away the time playing games and telling stories until we heard a voice outside our tent.

Peeking out, I saw Mutsuo standing in the rain holding an umbrella. "Want some breakfast?" he asked.

Sho and I happily accepted, racing through the downpour with him over to a pavilion, where Taeko was preparing the food. The four of us dined on *miso* soup, pork strips, rice, sesame paste and super-sour homemade *umeboshi*. Sho enjoyed the *umeboshi* so much that Taeko gave him an extra bottle filled with the red pickled plums.

We spent the morning chatting with the amiable couple, who entertained Sho with picture games and paper airplanes.

When the rain finally began to taper off and I loaded our bikes to leave, Taeko gave Sho a handful of stamps with Japanese cartoon characters, and Mutsuo gave him a 500 Yen coin (about five dollars). "Good luck on your journey. Be careful," they said as we rolled out of the camp.

We cycled through puddles and intermittent spitting rain for the next six hours before reaching the town of Muroran, which lies at the tip of one of Hokkaidō's many capes and was bombed at the end of World War II by a U.S. battleship. As dusk fell, we reached a *michi no eki* rest stop on a waterfront lined with marinas at the base of a towering bridge lit by a string of lights. The view reminded me of the George Washington Bridge in New York City.

We entered the rest stop and approached an office that was empty save for a middle-aged man dressed in a blue uniform. "Excuse me," I said, as he looked up. "Do you have any rooms for the night or a campsite here?"

"No," he said. "This rest stop doesn't have any accommodations."

"We have a tent," I suggested. "Is there anywhere out of the way we might set it up?"

He started to shake his head, then looked down at Sho and seemed to change his mind. "Follow me," he said, walking us outside and around the building. He led us into a small shack with a desk and a built-in cushioned couch along two walls. "Will this do? It's a changing room for guests of the golf course next door."

Sho and I nodded simultaneously, grateful to avoid another night in the rain.

"No one will use it before 9 a.m. tomorrow," he explained. "Just make sure you're out by then."

Early the next morning, light streamed into our cozy shack, strong winds gusted off the nearby waterfront, and the patter of rain tapped against the roof. I spent a couple hours writing in my journal and appreciating the changing hues of the cloudy early morning sky as Sho slept soundly beside me.

The downpour intensified soon after we began cycling from Muroran to Lake Tōya, and we donned our rain pants, jackets and booties, determined to go on despite the foul weather. The quickest route would have been over the looming bridge that had bathed us with its line of lights overnight, but it was crowded with zooming vehicles, and I decided not to risk a bike ride on that beast. The alternative route took us on a fifteen-mile detour.

We cycled through the mess all day. Every so often, the rain seemed to taper off, and the sun poked through a break in the thick cloud cover. We rejoiced at the end of the inclement weather several times, only to be greeted a few minutes later with another torrent mocking our premature celebration. The route was rolling, and as we worked up long inclines, I noticed a marked increase in Sho's strength since we had begun riding seventeen days earlier. At the end of the afternoon, we pulled up to the crowded Nakatoya Campsite, dripping and worn out. I had to ask for a towel before signing in at the camp office, for fear of ruining the guest book.

The rain finally stopped as we set up our tent and changed into dry clothes. We had hoped to watch the nightly summer fireworks display on the opposite side of Lake Tōya from the campsite, but clouds obscured all but the sounds of distant explosions. Sho and I fell asleep to the gurgling of a nearby creek.

I awoke at dawn, snuck quietly out of the tent, and took a few pictures of the mist settling over Lake Tōya. The rainstorm had long passed, and the azure sky, tumbling white clouds and surrounding forest reflected off the water. I sat on a rock, staring out over the lake, appreciating the calming sounds of softly lapping water and birds calling from within the trees overhead. I felt like I was inside a shimmering work of art. The life back home, filled with high-pressure, never-ending professional demands, felt far away. I could see its contours more clearly now that I was not caught up in the distracting minutiae and exhaustion that comes with a full-time professional job. I had the unmistakable sense that this trip was shaking something loose, that I was changing in a way that threatened to upend my old life.

As I stood, my thigh seized up in a cramp and I fell back down hard on the rocky edge of the lake. I straightened my leg and massaged the muscle, grimacing in pain. I had a sudden flash of anxiety that I would not be able to continue riding day after day like this. We were only a few days away from Hakodate, our last stop on the island of Hokkaidō. From there, we would take a ferry to the main island of Honshu. I would stick to the coast for as long as I could after that, but eventually our route would take us inland and across an entire mountain chain, the Japan Alps. Rubbing my tender thigh, I wondered if I would be up to the task. The anxiety I felt brought back memories from when I was thirteen years old and trying to figure out how to train for my first marathon.

It was the beginning of my summer vacation after seventh grade in 1981. My father and I were registered for a September marathon in Jackson, Tennessee, a couple hours west of our home in Nashville. I had competed throughout the spring on my junior high school track team in the mile and half-mile distances. The training consisted entirely of hard, fast, relatively short workouts and, with three months to go before the marathon, I knew that I needed to run longer.

I didn't really know how to prepare for a marathon and was too proud to ask for help. My father and I ran together a few times, and he gave me tips and encouraged me. But he made a conscious effort not to be an enforcer in a process that I had initiated. He was careful not to push me too hard, concerned about the effect heavy training might have on my still growing body. And then he left to spend the summer at an academic conference in Italy. I would have to train on my own.

I made a remarkable number of mistakes. I started off fast whenever I ran and viewed slowing down or walking briefly as failures, instead of opportunities to increase my body's ability to exercise for longer periods. I carried no food or water, despite running in hot, humid conditions. As a result, I could not run for more than 45 minutes or so before dehydration and exhaustion from the hard pace forced me to stop. I set a goal of running every day, but struggled against a lazy lethargy that came with being on summer break and undercut my attempts at self-discipline. I was also easily distracted by opportunities to socialize with my friends and missed many planned workouts. This was one case in which I benefited to some degree from my lack of discipline: running hard every day would have increased the chances of an injury.

As the summer wore on, I realized with increasing concern that I would not be ready for the marathon. And my friend, Alex, didn't help. He kept his stash of marijuana inside a hollow container of Mennon Sports Stick deodorant with his name scribbled on it in permanent marker. It was an ingenious hiding place, sitting openly in front of his unsuspecting mother and step father every time they opened the bathroom mirror.

Alex and I had met on the first day of seventh grade ten months earlier and quickly became good friends. He laughed easily, had a good sense of humor and a gentle face, topped by a thick head of black hair. We enjoyed one another's company, and when school let out, excitedly made plans to meet regularly over summer break.

It was almost noon on a hot, steamy day in early July. Alex and I had spent the morning playing tennis at a nearby court and were back at his condo. His parents were at work, and we had the run of the place. Setting down a half-finished, ice-filled glass of cold lemonade, I perused his album collection and pulled out "Foreigner 4." Carefully palming the edges of the twelve inch vinyl record to avoid getting finger prints on its surface, I placed it on Alex's turntable, confirmed that the rotation speed was set at 33 1/3 RPM, and carefully laid the stylus needle on the groove for the second song on the spinning black LP.

A second or two of crackle, then two large charcoal-colored mini tower speakers in each corner of his room filled the condo with music. *"Standing in the rain with his head hung low. Couldn't get a ticket. It was a sold out show . . ."*

Retrieving the glass of lemonade, I was humming along to "Juke Box Hero" and looking over Alex's motocross trophies when I remembered the post card from Italy I had received the day before. "Greetings from Perugia!" was splashed across the top of a photograph of an idyllic country scene. On the back, my father had written, "Hey Charlie! I hope you are enjoying the summer. It's been hot here, but I've gotten in several good long runs. How is your training going? Love, Dad."

I felt a knot in my stomach. The marathon was looming, and I could run for no more than an hour before I stopped from exhaustion. I knew that the race would take me at least four times that long. "I've still got time," I mumbled to myself, suppressing a nagging realization that my goal was beginning to appear less and less attainable.

Alex called me into the bathroom. The Mennon Sports Stick lay on its side on the counter, next to a pile of marijuana. He was carefully separating the seeds. Looking up with that great smile, he plucked one between his fingers and held it out to me. "Eat this man. It's a pot seed. More potent than smoking the leaves."

I had never tried pot and knew that my parents would not approve. But they weren't here, and Alex was my friend. I had to admit that I was curious.

"What's it like when you're high?" I asked, taking a sip of lemonade and ignoring his outstretched offering. I glanced down at the drink in my right hand, beads of sweat from the cold liquid clinging to the tall glass, refracting the harsh white light of the bathroom. One bead began to slowly roll down the edge of the glass until it rested against my finger, as if warning me that the decision I made in the next few moments would be consequential.

Alex shrugged, popped the seed in his mouth and said, "Man, it's great. You feel relaxed, like everything's gonna turn out okay, you know? And you laugh at random stuff, like the shape of a cloud or your friend's eyebrow. You get the munchies like crazy and crack up at the sound inside your head when you're eating a mouthful of chips. It's just fun, especially when you're bored."

I was tempted to give it a try and glanced down at the joint he was starting to roll. As he squeezed the pot leaves onto a small square of paper, rolled it up and sealed it with a lick, Alex continued, "Last week, I was totally baked at soccer practice. I kept cracking up for no reason, laughing at the sound of my shoes on the grass. And I was so uncoordinated, it was ridiculous. I couldn't kick the ball for crap. It was like everybody else was running in fast motion, and I got my butt kicked. Usually, I would have been pissed, but I was so high I didn't care. It was hilarious."

I was horrified. I already felt guilty about not training enough for the marathon. If I started smoking pot, I'd never have a chance.

"No, I'm gonna pass, man," I said, looking away and returning to Alex's room. "I'm in training."

"Suit yourself," he said, popping a few more seeds in his mouth and leaving me on my own to listen to Foreigner and worry about the marathon.

Sitting quietly beside a lake in northern Japan twenty-eight years later, I remembered the feelings of insecurity I had at age thirteen, overwhelmed by an ambitious goal, and how that insecurity had turned to resolve. I determined to do the same thing now and figure out how to make it to the end of Japan, mountains and all. I stood carefully, favoring the leg that had cramped, and returned to the tent where I found Sho starting to stir.

Our day's destination was the coastal town of Oshamanbe, fifty miles away. We followed Highway 37, which looked on my map like a reasonably flat ride along the coast, but soon we were chugging up winding climbs through tunnels and eventually above the cloud line. The day had started sunny and warm, but we donned jackets as we gained elevation and found ourselves surrounded by a chilling mist. We crossed a few dramatic bridges cloaked in fog. Staring into the obscured abyss, Sho observed, "Daddy, you know if we fell over the side railing we would be totally dead."

Despite the cool temperatures, sweat poured out of my helmet from the steep climb. My muscles ached, and I started to feel overwhelmed by the effort. "I'm not giving myself enough time to recover from each day's ride," I thought, as my right quadriceps muscle twitched and threatened to seize up again, as it had in the morning. I glanced back at Sho, who was gripping his handlebars tightly and pushing down hard on his pedals, head down and tongue hanging out. The climb up the unexpected mountain road took us two hours, and we both cheered when we reached the summit.

But my relief was quickly replaced with harrowing fear as we started the descent. Rapidly returning toward sea level down the mountainside, I squeezed the brakes with a desperate grip, afraid of losing control on the steep decline. We finally made it down safely, and although I was relieved, the tips of several fingers were completely numb.

In Oshamanbe, we found a *minshuku* Japanese inn with an *onsen* bath and the only coin laundry in town and splurged seventy dollars for a room. After a satisfying soak in the baths, where I tried to regain feeling in my fingertips by flexing them open and closed in the steamy water, Sho loaded the laundry machine with practically every piece of clothing we'd brought, both of us relishing saying sayonara to the mildew smell.

We had arrived too late to eat dinner in the inn, as is customarily provided for guests with a reservation, but the proprietor brought up two delicious crabs to our room. "You look like you could use some food," she said with a bow.

Sho and I devoured the delicious crabs before snuggling under thick comforters on our sumptuous futons. There are few pleasures to rival a good futon and comforter following a long day of cycling, and we relished the luxury.

"We totally deserve this," I said to Sho, just before settling into a deep slumber.

Chapter 21
The Wanderer

I AWOKE WITH A DEEP FATIGUE IN MY LEGS. MY CALVES twitched, not yet recovered from yesterday's long, steep climb into the clouds. Rain poured down outside, wind gusts slamming sheets of water against the small wooden window of our tatami mat room. I was thankful that last night we had chosen to sleep in a Japanese inn instead of our tent. Groaning at the prospect of riding in the storm, I crawled under the soft warmth of the comforter, snuggling close to Sho on our futons for a few minutes more before facing the day.

Sho, groggily coming to consciousness, had pulled the comforter over his head, so that I could make out only a mischievous pair of eyes peering out at me. He didn't want to relinquish the warmth of our futons any more than I.

"Good morning, buckaroo. I hope you slept well," I said, adding, "I love you."

Sho's eyes stared back, bunching up a bit at the corners, as he smiled from within his comfortable cave. He said, "I love you more." It was a game we often played, coming up with silly, competing metaphors.

"Oh yeah?" I teased. "You know, I love you more than this whole Japanese inn!"

"Well, I love you more than everything now or ever, including infinity," he responded.

"Hmm," I mumbled. Usually we let the game go on a few rounds before pulling out the big stuff like infinity. "Well, I can't top that. But, in all seriousness, I do want you to know that I love you unconditionally."

Sho eyed me suspiciously. "What does 'unconditionally' mean?"

"It means that no matter what you do, I will always love you for who you are."

"Really?" he responded enthusiastically, pushing himself up to rest on his elbows, letting the comforter drop off his head to drape across his shoulders. "So, if I whacked you on the head with a fish, you'd still love me?"

"Um, yeah. But that's a weird idea, and I wouldn't be happy with your behavior."

"What if I stabbed your foot with a knife? Or shot you in the leg with a gun?"

"I would walk with a limp and be very unhappy about what you did, but I would still love you."

"What if I chopped off your head with an axe?"

"Well, then I'd be dead. But you should know that up until that point, even as I was screaming desperately at you to put down the axe, I still loved you."

Sho laughed, then with a surprise attack—a pillow launched at my head—screamed, "Pillow fight!"

That got us moving, and after a few minutes of exhausting mutual destruction, our stomachs were rumbling. Donning soft cotton *yukata* robes—that had been neatly folded beside our futons, but thanks to the pillow fight, were now a disheveled mess—and wearing slippers supplied by the inn, we followed a hallway to a large tatami mat common room. About ten other guests, all Japanese, were already enjoying a hearty breakfast while seated on mats along an extended low table. A lone TV was perched on a raised dais like a deity at the front of the room, a news program by the public TV station NHK commanding most of the guests' attention.

Sho and I pulled off our slippers and lined them up beside ten identical pairs arranged in a tidy row in front of the room's entrance, and an elderly woman led us to a pair of mats placed on the floor beside the low table. She wore a casual kimono covered with patterns of bright pink cherry blossoms. Her skin was wrinkled, her hair speckled gray, and she walked with a slight bend in her back, perhaps from a lifetime of laboring over low tables and doing housework. Her eyes contained an engaging sparkle that complemented her genial politeness. As we settled down, sitting cross-legged on the mats, she shuffled around us, distributing various dishes prepared by the *minshuku* staff and describing each one. She gave Sho a sweet grandmotherly smile.

"Here's some *miso* soup—careful, it's still hot—grilled fish, a bowl of rice, fermented soybeans, pickles, and salad. Would you like some orange juice?"

"Yes, please," Sho responded, and the old woman beamed at him. "You're so polite." He returned her affectionate look, then began devouring the food. Hoping to delay our impending ride through the storm that raged outside, I told our waitress about our end-to-end bike ride across Japan and asked if we might stay a bit longer than the 10 a.m. checkout time. Maybe they would bend the rules for an eight-year-old adventurer.

But rules were rules. "Hmm, that's a little bit of an issue . . ." she responded, making a pained expression and sucking in her breath in a distinctive manner I had often experienced in Japan. Translation: "Ain't gonna happen." I accepted her response without protest, and checking my watch, decided to take advantage of the time we had left.

Sho and I finished off our meal, left the other guests still transfixed before the TV, and headed straight for the steaming luxury of the inn's onsen bath. There were two communal rooms, separated by gender, and for now we were the only guests using the men's section. Sho slowly inched his way back and forth in the water, while I stretched out my legs, closed my eyes and rested my head against the top of the tub, mini waves lapping my chin and steam enveloping my face. Relishing the luxurious sensation, I hoped to soak up as much heat as I could to counter the wet, cold ride to come.

We finally returned to our rooms, relaxed and radiating warmth, thirty minutes before checkout time. We had made a mess of the futons and comforters in our pillow fight, but folded them neatly and returned the room to pristine condition before leaving. I knew it was considered rude to leave a mess at a Japanese inn for the staff to clean up, and we didn't want to reinforce the stereotype commonly held in Japan that Americans are loud and messy.

"Only sometimes," Sho laughed, as he helped clean up.

Rain pounded the ground relentlessly just inches from our feet, as Sho and I loaded gear back onto our bikes under the inn's awning. I wrapped rain covers over the bike saddlebags, securing them as tightly as I could against the wind. Sho and I pulled on rain jackets, rain pants and covers for our shoes, as our friendly elderly waitress stood politely by the door to see us off. She bowed and offered a hearty "*Ganbatte!* Good luck!" as we said farewell, turned our backs on the comfortable inn, and pushed into the powerful storm.

The rain and wind put on an impressive display, and scarcely ten minutes into the ride, I pulled to a stop to capture the storm on video. We were cycling on a coastal road, powerful wind gusts spewing salty spray off crashing waves surging just to our left, menacing fingers clawing out from the forbidding, churning ocean overhung by columns of dark storm clouds.

"Man, this is friggin' ridiculous," I narrated as I stood astride my bike and cloaked the camera with my left hand to keep as much rain as I could off the lens. Sheets of rain slapped my face, and a waterfall streamed off the front of my helmet. I felt the lingering warmth from the hot bath fading quickly.

"Whoa, Daddy, check it out!" Sho screamed above the storm's cacophony, pointing toward a row of long silver poles with flags flapping violently, threatening to rip off their posts.

We rode through the mess for the next five hours, fighting to maintain momentum and stay upright against the powerful wind and steady rain. Our route eventually left the coastline, and we followed a narrow two-lane road that alternated between small towns and extended sections of forest. Finally, legs weary and soaked through, we had enough. As we entered Mori, a verdurous, park-filled town whose name means "forest", we rejoiced at the sight of a sprawling rest stop that included a grocery store, information center and several small restaurants. Parking our bikes beneath an overhang that protected our gear from the downpour, we tracked dripping brown water into a noodle shop and feasted on mounds of *soba* noodles in steaming hot broth. I had pushed hard while riding through the rain. My hands shook and I felt woozy as I buried my head over the bowl and slurped the steaming broth greedily.

"These are the best noodles I've ever had," Sho said through a mouthful of *soba*, and I grunted in agreement.

After our rejuvenating meal, we explored the visitor center and met a friendly woman selling produce at a stall who immediately took a motherly liking to Sho. She wore a gray apron over long white pants and a blue turtleneck shirt. I guessed that she was a local farmer selling food that she had grown herself.

"Do you know if there is an *onsen* around here?" I asked. "My son and I are on bicycles and would like to clean up a bit after riding through this mess all day."

"You do look pretty soaked," she said with a grin. "There's a public bath at World Ranch. It's a recreation area with a campsite about ten kilometers down the road from here."

"Sounds perfect. Thank you!"

"My pleasure. How far are you riding?"

I glanced at Sho and he answered, "To Cape Sata."

"Cape Sata!" she exclaimed. "You mean all the way at the bottom of Kyushu? I can't believe a kid would be able to ride so far," she said. "Hold on, let me get something for you." She pulled out a sack, filled it with five tomatoes and a carton of cherries and handed it to me. "Here, take this. It's on the house." Then, reaching into her pocket, she dug out a 500-yen coin (about five dollars) and handed it to Sho. "Good luck on your journey, young man."

We thanked her with an appreciative bow and returned to our bikes, singing "Rain, Rain Go Away." As if in response to our entreaties, the rain finally stopped as we set off toward the campgrounds. I removed the rain covers to let the wind dry off our gear as we rode. My legs had tightened up during the break, and they protested as we set off. I let out an involuntary middle-aged groan and hoped that the stiff muscles would warm up as we got moving along the rolling hills.

As we rounded a bend on a meandering rise through Mori's lush, forested landscape, we spied a lone figure plodding toward us on foot. A large conical hat concealed his face, and his flowing robes draped down over worn sandals. We stopped to say hello.

Taking off his hat, he revealed a gentle face with intense eyes and a shaved head wrapped in a white handkerchief. Peering at our connected bike set-up, he said, "I've never seen such a thing." We told him about our plans to cycle the length of Japan and he nodded, as if he weren't surprised. I asked him where he was headed.

"Cape Sōya, where you started," he answered, but he was only telling us half the truth. We learned that he was thirty-nine years old, a wandering Buddhist monk who carried no money and depended on handouts for survival. Only a thin leather strip between his big and second toes kept his modest sandals on his feet. Around his torso, he draped a thin blue plastic sheet, on which, he explained, he slept wherever he happened to find himself each night. Two small plastic bags were wrapped around his arm, holding what looked like a towel and a few other small items. He did not carry much else.

Sho and I exchanged glances with raised eyebrows, knowing how much food we had been consuming during our trip. "Walking all day? He must be hungry constantly," Sho whispered.

"Will you return home after reaching Cape Sōya?" I asked.

The monk smiled bashfully and responded, "No, I'll keep going along the coast around Japan."

"All the way around?" Sho asked.

"Yes, I am walking all the way around."

"How long will it take you?" I responded, astonished.

"It takes me about one year to complete a circuit. This is my sixth one so far."

"You've been walking for six years?" Sho asked incredulously.

"Yes, almost."

"That is remarkable," I said to the monk, shaking my head. "Your journey must be full of amazing experiences."

He smiled at my enthusiasm and said softly, "Walking continuously or not walking, traveling or not traveling, all experiences are both wonderful and mundane in their own way."

As he spoke, I couldn't help but think that walking endlessly in circles was foolish somehow. He had taken the concept of an adventure too far, left too much behind, drifted too far away from "normal" society. I thought back to people I had met in Bangkok when I was traveling around Asia just out of college. They hung out on the street, smoking pot, doing nothing and living on a few dollars a day. They had dropped out. One guy bragged that he had figured out how to live on less than $1,000 a year.

But even though he was wandering, the monk was not lost like the guys I'd met in Bangkok. By wearing this garb and living off handouts, he had grounded himself in a Buddhist tradition that provided a structure for his peripatetic life. Letting go of material ambition created the space for an altogether different engagement with the world. His comment about the wonder in all experiences, no matter how mundane, reminded me of a quote from Hermann Hesse's *Siddhartha*: "What could I say to you that would be of value, except perhaps that you seek too much, that as a result of your seeking, you cannot find."

I took the monk's picture and offered some of our food, which he accepted graciously. As Sho and I said farewell and the wanderer set off, I thought, "Life is like a gift, which you can celebrate or throw away. The choice is yours."

As we turned to go, I called back to him. "I'm sorry. I forgot to ask. What is your name?"

He paused, looked off, and answered cryptically, "It's better if I don't say."

We had only been riding a few minutes further when we heard shouts of encouragement coming from behind us, and saw our friend from the produce stand driving by. She waved at us out of the car window, smiling and shouting, "*Gambatte, gambatte*! Keep it up," her voice trailing off as she disappeared ahead in the distance.

World Ranch was a few miles off the main road, a sprawling country play-land designed for the whole family. In addition to its *onsen* hot baths and a modest campground next to the horses' stables, it boasted two eighteen-hole practice golf courses with billiard-size golf balls, an archery site, badminton nets, a large wooden maze, a collection of farm animals—including a curious "small dog" cage with one Maltese and one Chihuahua—and best of all, speakers hung throughout the farm doling out old time country songs from the American South. My favorite was a catchy but depressing tune whose title was probably, "Hillbilly Blues," followed a close second by a schmaltzy, twanging country ode to the merits of "prayin' for the Good Lord to save my wretched soul."

There was something both endearing and jarring about this particular soundtrack echoing through Hokkaidō's bucolic countryside, another example of the mix of modern and ancient that we encountered regularly in Japan. It reminded me of a visit to a traditional Japanese crafts store while we were in Tokyo. Sho and I had laughed as we heard

Jason Mraz's "Geek in the Pink" floating over the delicate lac-quer trays and refined silk screens.

We would enjoy World Ranch in the morning. It was already early evening, and we needed to set up our tent. We made our way to the campsite, propping the bikes against a table and unloading our gear. Although the rain had stopped, a seemingly endless line of dark, billowing clouds rushed by overhead, propelled by powerful gusts that sent us chasing after various items as Sho and I tried to set up the tent. To keep from losing it to the wind, I had to bundle the fabric into a clump that I could hold onto while securing one section at a time to the ground with stakes. Sho stood guard over our bikes, holding onto gear and shouting excited exclamations as the wind tried to rip open the saddlebags. We finally managed to set up the tent, secure our belongings and retreat inside.

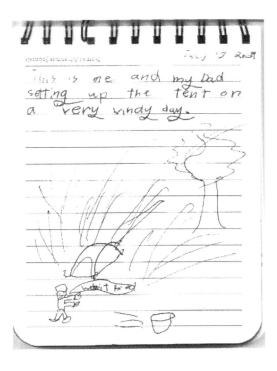

As I read Japanese fairy tales to Sho, engulfed in the darkness, the tent rattled and bowed and swayed around us, like the hull of a boat tossed in a boiling sea. Despite the racket, we were both asleep by nine, exhausted from the day's challenging ride. I woke up briefly just after midnight and emerged from the tent to a brilliant, clear night sky, constellations glowing against the black void, and the clouds and wind gusts long gone. Pausing to appreciate the peaceful night, I wondered where the Wanderer was sleeping. Then I snuggled back inside next to Sho, falling asleep to the sound of his soft snores.

Chapter 22

Animal Farm

AT 4 A.M., FIRST THE LOCAL DOGS BEGAN TO CALL TO ONE another, presumably to see if anyone was still sleeping. Then several goats joined in, making it necessary for the crows to proclaim their presence. Finally, the horses in the barn next to our tent complemented the cacophony with a round of impressive neighing. I thought the noise would end shortly, but this was apparently a contest expected to last well after sunup.

Sho stirred only briefly, while I spent the next two and a half hours attempting to return to unconsciousness, as I lay inside our tent and created a mental sound map of the local animal population.

At 6:30, Sho abruptly sprang up and asked excitedly, "Daddy, can we play golf at World Ranch?"

"As soon as we get the tent broken down and our gear loaded on the bikes." Sho helped complete these tasks in record time.

We took advantage of all the major attractions at World Ranch, which was spookily empty, save for some bored attendants.

"Why isn't anyone here, Daddy?" Sho asked as we wandered around.

"Early on a Tuesday morning isn't the most popular time for people to visit a place like this."

After eighteen holes of practice golf, we tested our archery skills (not so impressive), made it through the country maze in thirty-two minutes ("pretty average" commented one of the workers), sampled a few video games, and drank some "orange juice" that was really orange coloring added to water, mixed with high fructose corn syrup. Sho was in heaven.

July 14 2009

This is me doing archery with my dad.

Nomad Adventure Journals

Today's destination was Hakodate, a coastal town on the southern edge of Hokkaidō that would be our last stop on the northern island. From Hakodate, we would take a ferry to Aomori, a city on the northern tip of the main Japanese island of Honshu. I smiled at the prospect of an easy two-and-a-half hour bike ride to Hakodate that included some comfortable downhill coasting through the thick forests of Onuma Park, a nature preserve designated by the Japanese government as "a place of natural scenic beauty."

In complete contrast to yesterday's storm-drenched ride, we pedaled in shorts and short-sleeved shirts under a brilliant sun. Cycling on a lightly trafficked road beside a deep green forest, I felt a sense of peace and rejuvenation. Sho hummed into the wind. Small hardy wild flowers flapped at the road's edge, and the lovely calls of yellow-breasted buntings floated around us.

"This is so much better than sitting inside a car," I said to Sho, taking a deep breath of the fresh country air. "Have you noticed how many people think we are crazy just for trying to cycle across Japan?"

"It's not nearly as hard as being an Ainu hunter," he said. "Think about how tough it would be to track down a bear in the forest and kill it with a spear."

We glided down a gentle hill and didn't speak for a few minutes. Then Sho said, "Daddy, I want to have a kid to play with when I grow up, but not a wife. Too many girls are in love with me, and it's really annoying. Maybe I could find an orphan to adopt."

I immediately pulled over our bikes and took out a note pad. Sometimes I just had to write this stuff down.

The bucolic countryside soon yielded to suburbia and heavily trafficked roads. Perhaps still enraptured by nature's spell, I did not see the sign explaining that the country highway we were on would soon turn into an interstate. Instead of taking the well-marked exit, I continued straight, riding up an elevated ramp. I quickly realized I had made a mistake when it morphed into an intimidating six-lane monster with cars whizzing by at seventy miles per hour.

"What the hell . . . ?" I wondered aloud. I considered turning around, but the shoulder was narrow and our long connected bikes would have looped out into oncoming traffic. I decided to continue riding on the far left of the road, pressing down hard on my pedals to reach the next exit as quickly as I could, about a half-mile ahead. A driver slowed down beside us and yelled out his window, "No bikes allowed on the interstate!"

"I know, I know!" I yelled back, lowering my head and hammering the pedals with all my strength.

I felt adrenalin course through me, and my heart was probably going at 180 beats per minute. The roaring cars seemed like a marauding herd of wild beasts snarling at us from only a few feet away. We were so vulnerable. My legs burned, my shoulders were tense, and I gripped the handlebars tightly as I panted and wheezed, head down. "You're an idiot, you're an idiot," I said to myself.

When we finally left the interstate and coasted to a stop at the bottom of the exit, I looked back at Sho and said, "Sorry about that."

"No problem. It was crazy cool."

"No, just *crazy*. I promise I'll never do that again."

I used the GPS to find a more bicycle-friendly route into Hakodate. I immediately liked the town, with its broad streets, beautiful ocean views, historic landmarks and the looming Mt. Hakodate in its midst. We found our way to the heart of the city, stopping at the main train station to get information about hotels and a ferry to Aomori. The next day we would take a break from cycling, and I booked two nights at "Smile Hotel," just around the corner from the station.

Leaving our bikes locked up safely at the hotel, we rode a tram to the base of Mt. Hakodate and took a cable car to the summit. The mountaintop was blighted by an awful collection of TV towers that looked like giant spears grinding into a majestic wild beast, but we enjoyed the impressive view of the busy town and harbor sprawled far below us. As Sho and I peered across the sea toward the southern horizon that hid the invisible landmass of Honshu, I relished a sense of accomplishment. We had just completed the first major section of our ride, the northern island of Hokkaidō.

"Congratulations," I said, wrapping my arm around Sho's shoulders. "Three weeks down, seven to go."

Sho nodded. "Two years from now, when I am ten years old, I'll be ready to ride across Japan on my own bike. You can put Saya on the trailer cycle for that trip."

"I love your confidence, but we've still got a long way to go. I'm not sure if I've got the strength to cycle over the Japan Alps."

"Don't worry, Daddy. I'll push really, really hard, and make sure we get over every mountain."

I mussed his hair and worried if I were setting us up for failure.

Chapter 23
Industrial Sludge

A STRONG BREEZE SPLATTERED HEAVY DROPLETS OF RAIN against our hotel room window the next morning, and I was relieved to have the day off from cycling. As we headed out of the hotel lobby to find breakfast, Sho noticed a vending machine by the door. "Look Daddy. You can buy an umbrella from a machine. Can we get one? It's only five dollars."

"Great idea," I said, handing him a 500-yen coin.

We huddled under the compact umbrella and stepped out onto the sidewalk. A wind gust immediately slammed into us, spraying rain in our faces and threatening to rip the umbrella from my hand. I held on tightly to the handle, fighting to keep the clear plastic dome over our heads with the wind whipping around us. As we crossed the road toward the train station, swirling gusts turned the umbrella inside out and ripped the plastic away from the thin frame. By the time we reached the other side of the road, the low-quality umbrella hung in a ripped tatter.

"That was the worst 500 yen I've ever spent," I complained, tossing the useless remains into a garbage can.

We pulled up our jacket hoods and ran through the mess into the wide entrance of a nearby building that was bustling with people. A large sign overhead read, "Asa-ichi Morning Market." Sho and I shook off the rain and joined the crowds inside. Vendors selling freshly caught seafood were crammed together, filling up the large warehouse with a multitude of ocean creatures on display, waiting to be eaten. Sho appreciated the dexterity and speed of several squid darting back and forth in a large tank, and he made up an impromptu "squid dance" that had me laughing out loud. We ate raw sea urchin, crab and salmon roe over rice, relishing the fresh food that had been brought in from the ocean just hours earlier.

As we waited out the rain, I called our cycling buddy, Mr. Saito, to check on his progress since we had last seen him huffing and puffing up to Shiretoko Pass.

"Hey Saito-san, where are you?" I asked.

"In Mori. I'm riding to Hakodate today and have a 5 p.m. reservation on a ferry to Omu."

"That's perfect!" I said. "We can see you off at the ferry terminal."

Sho and I were waiting in front of the terminal building that afternoon as Mr. Saito pedaled into the parking lot. He looked fit and had a cycling tan from mid-bicep to wrist and mid-quadriceps to ankle. He bowed in greeting, then took a closer look at me. "You're looking rougher," he said with a smile. I had not shaved for three weeks and sported a light beard and mustache.

"Yeah, I was going for the Greek demigod look."

"I think he looks like a scraggly weirdo," Sho said, making us all laugh. We were in high spirits as we sat down in a coffee shop with sunlight streaming through large windows that overlooked the ocean.

Mr. Saito took out his camera and scrolled through pictures, telling us about his adventures for a while before asking us to share some of our stories. Sho told him about this morning's umbrella fiasco and complained about the lack of game rooms so far on our trip. As I was excitedly telling Mr. Saito about meeting the Wanderer, a gruff voice yelled out, "*Urusai!* You're being too loud! Keep it down over there."

A silver-haired man, perhaps in his seventies, was seated alone a few tables away from us. He was wearing a suit and had a newspaper spread out on the table before him. He wore the aggrieved expression of someone righteous in indignation at having been wronged. I probably had been speaking a bit too loudly in my exuberant storytelling and realized with an internal groan that I had just played into the stereotype of the noisy, inconsiderate American. But I was annoyed that he chose to yell first, rather than ask politely. I looked him directly in the eye without apologizing. Mr. Saito immediately bowed to the man and said, "Please excuse us."

The old man, sporting a smug look, returned to his newspaper with a "harrumph."

"I'm sorry," I said, turning to Mr. Saito. "I'm enjoying the chance to catch up with you and got carried away."

"Don't worry about it. He's just a grumpy old man. It's about time for me to board the ferry anyway. I hope we get a chance to see each other again."

Sho and I planned to cycle along the west coast of the main island of Honshu starting in Aomori, while Mr. Saito's route followed the east coast starting in Omu. We had no idea, of course, that he would ride through towns that would be devastated by a horrible tsunami a year and a half later. Our routes would converge on the island of Shikoku, and we made plans to reconnect there five weeks later, if our schedules overlapped.

We waved goodbye as Mr. Saito rolled his bicycle onto the waiting ferry. "Will we see him again?" Sho asked.

"I doubt it. The odds are low that we will arrive in the same place at the same time over a month from now."

"Aw," Sho complained. "He's such a cool dude. Other people keep saying this trip is too hard for a kid, but he knows I'll make it all the way. And he takes way better pictures than you, Dad. No offense."

Less than twenty-four hours later, Sho and I were back at the terminal standing before a towering, sturdy 1,777-ton craft. "Hayabusa", the ship's name, was painted prominently in large blue characters on its weathered hull. A line of trucks, including one carrying a group of docile cows, waited in front.

Several uniformed workers led us into the ferry's yawning belly ahead of the vehicles. As we followed, I stepped in a mound of fluorescent green goo, rolling the bike wheels through it as well. The stuff looked like quick-dry concrete that had just been applied to fill gaps in a long narrow speed bump on the floor. I handed the bikes to the workers, who secured them to metal loops on the wall with old rope and covered them with heavy, dirty blankets. As Sho and I walked toward the stairwell, I tried to get the dangerous looking material out of my bike shoe cleats before it hardened. That spread the goo onto my hands, and I anxiously climbed the stairs from the ship's hold and found a bathroom, Sho trailing closely behind. I tried to wash off the strange, sticky substance, but after several thorough scrubs with soap, my hands retained a green pallor, complemented by streaks of the goo lodged under my fingernails.

"Cool, Dad. You're like the Hulk."

"Yeah, green and contaminated. *Cool.*"

I imagined the product label declaring, "Do not allow contact with the skin of any carbon-based organism." For the rest of the trip, the wheels on our bikes and the bottom of one of my shoes would host the crusted green remains of this industrial sludge.

In *Travels with Charley,* John Steinbeck wrote that traveling with a dog was the best way to meet strangers. The dog was usually the cause for an apology of some sort, which opened up an opportunity for a conversation. "A child can do the same thing, but a dog is better," he wrote. Whether you come down on the side of the dog or the child, the maxim holds true. Sho was testing his strength against the wind on the ferry deck when he nearly bumped into Kenji and Naoko Aoyagi, a couple who looked to be in their 30's or 40's.

"Sorry about that," I said, asking Sho to apologize, too.

"No problem," Kenji said. "Looks like he's having fun." We began chatting while sharing the ocean view, and Kenji explained that they were traveling around Japan in a minivan with their dog, Vino.

"We started from our home in Saitama, near Tokyo. So far, we've driven through northern Honshu and all of Hokkaidō. We're headed back home for a brief pause, then will continue south."

"Where is Vino?" Sho asked, looking around the deck with some concern. A small dog could easily slip through the railing into the churning waters.

"Don't worry. He's safe inside our minivan in the ferry hold." He added, "It's a bit of a challenge to travel with Vino. We wanted to stay in campgrounds on our trip, but most do not allow dogs, so we usually just sleep in our van."

"That's not fair," Sho said, clearly outraged. "I love dogs, but my dad won't let me get one." He gave me an accusing look.

"We have a cat . . ." I said lamely. I had grown up with dogs, but I didn't want the added responsibility at this stage of my life.

Kenji said, "I was bitten by a dog when I was a boy and never liked them, but my wife Naoko convinced me to get Vino."

She gave him a nod and said, "That's right."

Kenji smiled at her and said, "Well, Vino is the one dog I like."

"Have you ever read *Travels with Charley*?" I asked.

"That was our inspiration for this journey!" Kenji said. "I spent nine months in Paris during my last year of college, waiting tables and hanging out in a bookstore. I assumed that I would return to Japan and become a *salaryman* in a company, but that future just felt wrong. While in Paris, I came across a book of photography by a Japanese man and realized that might be a viable career option.

"I started traveling the world with my camera. I was in China during the summer of 1989, just before the Tiananmen Square massacre, and my photos were published in a Japanese magazine. I've been coming up with ideas for photo travelogues ever since. Naoko and I thought a Japanese photographer's version of *Travels with Charley* would be interesting."

Kenji and Naoko invited us inside the covered ferry hold to play cards. We sat across from one another on a carpeted floor surrounded by passengers lounging at a few tables and worn couches, the smoke from their cigarettes turning the air gray. After I had played only a few games, I began to feel nauseous.

"Sorry, but I need to go outside to get some fresh air," I said, setting down my hand mid-game.

Sho, impervious to motion sickness, chose to keep playing cards with our new friends. In the strong, cool wind, I felt better immediately and spent the final thirty minutes of the trip watching the Tsugaru Peninsula take shape on the horizon. The city of Aomori finally came into view, the capital of the northernmost prefecture on the main island of Japan. Much of the city was destroyed near the end of World War II, and the rebuilt downtown area had a decidedly modern look. The Aomori Prefecture Tourist Center, a large pyramidal building, dominated the downtown waterfront beside the dramatic Aomori Bay Bridge. The bridge's suspension cables and the triangular tourist center were each designed to look like a giant letter A.

Sho and I disembarked from the ferry, said goodbye to Kenji, Naoko and Vino, then found food—delicious raw scallops over rice—and a place to sleep.

Aomori boasts an archaeological site of a village that dates to the Jomon Period thousands of years ago, when early humans likely migrated across an ice bridge connecting Siberia and northern Japan. The ancient village was discovered by chance during a land survey and includes hundreds of homes, storage sites, burial pits, tools, pottery and artwork.

An impressive art museum stands next to the archaeological site. The museum's design mirrors an actual archaeological dig—its displays laid out in trenches dug into the earth—and includes a statue of a dog over twenty-five feet tall and three Marc Chagall paintings that are so large they must be displayed in a room sixty feet high.

Unfortunately, I saw none of these places. We were already five days behind schedule due to our mechanical problems and my decision to change our planned route in Hokkaidō. I felt pressed to get under way and had only allocated two hours the next morning for sightseeing in Aomori.

But instead of exploring the city, Sho convinced me with some impressive begging to spend that time in a game room. We immersed ourselves in the cacophony of one hundred yen-sucking machines featuring battling dinosaurs, Pokemon proxy wars, taiko drums and frustratingly flimsy claws grabbing for candy. My ears were ringing as we cycled out of town.

Two hours later, our trip across Japan nearly came to a disastrous end. Beside the road, Sho spotted a large field dotted with playground equipment. The difference in adventure cycling with a child comes into starkest relief during roadside breaks. A rational adult would consider this an opportunity to rest from hours of riding. But Sho was only interested in testing out everything the playground had to offer. I eyed a comfortable-looking bench longingly but succumbed to his urgent pleas to join him in the fun.

Jungle gym. Trapeze rings. Swingset. Seesaw. Slide. Obstacle course. Merry-go-round. Chin-up bars. We did them all, not just once, either. Sho turned into a taskmaster, "No sitting out, Daddy! This is the best playground in my life." Finally I had enough and said that it was time to return to our bikes. But Sho asked me to join him on one final piece of equipment.

The zip-line consisted of a pulley attached to a cable running between two tall wooden A-frame platforms. A long hardwood two-by-four served as a crossbeam supporting the platforms. I lifted Sho over my head and he grabbed the pulley, immediately zipping along the length of the cable before coming to an abrupt stop as he reached the end and fell to the ground laughing.

"Daddy, you've got to try it!"

I retrieved the pulley and hoisted myself up on the platform. Holding on with both hands, I leapt forward and swung my legs to generate momentum. I was surprised at the speed and realized my mistake a moment too late. The cable ended just a foot in front of the wooden A-frame platform, which did not have any padding. I should have let go early and fallen to the ground. Instead, I flew through the air like an out-of-control Tarzan, arms stretched overhead, feet flailing as the pulley slammed into the end of the cable. Momentum whipped my legs forward and my right shin slammed into the sharp edge of the wooden crossbeam so hard that I thought I heard my tibia snap. I fell to the ground groaning in pain and biting my knuckles to keep from screaming out.

Chapter 24

In Need of Help

SHO RAN OVER. "ARE YOU OKAY, DADDY?"

"One second," I grunted, my face buried in the grass, my body still. I did not want to look at my leg, which was numb and throbbing painfully. I imagined the embarrassment of explaining this ridiculous accident to my family, the people following our blog, and the TV Japan program that was producing regular features on our progress. Worst of all would be telling Sho that the trip was over.

I tried to flex my right foot and grimaced as painful jolts shot through my shin, but my foot did move. I took a peek at my leg and didn't see a bone sticking out. I tentatively ran a hand lightly over my right shin, and my fingers traced over an impressive lump. I squeezed around and breathed a sigh of relief. The injury was going to be painful for a while, but I had not broken a bone.

I lay on the grass staring up into the midday sky, calming my breath as the pain slowly subsided. Sho sat beside me, concerned. I rested for a while, then hobbled back to the bikes, Sho holding my hand and repeatedly asking if I was going to be all right.

Searing pain shot through my shin as I pressed down on the pedal and twisted my right foot into the toe clip. I felt nauseous and closed my eyes briefly, waiting for the pain to subside.

"Daddy, are you going to be able to ride?"

"It's just pain. I'll be fine."

"But when something on your body hurts, doesn't that mean you're not supposed to use it?"

"Usually. But we're already behind schedule and need to cover some distance today. It's just a bad bruise, so cycling on it shouldn't make the injury any worse. And anyway, I'm not going to sit around whining."

Sho looked at me skeptically. "Okay. I just hope your leg doesn't fall off."

We rode south on Route 101 for a few hours. As we neared Tsugaru City, I noticed periodic billboards advertising "Japan's oldest apple tree ahead." When we reached a sign for the famous tree directing us off the main route, I decided to see it for myself. We rode down several small roads that cut through sprawling rectangular plots of rice paddies, then rolled into a rural suburb. As we came to an intersection, I stopped the bikes and looked around. Sho asked, "What's wrong, Daddy?"

"I'm not sure where to go. I must have missed the last sign."

I saw an old man cleaning his tractor in front of a barn and rode over. "Excuse me?"

He looked up with a friendly smile framed by elderly wrinkles.

"Sorry to bother you. Do you know where Japan's oldest apple tree is?" I asked.

"Yes, I do," he answered, standing up. He wore tan pants, a blue baseball cap, and a light blue short-sleeved button-down shirt. His dark blue shoes were stained with dried mud. He was short and wiry with muscular forearms, and his skin glowed with the healthy look of someone who spent much of his time working outdoors.

"Would you mind telling us how to get there?"

"Sure. In fact, I'll take you there. Wait a minute while I get my bike."

He returned pushing an old black bicycle with a basket on the handlebars and handed me a picture of the apple tree. "Here, I tore this off a calendar inside. You can keep it. I'll show you the tree, but first tell me about your bicycle. I've never seen a connected one like this."

After I told him our story, he said to Sho, "You're an impressive kid. I'm glad you stopped by. An end-to-end trip across Japan wouldn't be complete without a visit to the country's oldest apple tree." His name was Waichirou Kosaka. When I asked if he had grown up in the area, he pointed across the road at a house and laughed, "I was born right over there."

He pedaled at a leisurely pace, greeting neighbors along the way, letting his eyes linger over a small construction site, a man at work under the hood of a car in his back yard, and the local graveyard. I imagined that his parents and probably some friends were buried there and that he thought of them every time he passed by. I could feel the deep connection that he had to this community and imagined the benefits and boredom that come from having deep roots in a small town.

We soon arrived at the famous apple orchard, walking our bikes up a small path to a comfortable home surrounded by apple trees and bursting with a large family of playful cats. Mr. Kosaka introduced us to "Ms. Kosaka, my relative who runs the place." I did not catch exactly how they were related, but I guessed that she might be his niece.

Ms. Kosaka, a middle-aged woman wearing jeans, a blue apron over a long-sleeved shirt, and a pink scarf wrapped around a wide-brimmed cap, walked us to the tree in the middle of a grove. Surrounded by a short wooden fence, its three fat trunks emerged from the ground like curling tentacles and created a low green canopy overhead. "Here is the oldest one. It's about twenty-five feet tall. The tree was brought over from America in 1878 with two others and still produces thousands of apples each year. It was designated a Natural Cultural Treasure by the prefectural government."

She and Mr. Kosaka swapped gossip about family members while Sho and I took pictures of the tree from various angles and started a game of catch with some fallen apples. When she spoke to us, Ms. Kosaka used clear standard Japanese, but I could only understand a small portion of her conversation with Mr. Kosaka, as they switched into a local dialect that even native Japanese speakers from other parts of Japan would not have understood fully.

Ms. Kosaka sent us off with two green apples from the famous tree, suggesting that we wait two days for them to ripen. "And clean them thoroughly. I recently sprayed the tree

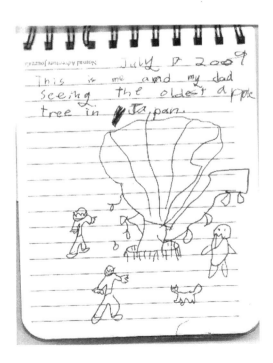

with insecticide. These apples are nice and sour. They taste particularly good if you dip them in soy sauce."

We returned to our bikes, and Mr. Kosaka led us on an enjoyable, meandering fifteen-minute ride through his quiet village, plodding along steadily until he brought us to Route 101. He gave us a polite bow and turned back toward home, pushing off slowly and not looking back.

That night, we slept in a roadside field, our tent set amid yellow wild flowers and lush grass. We awoke to the sounds of birdsong.

The purple-streaked, golf ball-size lump on my right shin throbbed when I flexed my foot, but would turn out to be merely a nuisance on the day's fifty-mile ride to Shirakami Sanchi. The name means "white god mountain area," which is a fitting moniker for what my guidebook described as the "last remaining virgin stand of Siebold's beech forest in Japan . . . The wilderness is almost completely undisturbed by human activity." I hoped to camp at the edge of this primeval, unspoiled forest and hike a short distance into the interior with Sho.

We rode along the beautiful coast, stopping frequently to capture shots of the impressive rocky shore and quaint fishing villages tucked between sharp cliffs. We were in the northwestern edge of the Tōhoku region, a rugged, storm-swept part of Japan known for its stunning scenery and unforgiving climate. The temperature was mild, and the sky, though covered with clouds, was benign.

The beach proved irresistible to Sho, and we spent an hour horsing around in the waves after eating lunch at a small noodle shop by the sea. A group of kids were playing in the surf, and I encouraged Sho to join them. But when he approached, they pointedly ignored him. He tried several times, offering to toss a ball and asking their names, but got nowhere.

"What's their problem?" Sho complained as he returned to me with a scowl.

"I think we've been spoiled on our trip by so many friendly people. We're probably due for some less magical encounters."

Before leaving the beach, I called Eiko. When I told her about the playground zip-line accident, she said, "Oh, no. That sounds horrible. Are you sure you can keep riding?"

"Yeah, it's just a bad bruise. When it first happened, though, I thought the ride was over."

"That must have been distressing. By the way, are you sure you work for Intel? You're not impressing me with your intelligence."

"Ha ha. Leave me alone. It was a freak accident."

"It sounds like something you could have anticipated. Try to be more careful, please. You're making me worry about your judgment."

"Only now?" I teased.

"Good point. When I first met you and we began dating, I could tell right away that you weren't like most other guys."

"I'll take that as a compliment."

"You are free to interpret my comment as you wish," she said with a laugh. Having spent half her childhood in international schools learning British English, Eiko still spoke with a certain formality. "Let me talk with Sho for a minute. I really miss him."

"Hi Mommy," he said, cradling the phone to his right ear with both hands and meandering away from me along the beach to talk with her in private. Since Eiko and Saya had left us two weeks earlier, Sho had not complained about missing them. I knew he did, but he probably worried that I would tell him to stop whining and just deal with it, the way I often treated any form of discomfort. His small form was a silhouette against the wide expanse of ocean, and I tried to empathize with how difficult it must be for an eight-year-old to be apart from his mother. After a few minutes, he returned within earshot and I heard him say, "Mommy, we saw a beautiful sunset the other night. You'd've loved it."

After saying goodbye to Eiko, we got back on our bikes and made our way toward the wilds of Shirakami Sanchi. As we neared our destination, the formerly benign clouds darkened and became a swirling malevolent mass. The first droplets began to fall, and we threw on light jackets and protected our gear with rain covers. By the time we turned onto a road leading into the forest an hour later, we were in the midst of a monster deluge of water and wind. Rainwater pooled on the top of my helmet, spilling out in a mini waterfall that ran in rivulets over my mouth and eyes. Sho laughed behind me, drenched and dripping, and shouted through the raging storm, "I love it!"

The coastal ride had been rolling, with short, manageable climbs. But when we took the sharp left turn toward Shirakami Sanchi, the road pitched up immediately. A sign warned of the challenging ten percent grade. Sho and I pedaled hard, like salmon fighting against the current as we rode through a fast-moving stream of water rushing down the

mountain road's edge. My legs burned with the effort as we crawled upward at a few miles per hour, pelting rain slapping our faces. The bruise on my shin ached as I pressed with all my weight into the pedals.

After twenty minutes of hard pedaling through the driving storm, we pulled into a visitors' center. The place was abandoned, save for a lone clerk, who explained that the campsite was another six miles up the mountain. It was 5:30 p.m., and the heavy forest canopy already cast the road in shadows. I didn't like the idea of riding in the midst of this storm up a steep mountain in the dark. I calculated that it would take us at least two hours to reach the campsite and worried about the risk of being hit by a falling tree or a car, or surprising a bear. I asked the clerk to help me come up with a creative solution. She pointed us across the road to a sprawling resort. "Try there," she suggested.

We cycled into the resort. Rows of bungalows lined pleasant streets that were laid out like a crowded residential community. We spotted a building with a "Check In Here" sign out front. Sho and I trudged up a flight of stairs and entered a pristine lobby. Fastidious, uniformed employees stood behind a polished mahogany counter helping several customers check in. I self-consciously looked down at a small pool that was forming at my feet from my dripping cycling clothes, and realized that I must look like a vagabond.

I stepped up to the counter. The clerk nodded to me politely, but could not hide a brief, barely perceptible raised eyebrow. "I'm really sorry to bother you," I said. "My son and I were caught in the storm and wondered if we could stay here. I'll pay for a room, or we could just set up our tent on your property."

"I'm sorry," he said with a sympathetic glance at Sho, who still wore his helmet and reminded me of a soggy Muppet. "We are all booked up. Typically you need to make a reservation at least six months in advance here. And the only place you are allowed to put up a tent is on the campsite up in the woods."

"Yes, that was my plan, but the camp is ten kilometers up the mountain, and I don't think it's safe for us to ride our bikes through the dark in this storm."

He breathed in audibly through his teeth and shook his head. "Sorry. You just can't stay here. I don't know what else to say."

Outside the storm raged, spraying sheets of rain against the window, and the sky was growing darker. I looked down at Sho and said, "We're in trouble."

Chapter 25

Shirakami Snake Charmer

THE CLERK'S REJECTION COULD NOT HAVE BEEN CLEARER, and I knew that it would be rude to press him, but I did anyway. "I understand," I said, looking him directly in the eyes and speaking slowly. "But I need to protect my eight-year-old son." I explained that we were attempting to cycle across Japan, mentioned our work with the United Nations, and finally offered, "I know you cannot give us a room, but perhaps I could speak with your manager to see if we can find a creative solution?"

He nodded tersely and said, "Please wait a moment" before disappearing into a door behind the counter. I tried unsuccessfully to get rid of the pool of water at my feet by sliding my foot back and forth. Sho stood nearby dripping into his own puddle.

The clerk returned with a man in a dark suit who smiled at Sho and addressed me in polite Japanese. "Please step over here," said the manager, motioning us toward the door. For a moment, I worried that he was going to try to hustle us out of the building. But he pointed out the window and said, "So those are your bikes? I've never met a father and son attempting to cycle the length of Japan. Sounds like a crazy idea. Tell me more about it."

We chatted for a few minutes, and he said finally, "I'm sorry I can't offer you a room, but I do want to help you. First, get cleaned up in our *onsen* baths, which are in the building over there. After that, have dinner in our dining hall, which is next door. Don't worry about paying—it's on the house. Then when you're ready, come back here, and I'll have my guys drive you and your bikes up to the camp site."

A deep sense of relief washed over me. I bowed, thanked him and offered to pay, but he refused and said, "I'm glad to help. Good luck on your trip."

Later, we were driven in a van to the campsite, the din of heavy rain pounding the roof. The steep, narrow road meandered up the densely forested Shirakami Mountains and was even more frightening than I had imagined. Once at the campsite, we set up our tent on the wooden floor of a raised pavilion that mostly protected us from the driving rain. The van driver helped us unload our gear and as he turned to go, commented, "This is highly atypical weather. It's usually a great time of year to visit. I'm sorry it wasn't better for you."

That night, I awoke several times, a powerful whirling wind screaming through the forest and slamming our tent mercilessly, shaking us with impressive wrath. At one point in the middle of the night, Sho sat up amidst the cacophony and, eyes still closed, said with a groggy smile, "Now, THIS is a real adventure!"

The next morning only a mild drizzle remained of the violent storm, like the remorseful tears of a child following a temper tantrum. Sho and I sat on the edge of the pavilion and nibbled on the rations remaining in our snack bag: some soy bars, peanuts, crackers and one of Japan's oldest apples. The surrounding trees slow-danced to a gentle breeze, and the trill of thrushes and melodic calls of jays gave the early morning a peaceful feel.

We set off to explore a tiny slice of the Shirakami Sanchi forest. Hiking toward Kanayama Lake, we slogged along a narrow trail, jumping over mud puddles and pushing through dripping fronds and bushy plants that crowded the path. Sunlight danced on the drops of rain that covered the greenery. The rounded crowns of Siebold's beech trees towered above us, some reaching over one hundred feet and probably more than three hundred years old. Their light gray bark was smooth, and their orange, yellow and green leaves formed a dense canopy winking in the sunlight far overhead.

Mixed in the forest were much shorter Smooth Japanese Maples, almost more of a deciduous shrub than a tree. Some were shaped like domes of colorful multi-pronged leaves hanging over trunks splitting off close to the ground. And Japanese Walnuts soared overhead, the trees' distinctive symmetrical outline and large elaborate dripping leaves competing for sunlight with the beech trees and giving the scene a tropical feel.

A striking bird the size of a sparrow with an exaggerated red beak hopped onto a branch a few dozen yards away. I managed to capture the animal briefly on my video camera before it fluttered away.

The forest seemed to breathe around us, its powerful presence looming and mystical. It whispered secrets of a long-forgotten past and hinted at unseen dangers for the careless wanderer. We encountered no other hikers during our two-hour trek to Kanayama Lake. The calm water sparkled beneath a morning mist that streamed off the dense forest surrounding the lake, and we sat quietly by the water's edge, listening to the soft lapping water and enjoying the glorious view. Reflected images of passing clouds overhead rippled on the gentle undulations, and although the moment was peaceful, I felt the unnerving indifference of nature. Kanayama Lake was there long before I was born, and it would be there long after I died.

Sho shook me out of my reverie, saying he was hungry, and we began to make our way back to our campsite. As I led the way, pushing through the dripping plant cover that leaned over the trail, I suddenly shouted, "Sho, don't move!"

A brown, spotted snake about three feet long was draped on a branch across our path. It was not moving and had a slight crook in its neck, presumably to allow for a quick strike, if needed. There was no getting around the snake on the narrow path.

"Shoo snake. Go away!" Sho commanded. "Daddy, should I hit it with a stick?"

"No, don't go near it!" I put my hand on his chest. "Stand still, and let's see if it will move off on its own." We waited. The snake remained motionless, its tongue flicking the air. I slowly took out my camera and snapped its picture.

"I think he wants *us* to go away first," Sho observed.

"He's blocking the only route I know back to our campsite."

After a few minutes of the standoff, I retreated and found two long sticks. As I slowly approached the snake, sticks outstretched, it made a subtle, but unmistakable, shift as if preparing to strike. I froze.

"Daddy, be careful!"

The snake and I appraised one another. It seemed utterly confident, while my pulse was quickening and my palms were beginning to sweat.

"Why did you stop?" Sho asked. "Is he hypnotizing you?"

Keeping my eyes on the snake, I whispered over my shoulder, "Quit distracting me."

"Sorry," Sho said with an exaggerated sigh.

"There you go," I cooed, as I placed the end of one stick at the edge of the snake's neck, and the other at its middle. As the sticks touched its scales, the snake seemed to relax. I gently lifted it off the branch and quickly moved it to the grass a few feet off the trail. The snake immediately disappeared in the underbrush.

Sho stayed close as I used the sticks to prod the hanging bushes draping the trail the rest of the way back to the campsite. But we ran into no other wildlife. After loading our damp belongings onto our bikes, we rode down the steep, wet, narrow roads through the forest, stopping frequently to let cars and busses pass us safely. My hands and forearms ached from gripping the brakes on the dangerous descent, and several times I had to stop to shake them out.

Before returning to the coast, we visited the Shirakami Ecology Center, a modest museum describing the surrounding mountains and forest. Sho excitedly pointed out an exhibit that tested our knowledge of various animal poop. He laughed when I kept guessing wrong. "Daddy, you really thought that was bear poop? It's so obviously fox poop."

We had the museum to ourselves, and a friendly guide gave us the day's first screening of a short film depicting the nature preserve in each season. The wilds of Shirakami are genetically diverse, hosting nearly one hundred species of birds, including the endangered Golden eagle and Black Woodpecker. Asiatic black bears and wild boars live alongside seven reptile and nine amphibious species. The area was designated a World Heritage Site by the United Nations because it holds "the last virgin remains" of a Siebold's beech forest in Japan—one of only a few remaining in East Asia. Japan used to have many beech forests, but as the country embraced a dizzying industrialization in the twentieth century, most were cut down.

Sho asked, "Is this really the last forest in Japan?"

"It's not the last forest. It's the last of a certain type of forest in the country. What makes it special are the unusual trees and the fact that people decided to let the place remain in its natural state. We are living in a time when wilderness areas around the world are disappearing rapidly, and many people are trying to figure out ways to preserve them. A few hunters go into Shirakami Sanchi every now and then, and you can get a hiking permit. But there are no man-made facilities or access trails into the interior."

The museum guide approached us. "Did you like the film?"

"Very much. We captured a little bit of the forest ourselves," I said and showed her the brief video of the red-beaked bird. She exclaimed, "That's an *akashobin* kingfisher!" Looking at Sho, she said, "Don't you think it's cute with its dumpy body, short tail, big head and long beak? The bird is reclusive, so you are lucky to have come across it on a short hike."

"Show her the snake, Daddy."

She took a close look at the picture and raised her eyebrows. "You know that's poisonous, right? A bite would not have killed you, but it would have been a serious problem. You two *really* are lucky."

We spent the next three days riding past crashing waves and towering cliffs along the coast. We met a few other cyclists, including an eighty-two-year-old man in racing gear who said, "I started riding bikes when I was a kid and never stopped. I still ride all the time." I said that I wanted to be him when I grew up.

Sometimes it rained. Sometimes it was dry. We rode regardless of the conditions, set up our tent at night by the water and enjoyed several memorable sunsets and evening bug hunts.

As we took a break on the side of the road one day, a grasshopper jumped onto one of the rear saddlebags. Sho immediately became attached to the friendly little guy who clung to the saddlebag as we began riding again, antennae flapping happily in the wind. The bug stared up with a mellow expression peculiar to grasshoppers, and Sho was smitten.

"He's going to sleep in a special box I'll make just for him," Sho said, gazing longingly at his new pet. "Daddy, do you think the airlines will allow a pet grasshopper to fly back home with us?"

"Hmm, we'll have to check." I saw a beautiful rock formation off the coast and stopped our bikes to snap a picture.

And then, just like that, the grasshopper was gone. I had only stopped the bikes for a few seconds, but that was enough for the insect to escape into the grass next to the road. Sho blamed me for the loss. "If you hadn't stopped, Grasshopper wouldn't be gone," he complained, tears welling up in his eyes. For the next hour, Sho sulked in silence refusing to pedal. In our blog, I entitled that day's ride, "Grasshopper Blues."

On another afternoon, we passed a group of young children wearing school uniforms and carrying backpacks on the sidewalks of a small coastal town. Sho asked, "Are they walking home from school?"

"Looks like it," I said.

"Aww man. No fair."

"What's the problem?"

"Those kids are younger than me, but they can go to school by themselves."

Our apartment in New York City was in a high rise next to Sho's elementary school. I usually walked him to school, which entailed an elevator ride and a few steps across a dead end street. A few times Eiko and I had let him go on his own. "You've walked to school by yourself before," I said.

"That doesn't count. It's like five feet away. When we get back home, can we move to an apartment that's far away from school, so that I can really walk there by myself?"

"Interesting proposal, Sho. I'll ask Mommy what she thinks."

Later that day, I heard a grating sound coming from my front wheel and saw that the top screw on the rack holding the front left saddlebag had snapped off again. The saddlebag was leaning out, its bottom side knocking against the tire spokes. Looking up, I saw a Bridgestone car repair center across the street. No longer in the sparsely populated wilds of Hokkaidō, where finding a screw required a multi-day search, we knew help was easily accessible. We crossed the street, and twenty minutes later, the rack was re-attached using a spare screw scrounged up by one of the Bridgestone mechanics.

The next evening, we found a beachside campsite in a small fishing village. A group of about twenty teenage boys on a school trip occupied several tents nearby, and Sho excitedly watched them set off fireworks against the dark night. Despite standing nearby and making it obvious he'd like to join the fun, the teenagers pointedly ignored him. After a while, we returned to our tent to conduct an interview via cell phone with TV Japan.

"Are you making lots of friends?" the interviewer asked Sho, having kept up with the many friendly encounters documented in our blog. Annoyed by the teenagers, Sho answered, "Not really."

The interviewer tried a different approach. "So, what's it like on the road?"

Sho grumbled, "I like the beaches, but I'm not getting enough game rooms out here!"

Chapter 26

New Friends in Niigata

THE MORNING SUN'S GLARE OFF THE OCEAN SURFACE HAD US up early, and we were soon on the road with plans to cycle sixty-eight miles to the city of Niigata. As we rode, Sho asked to listen to the *Billy Elliot* soundtrack. I would have preferred not to spoil the enjoyable sounds of ocean waves and wind, but sympathized with Sho's desire for a distraction from the many hours on the bike. He asked me to play "The Letter" and immediately began to sing along. The song dramatized a letter written to Billy by his mother shortly before she died. It was the most moving part of the musical and had made me cry.

As we cycled beside the ocean, Sho sang about a mother's love for her son and her hope that he would always be true to himself. As the song ended and his tender voice trailed off, Sho said, "I really miss Mommy."

"I know. I do too. Want to know a secret?"

"What?"

"There's a care package waiting for you in Niigata from Mommy. She sent something special for you, care of Sato-san. Remember him? Don't confuse him with Saito-san, the nice guy who is cycling around Japan. Sato-san is the ultra marathoner we met in Lake Saroma on the third day of our ride."

"Yeah, we shared a room with him at that place with the train."

"Exactly. He lives in Niigata, where we're headed today. You'll have to wait until we meet him to find out what Mommy sent though."

"That is so unfair!"

As we approached Niigata, our route left the coast and wound through forests and small towns. The road did not have a shoulder and unfortunately seemed to be a preferred route for trucks spewing exhaust and hemming us in so that we had to ride over debris along the road's edge. The closer we got to the city, the more vehicles crowded us on the road. Soon a constant procession was roaring by. I kept the bikes in as straight a line as possible, dealing with a margin of error of about a foot. If I swerved out much farther than that, I risked getting whacked by a truck's side mirror. My shoulders and forearms began to ache from the strain. Our truckers' route eventually ended in a ramp leading onto an interstate. Unlike my mistake on the outskirts of Hakodate, I recognized the transition and pulled to the side of the road.

"We gotta find another way into Niigata," I said to Sho. The GPS showed a complicated grid of what looked like neighborhood streets nearby that seemed to lead into the city. These turned out to be paved paths through rice paddies and farms populated by cows, chickens and even a few ostriches. We had to double back several times when the road turned into a driveway leading to someone's home or simply ended in the midst of a field. But we eventually found our way into the downtown area.

We slept that night in a small hotel and met Mr. Sato in the lobby the following morning. He was wearing blue jeans and a pink short-sleeved collared shirt, which hung loosely on his slender, athletic frame. His left hand was wrapped in a cast. He bowed to us in greeting, then handed Sho a wrapped box. "This is from your mom," he said. Sho promptly began to tear away the wrapping paper, letting it fall to the floor.

"In Japan, people usually carefully remove wrapping paper and fold it neatly," I said with a frown. "It's much more polite than tearing it to shreds."

Sho ignored me and pulled out the gift, a Nintendo DS Pokemon game. He yelled out, "Yes!" and pumped his fist as if he had just won a championship.

"I see your mother knows what you like," Mr. Sato said with a smile. Turning to me, he added, "These gifts are nothing special, but I brought you this fan and a pouch my wife made."

I thanked him and asked about his wrist. He shrugged and said, "Oh, it's nothing. I took a tumble and sprained it."

Mr. Sato offered to drive us around on an extended tour of his hometown and even help us run errands. I accepted his offer happily. I mailed a package of items back to the U.S. to lighten our load and bought new bike gloves to replace the old pair, which was starting to disintegrate. At a sporting goods store Sho found a collapsible fishing rod that would fit in a bike saddlebag. I was so used to cycling that, as we drove around, I had the urge to stick my legs through the floor and propel the vehicle forward like Fred Flintstone.

Later, we stopped at a rocky strip of beach with piles of boulders and massive hexagonal concrete blocks jumbled together and jutting out like piers. Several other lines of boulders served as breakwaters further out from the beach.

"I thought you might enjoy this spot," Mr. Sato said.

Sho jumped out of the car and ran to a short wooden fence between the parking lot and the beach. A twisting wind surging off the ocean whipped up his hair, and he framed his face with cupped hands to protect his eyes, squinting out at the sparkling waters. I joined him, wrapping my arm around his shoulder and staring out to sea.

Mr. Sato stepped beside me and said, "This is where I do swim training for Ironman triathlons. You have to be careful climbing over the rocks though. They can get slippery. That's why I'm wearing a cast. This is where I slipped."

"That's terrible," I said.

"My dad almost broke his leg last week," Sho said.

Mr. Sato looked at me with an inquisitive expression, and I said, "Playground accident. I also nearly got bitten by a snake while hiking in the woods. I think we'd be safer if I just stayed on the bike."

Mr. Sato laughed and said, "You and I need to watch ourselves! I dive in the ocean for Japanese oysters and was going to get you some as a special gift. But with this cast, I can't go in the water."

I thanked him and marveled at the amount of trouble he was willing to undergo for us. We had only spent a short time together the evening before his ultra marathon and, in my mind, we did not deserve this star treatment.

"What are the big blocks for?" Sho asked.

"They help prevent erosion," said Mr. Sato. "This used to be a sandy beach, but it was all washed away. This is also where North Korea abducted Megumi Yokota in 1977. She was only thirteen years old, and apparently she was taken to a waiting submarine offshore."

Sho looked up, astonished. "Why would they do that?"

"I don't know. North Korea kidnapped dozens, probably hundreds, of people in the 1970's and 80's. The press speculated that the abductees were forced to teach Japanese to North Korean spies. The country's leader Kim Jong-il finally admitted to it in 2002, but said only thirteen Japanese had been taken—not sure if I believe that number. A few of them were actually allowed to return to Japan."

"Did Megumi come back?" Sho asked.

"Unfortunately, no. The North Koreans said that she committed suicide in the 1990's."

Sho looked down at his feet.

"Sorry to bring up such a sad story," Mr. Sato said. "Let's change the subject. If you walk out onto those boulders, I bet you can find some interesting creatures. Want to see what you can find?"

Sho nodded enthusiastically and within minutes had found some tiny crabs, about the size of a dime, and dozens of water bugs that looked like centipedes with rough, gray exoskeletons.

After about an hour, Mr. Sato said, "I'm going to take you back to your hotel now to get your bikes."

"Why do we need our bikes?" I asked.

"I want you to show them to someone special."

A half hour later, we were standing before Kenichi Suzuki, the owner of Attack Bike Store. The place was crammed with bike paraphernalia, tools and parts haphazardly strewn about. The messy space looked more like a workroom than a store, and I suspected that Mr. Suzuki was more interested in the bike than the business.

Mr. Sato whispered, "Don't judge the store by its appearance. Suzuki-san is brilliant. He's run this shop for over thirty years and builds his own bikes. This is, no doubt, the favored destination of the local cycling and triathlon community."

Exactly the person I wanted to find! I handed our bikes over to Mr. Suzuki, who inspected them like a doctor carefully examining a patient. "You've worked them hard, I see. If you're going to ride all the way to Cape Sata, you'll need a little extra help."

He fished around in a nearby drawer and pulled out a small, unmarked plastic container with a thin tube sticking out the top. "This is magic oil," he said, holding it out for Sho to inspect. "We want to make sure the screws and points stay well lubricated so they can manage the constant exposure to the elements."

After he finished lubricating the bikes, he said, "Sato-san told me that you are planning to ride over the Japan Alps?"

I nodded, and he said, "Let's swap out your brake pads then. You'll want a fresh pair, so that your brakes don't fail on the long, steep descents." My chest suddenly tightened as I thought about cycling over the mountains. Of all the risks on this ride, crossing the Japan Alps intimidated me the most.

The collection of three mountain ranges included several peaks reaching over ten thousand feet, taller than every other mountain in Japan save Mt. Fuji.

Mr. Suzuki seemed to sense my tension and said in a reassuring voice, "I'm sure you'll be fine. Just be careful." Then he added, "Many people just ride along the coast. It's much easier."

"I know," I said. "But I want to visit several World Heritage Sites that lie on this route: Shirakawa Go, Kyoto and a Buddhist temple in the Kii Mountains."

He laughed, "Well, you've given yourself no choice but to cross about eight mountain passes then." He looked down at Sho with admiration and said, "I see a lot of athletes, but you guys really impress me."

After Mr. Suzuki finished working on our bikes, we took his picture and tried to pay him for his services. But he refused. "It's an honor to help out two adventurers. Good luck."

We cycled back to our hotel on fabulously smooth machines.

Mr. Sato had planned to take an overnight ferry up the coast later in the day to go on a 150-mile training ride, but canceled his plans. "Two of my friends have invited you to dinner tonight. I'll pick you up at your hotel at six."

"That gives us time to find some fireworks!" Sho said excitedly.

That night, Mr. Sato drove us to the home of Seiki Yanigasawa in the suburbs of Niigata. Mr. Yanigasawa met us at the end of his driveway with a hearty welcome. He looked to be in his sixties, his black hair slightly thinning at the top, and his light beard and mustache were gray. The summer heat from the day lingered, and he wore a white short-sleeved button-down shirt and cargo shorts that showed off the powerful calf muscles and forearms of an athlete.

By his side stood Chikako Seida. Her legs were similarly muscular beneath gray, knee-length pants, and her black tank top revealed toned biceps.

Mr. Sato introduced us. "Seida-san is training for an Ironman on Sado Island next month. She's one of the top female athletes in the area. And Mr. Yanigasawa has been racing for decades. He heads up the local Ironman triathlon club and also runs ultra marathons."

Mr. Yanigasawa bowed. "Nice to meet you. Thank you for taking the time to join us for dinner. We are amazed by your effort to cycle across Japan." Turning to Sho, he said, "Especially you! Come inside. We've prepared some food that we hope will give you stamina for your hard journey."

The spread was amazing. Alongside two large round trays of about fifteen different types of sushi were plates of sliced marinated cucumbers, grilled *gyoza*, bell pepper salad, chunks of grilled chicken, raw oysters, edamame, and bowls of rice. Mr. Yanigasawa poured me a beer and gave Sho some orange juice.

"Wow, Daddy. This is the best meal we've had on the trip," Sho said to appreciative smiles from our hosts.

The conversation was lively, ranging from stories about our ride to details of their Ironman races. I noticed that each person was modest about his or her own accomplishments while effusive in praising the other people at the table. As the beer flowed, we all became more boisterous.

While telling a story about a recent competition, Ms. Seida shook her head and said, "I'm not very good at riding the bike, but I had a good race that day."

Which prompted Mr. Yanigasawa to interject, "Not true! When you pass me on the bike, my beard rustles in the wind."

"You're such an exaggerator!"

We ended the day sitting in the empty suburban street in front of the house, shooting off the big package of fireworks Sho had brought. "I haven't shot fireworks here since my kids were Sho's age, over twenty years ago," Mr. Yanigasawa commented wistfully, as Sho performed a silly dance while holding a sparkler in each hand.

We left Niigata the next day with plans to ride fifty miles to Kashiwazaki, known for a popular *onsen* public bath and a special summer fireworks festival. Reading through our guidebook the night before, I noted that it was also the site of two more North Korean abductions in 1978.

About fifteen miles into the ride, Sho spotted a sandy strip of beach next to a campsite and restaurants and pleaded to spend the rest of the day playing there. It was sunny, about seventy-five degrees, and I agreed. I wanted him to enjoy some time on the beach, but I also appreciated the chance to procrastinate a little more before heading into the mountain chain. We spent a few hours body surfing, kicking a beach ball, and jumping over puddles.

When I had had enough, I retreated to a nearby restaurant with a view of the beach to write while Sho continued to

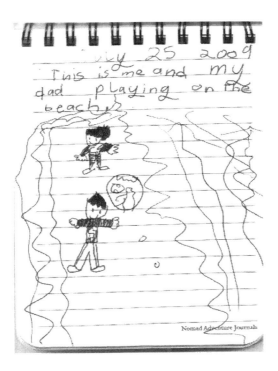

play by himself. I could see him through the window, tracing designs in the sand, kicking at the water and conducting an ongoing monologue. He looked utterly happy.

Sho finally joined me near the end of the afternoon, and as we ate dinner, the sun began to dip into the ocean, spreading colors across the surface like a painter's melting palette. I wanted a re-fill of water, but chose not to interrupt our waiter, who was perched by a nearby window, snapping pictures on his cell phone of the dramatic display. The ocean turned into a shimmering kaleidoscope of orange and red that was slowly swallowed by darkness.

We must have been worn out from the beach play, because we both slept for eleven hours that night. After breaking down the tent and loading gear onto our bikes the next morning, we were on the road toward Kashiwazaki by 8:30, rolling up and down hills on the coastal highway, passing broad sandy beaches dotted with frolicking families and occasional groups of wetsuit-clad surfers. Suddenly I heard, "Charles-san!" from behind, as a group of cyclists overtook us.

It was Ms. Seida and Mr. Yanigasawa, the Ironman tri-athletes we'd shared dinner with two nights earlier. They were with a group of eight cyclists out for a hundred-mile training ride. The nimble riders bounded past us on light, carbon-fiber racing bikes, easily zipping up a long climb, as Sho and I plodded along at a crawl on our heavily encumbered rides. We agreed to meet for a mid-morning snack at a park not far ahead.

The group was seated on the grass by the road, their bikes leaning on a guard rail, waiting patiently when Sho and I pulled up to join them. We answered questions about our trip and showed off the connected bike set-up to the appreciative group. Sho beamed as the super fit athletes praised his stamina and shook their heads at the thought of an eight-year-old riding the length of Japan.

Mr. Yanigasawa told us about a road closure not far ahead, due to an earthquake two years earlier that sent part of the road crumbling into the ocean. The detour was relatively straight forward—an inland run for about ten miles before returning to the coast. But knowing what to expect was a relief. After everyone had finished snacking, we took pictures and said goodbye to our ultra athlete friends, who sped off to continue their hard training.

Sho and I arrived in Kashiwazaki at 3 p.m., just as the rain started to dump on us, and we headed straight for an *onsen*. The popular spot was packed with people waiting to bathe, and we took a number in the lobby and waited our turn. Once inside the baths, we soaked in the outdoor *rotemburo*, letting the heavy rain pound our heads as we relaxed in the steaming hot bath. After cleaning off, it was a shame to put on our wet bike clothes and roll back out into the driving rain to find a place to stay for the night. We got a single room in an inexpensive business hotel, which had a coin laundry for our wet belongings.

After cleaning up at the hotel, we joined a throng of people filing down Kashiwazaki's broad main street toward the beach. The rain had finally let up, but we carried umbrellas just in case. Tonight was the last night of a three-day fireworks extravaganza over the ocean, and we enjoyed two hours of incredible displays in the sky: sparkling waterfalls, raccoon-shaped explosions, mini-Saturns, etc. Every fifteen minutes or so was sponsored by a local business, whose name was announced over loud speakers to the thousands of onlookers.

"What a great way to celebrate summer!" I said as Sho and I walked hand-in-hand through the energized town back to our hotel.

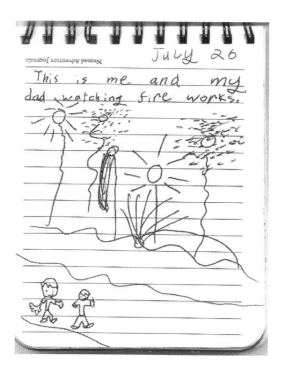

Chapter 27

Mountain Climbing

ABOUT SEVENTY PERCENT OF JAPAN IS COVERED BY MOUN-
tains, and some of the highest are concentrated in central
Honshu. In his 1941 *Climber's Book,* Walter Weston, an
English missionary, dubbed this area "the Japan Alps," and
the name stuck. There was no going around them if Sho and
I wanted to see Shirakawa Go, the third World Heritage Site
on our itinerary.

We spent the morning in Kashiwazaki, hanging out in a
game room, where I wrote in my journal, interrupted occasionally by Sho coming over to recount his exploits fighting
electronic monster bugs and dinosaurs. We finally cycled out
of town on a highway beside the glittering ocean.

At one point, Sho squinted out at the water and said in an
urgent voice, "Daddy, I see something!"

"What is it?" I asked over my shoulder, wondering if I
should pull over the bikes.

"I think it's a submarine from North Korea . . ."

I tried to appreciate the beautiful coastline, knowing that
we would leave it soon. At Kakizaki, we turned inland, and
Sho blew the ocean a kiss. "See you on the other side of Japan!"

Craggy, intimidating mountains loomed in the distance, and I wondered if we would be able to manage the many climbs ahead. Had I been alone on my light, carbon-fiber racing bike, I would have been confident. But seventy-five pounds of gear and an eight-year-old changed the equation. Sho and I had managed to ride almost every day for over a month, including some serious climbs, but we had never tackled anything approximating the series of mountains we would encounter over the next week. I wondered if our bodies and spirits could handle it, but kept my anxieties to myself, telling Sho to "get ready for some awesome mountain climbing!"

Happily, the route from the coast to Arai followed a flat road through rice paddies and farms nestled in a broad valley at the base of the mountain range. Rain pelted us early on, but the sky soon turned cloudy, around seventy-five degrees, making the ride a genuine pleasure for some five hours. By the time we reached Arai, the flat valley was beginning to morph into the base of a mountain chain, and I knew that our easy cycling was over. We found an *onsen* and a hotel room, hoping for a good night's rest before tomorrow's mountain adventure.

After Sho fell asleep, I lay on my back unsuccessfully trying to slip into unconsciousness, anxiety over the following day's route keeping me alert. As I breathed deeply and tried to relax, I had an unsettling flashback to the marathon I ran with my father at age thirteen, a lesson in the harsh reality of physical limits.

It was an early September morning in Jackson, Tennessee and already hot and humid, as my dad and I lined up in the middle of a crowd of runners at the marathon starting line. I could see sweat glistening on my father's forehead, although we had yet to begin the race. Looking around at the adults dancing nervously in place, shaking out their arms and legs, I turned to my father and said, "Dad, you know I'm the youngest person in the race?"

"Yeah, that's really something."

"This is going to be quite an accomplishment for a thirteen-year-old," I said confidently.

"It sure will be. Now don't go out too fast," my father counseled, and the starting gun sounded. After months of anticipation, I was finally running the marathon! I excitedly took in the sound of hundreds of feet shuffling around me, and I settled in next to my dad, matching his steady pace of eight minutes per mile. I felt strong.

After the second mile, I said, "This feels easy, Dad."

"Good. Just stay relaxed. We've got a lot more ahead of us."

He was right. After an hour, I realized that I could not keep up with my father and told him to go ahead without me. "You sure you're okay if I go on?" he asked.

"Yeah, I'll be fine, Dad."

"Hang in there, Charlie," he said and slowly drifted away.

My legs felt heavy, and a steady stream of runners began to roll past me as my pace slowed. By the fifteenth mile, I was in last place. I wanted to maintain a steady jog, but had to walk every few minutes. I wasn't injured, as far as I could tell. I was just TIRED. Dog tired, as we say in the South. I imagined a helicopter appearing overhead, a heavily armed gunner hanging out the window and filling me with bullets. At least then I would be able to lie down in the comfortable-looking ditch by the side of the road.

I heard an engine and glanced overhead. But instead of a helicopter, a van with race volunteers pulled alongside and a kind-faced young woman leaned out the window. "You want a ride in?" she asked, in a pleasing Southern drawl. "It's no problem, kid. You gave it your all and did great to make it this far."

"I'm good," I responded and picked up the pace for a few minutes.

Mile Eighteen loomed ahead at the intersection of two empty rural roads. The oppressive heat created a shimmering effect on the surrounding sprawling farmland. As I neared the intersection, I saw my family's yellow Toyota Tercel parked by the road with its engine running, no doubt for the air conditioning. My mother threw open the driver's side door and bounded toward me with a bag of sliced oranges and a worried look on her face. She wore a colorful summer dress covered with images of yellow sunflowers, and her dark hair was pulled up in a bun to allow the faint breeze to cool her neck. As she reached me, I stopped and greedily took the oranges from her.

Our eyes met for a moment, and I felt an urge to cry. I could no longer deny the truth: running a marathon was too much for me. The volunteer van was trailing a few dozen yards behind, keeping an eye on me, the race's last place runner, from a respectful distance. That van sure did look comfortable. I knew the prudent choice: just give up.

Then I imagined what "just give up" would feel like, and I didn't like it. It would take away the physical discomfort, but that short-term relief would be replaced with something much more painful: disappointment. No one had told me to do this race. I'd chosen it, I'd set the goal. Bumping up against my physical limits was humbling but also strangely empowering. I was tired and wanted to stop, but I realized I could still go on. I could fear the discomfort—or accept it. I still had a choice in the matter. And I decided, as long as it was up to me, I wouldn't quit.

"You sure you don't want a ride in?" my mother asked, glancing back at the kind-faced young woman peering at us through the windshield.

"Nope," I answered, talking with food in my mouth as I greedily finished off the fruit. And then, without saying thanks, I turned my back on my mom and kept jogging.

The last image I remembered before finally falling asleep next to Sho was that farewell to my mother.

Sho and I were up early the next day. It was already sunny and in the mid-eighties—pleasant for a relaxed stroll, but hot for a full day of cycling uphill. We covered the forty-three miles from Arai to Nagano in about five and a half hours, most of which was a steady climb. Our combined weight and heavy saddlebags kept us chugging along at a slow pace, but we were able to ride steadily. We had to rest frequently, because of the heat and humidity, drinking often to ward off dehydration. Sho and I dubbed the infrequent flat sections "gifts" from the mountain. Whenever the steady climb flattened out slightly, Sho yelled out, "Thank you, Mr. Mountain!"

We took a break from riding at a rest stop, throwing a hacky sack we'd brought along. Sho came up with a series of games for us to play, borrowing terminology from baseball, but taking massive liberties with the rules.

The final nine miles of the day's ride into Nagano was a steep downhill on Highway 18, and I held onto the brakes tightly. I couldn't decide which was more uncomfortable: lugging our heavy load up a long, steep climb for several hours or trying to maintain a grip on the brakes on a steep mountain descent, as my forearms burned and my fingers went numb. Every ten minutes or so, I had to stop in the middle of the downhill to shake out my arms until feeling returned to my fingertips.

As we rode along a busy route into Nagano's urban sprawl, Sho spotted a large game room with a batting cage. We spent an hour there, Sho playing games, while I tried to figure out where we would sleep for the night. It had started to rain, so I decided to stay in a hotel I found nearby. We washed our grimy, soaked clothes in the hotel's coin laundry, then I read Rudyard Kipling's "How the Camel Got His Hump" to Sho before we both drifted off, relieved that the first day in the mountains had been manageable.

Nagano, host of the 1998 Winter Olympics, is also home to Zenkō-ji, a Buddhist temple that is over 1300 years old. The temple is famous in Japan as a pilgrimage site, but it also gained some notoriety just before the 2008 summer Olympics.

The temple had been part of the opening ceremonies for the 1964 Olympics in Tokyo, the 1998 games in its hometown of Nagano, and was slated to host a torch relay ceremony for the 2008 games in Beijing. But after Chinese troops killed over 150 Tibetans protesting China's rule, the monks in Zenkō-ji decided to demonstrate their solidarity with their fellow Buddhists and refused to be part of the ceremony.

As with many temples in Japan, visitors pay a modest entrance fee of about five dollars to visit Zenkō-ji. And there are many other opportunities to give more money to the temple. It is common practice to throw a coin into a waiting receptacle before praying. You can also purchase fortunes or simply place donations in widely available containers. Sho and I did our part to support this ancient business model.

The temple houses a statue of the Buddha brought from India to Japan in the year 552. It is believed to be the earliest image of the Buddha to arrive in Japan and is kept in a secret location. Not even the head priest of the temple is allowed to see it. But every six years in the spring, a replica of the statue is displayed for the public.

As I read a pamphlet out loud to Sho that explained this history, I said with disappointment, "The replica was shown in April and May of this year. We just missed it by two months! Now we'll have to wait another six years to see it."

Sho said, "Wait a minute. If even the head priest isn't allowed to look at the original statue, who made the replica?"

It was a good question.

Sho and I spent the morning exploring the temple, including an exciting search for the "key to paradise" in the *Okaidan,* a completely dark tunnel underneath the main temple's inner chamber. We descended a narrow staircase and groped our way through the darkness, running our hands along the stone wall, feeling for the famous key.

When we emerged from the other end of the black corridor, blinking as our eyes adjusted to the light, an attendant approached Sho and asked, "Did you find the Key to the Western Paradise of the Amida Buddha?"

"I don't think so," he said. "But I bumped my head in the dark."

As we walked away, Sho asked, "What did she mean?"

"They say that, if you find the special key in that dark tunnel, you will achieve enlightenment."

"What does *that* mean?"

"It's hard to explain. But my guess is that enlightenment is kinda like being happy with who you are and knowing the truth of the world."

"Then I already have enlightenment!" Sho announced. "I'm happy with who I am, and I know that, when you're dead, you're dead."

"I think there's a little more to it than that," I said with a laugh. "I've been thinking that this bike ride across Japan is like a first step toward living a more enlightened life."

"That doesn't make any sense, Dad. You don't take a step when you're on a bike—you roll."

"Thank you, Mr. Literal." I waited to see if he would ask me what that meant, but he was walking ahead.

"Look, Daddy!"

Tucked away in the back of the temple grounds was the Kamikaze Special Attack Corps Monument. It featured a plaque commemorating Vice Admiral Takijiro Ohnishi, the creator of the kamikaze force. The plaque read:

On October 20, 1944, past 1 p.m., at Clark Air Base in the Philippines, Navy Vice Admiral Takijiro Ohnishi, Commander of the First Air Fleet, gave his consent with tears in his eyes to the young officers and men who desired to carry out sure-death, sure-hit body-crashing battle tactics in which they would burst into flames. On the next day, the 21st, two planes of the Yamato Unit of the First Kamikaze Special Attack Squadron took off. After that date until August 14, 1945, 2,525 young men with promising futures plunged their bodies like artillery shells one after another in order to defend the mountains and rivers of their beautiful homeland that they yearned for in their dreams. Inscribed on this monument is the last letter of Takijiro Ohnishi, who was Deputy Commander at naval command headquarters at the time. He wrote it as he faced death by using his sword on himself at his official residence on August 16, 1945. We believe that the noble spirits of the Kamikaze Special Attack Corps members, with their deep feelings of love for their country and its people, should be recorded forever in history. Here we erect this monument on the 17th anniversary of their deaths in order to console the spirits of these young divine eagles and to make known forever the work they left unfinished as a foundation for world peace.

I shook my head sadly, and Sho asked what was wrong. I pulled him close and said, "I just hope that you never experience war."

On our way out of the temple, we stopped by a rotating stone wheel at the Rinneto Transmigration Pagoda. Built into a rectangular stone column, worshipers who spun the heavy wheel were supposedly "saved from pain and suffering." Sho eagerly reached up and gave the wheel several good turns.

I patted his head and said sympathetically, "We're about to cycle forty-three mountainous miles from Nagano to Matsumoto. You can rotate that wheel all you want, but I don't think we can avoid pain and suffering on this ride."

We ate some muscle-stimulating *yaki zakana* grilled fish and then hopped on our bikes. Yesterday's ride had been a challenging steady climb, but today's was straight up a mountain. We rode for six and a half hours in total, including a two-hour climb into the clouds, up ten percent grades with no relief from the steep pitch. Rain came and went as we passed through cloud lines, chugging steadily up, up, up. An expansive view of glistening leafy forests and mountains opened up to our left, while the sheer mountain side hemmed us in to the right on the narrow road. The pull of gravity was relentless, and we crawled along at a ridiculously slow pace, struggling to keep the bikes from falling over or weaving off the road and over the short guard rail into the yawning abyss. Few cars joined us on the route up to Sarugababa Pass, so we often rode up the centerline.

My legs burned, and sweat mixed with rainwater constantly dripped off the tip of my helmet. We rested every fifteen minutes or so, as I shook out my numb hands. As I leaned over my handlebars catching my breath, Sho took the chance to come up with impromptu silly dances.

"Aren't your legs tired?" I gasped.

"Yeah, they're tired," he answered, still dancing.

Re-starting on a ten percent grade hill was a struggle, as I had to push down several times on the pedal with one foot to get enough momentum to jump on the bike with my other foot. Sometimes I lost balance and had to quickly unclip my bike shoes from the pedals and slam my foot back down on the road to keep from toppling over.

Birds hidden in the forest canopy trilled sweet songs that echoed through the mountain side. The sound of rushing water from a nearby stream wafted over us, as a forested vista opened up dramatically the higher we climbed. The mountain chain continued for as far as I could see, and our own mountain loomed overhead, like a playground bully straddling his victim. And we struggled and struggled.

At first, I was intimidated by today's extreme physical challenge, fearing the mountain and waiting for my legs to seize up. But as we continued up the monster climb, I began to gain confidence. Cycling through the Japan Alps was brutal, no doubt, but I was convinced we could do it. The key was to take frequent rest breaks, eat and drink regularly, and keep a positive attitude.

I came up with a mantra that calmed my mind as we crawled around switchbacks with no end in sight: "Today,

I *am* Climbing." My identity was taken over by the act of climbing. I should expect only to ride ever higher, straining against gravity. Strangely, this simple thought made a big difference. Rather than complain about the exhausting effort or wonder when it would end, I simply became lost in the effort. The burning in my legs and back and forearms, the numbness in my hands, the steady ache in the bottom of my feet as I pressed down hard on the slowly rotating pedals, became an unquestioned part of who I was. Climbing became a state of being.

Sho helped too, especially when my breathing became labored and he could tell I was hurting. "Don't give up, Dad. I know you can do it."

When his legs gave out, and he had to stop pedaling and just be pulled along, the full load slammed my quadriceps. Although I was exhausted and breathing hard, five weeks of regular cycling provided a good enough base to keep going hour after hour up the mountain.

When we finally reached the Sarugababa Pass, Sho and I gave each other high fives and rested a bit. I had to wait a few minutes for the loud thumping of my heart to stop drowning out the peaceful mountain sounds.

The descent was nearly as challenging as the climb. We navigated sharp, steep switchbacks threatening a dangerous fall if we slipped off the narrow road's edge. My shoulders ached, my forearms burned, and my hands went numb once more from the tight squeeze I had to maintain on the brakes. I wanted to steal more than brief glances at the beautiful view but needed to stay focused on making a safe descent.

Once we were off the nearly deserted mountain road, we cycled along a busy Route 19 into Matsumoto. Exhilarated from the climb, we hammered the final hour of gently rolling hills to Matsumoto Train Station, pulling in at 6:45.

A smiling Takeo Sugishita was waiting for us there. I had met Mr. and Mrs. Sugishita and their son by chance on a flight in the U.S. the previous year. I'd told them about my plans to cycle across Japan with Sho, and they'd invited us to spend the night in their home during the trip. Mr. Sugishita and I unloaded the saddlebags and threw the bikes in the back of his truck.

Their home was a beautiful dwelling in the traditional Japanese style, with bamboo sprouting in a well-maintained yard. They laid out futons for us in their tatami mat guest room, and we spent the evening enjoying a delicious meal prepared by their 34-year-old son, Yuki. The Sugishitas were wonderful hosts, and I felt the stress of today's strenuous ride dropping away. Sho enjoyed playing with Yuki, who was a natural with kids and who patiently humored Sho's desire for endless Pokemon card battles.

Yuki explained that he had lived for twelve years in the U.S. and only recently returned to Japan to live with his parents. "I've had some trouble with my liver and came home to recover."

At 10, Sho and I took a bath and retired to our futons. I read "The Elephant's Child," by Rudyard Kipling, to Sho, and he laughed hard when I held my nose as I read the line where the crocodile has clamped down on the elephant child's trunk. My older brother, Stuart, memorized this story when I was a teenager, and as I read it, images rushed back of my brother reciting lines in the family room of our childhood home in Nashville. The teenager I was then, listening impatiently to my brother practice the story over and over, would not have guessed that the next time I would read "The Elephant's Child" would be to my eight-year-old son in Matsumoto, Japan, almost thirty years later.

Chapter 28
More than We Bargained For

MRS. SUGISHITA FILLED US UP WITH A DELICIOUS BREAKFAST. Sho and I ate heartily and after the meal, thanked the family for their generous hospitality. We then followed Yuki on his bike to nearby Matsumoto Castle. It was an impressive structure towering above the surrounding town and encircled by a koi-filled moat glistening in the warm sun.

As we stepped onto a wooden bridge with a red railing that crossed the moat, Yuki explained, "The castle was built in the 1500's and is nicknamed the "Crow Castle" because it's black and sort of looks like a crow spreading its wings. It's designated a National Treasure in Japan."

"Wow! I would go here every day, if I lived in Matsumoto," Sho said and ran ahead toward the entrance.

Yuki said, "This is actually the first time I've been back here since a field trip in elementary school."

We explored the old castle, peeking out of slits designed to shoot arrows at attacking armies, climbing up ridiculously steep staircases, and studying displays of firearms from the nineteenth century. Sho loved the place and excitedly ran ahead and back, reporting on the upcoming exhibits.

When we reached the top of the enclosed keep, Sho set off to walk the perimeter while Yuki and I stared out a window, enjoying the view. The red railings of the wooden bridge stood out like a beautiful bow on the shimmering moat far below.

"I read that just after the Meiji Restoration in the 1870's, the castle was slated to be torn down so the area could be redeveloped. But a group of citizens lobbied successfully to preserve the castle."

"You know more than I do," Yuki responded with a laugh. "I guess I've lived in the U.S. too long and forgotten my Japanese history."

"Are you planning to return to the States?"

"I don't think so. I'll look for a job here." His expression was suddenly stoic, and I could tell that this had been a difficult decision. He added, "It feels strange to live in Japan again after so many years."

I nodded, and he continued. "I drank too much alcohol when I was in the U.S. and ruined my liver. I'm going to live a healthier life from now on."

We stared out in silence until Sho returned.

"Now that you've seen the castle, do you want to go to a game room?" Yuki asked.

"Yes!" Sho shouted, jumping up and down.

Sho and Yuki spent the next hour hammering out beats on taiko drums, and battling digital beasts. I found a stool in a corner of the game room and wrote in my journal, the nonstop cacophonous clanging and beeping of the machines all around testing my concentration.

When it was time to go, Yuki followed us outside to our bikes. Pointing down the road, he said, "Narai is that way. Be careful—you've got some steep mountains after that. I'm heading back home in the other direction. Good luck on the rest of your trip."

I thanked him, and Sho gave him a hug.

As we cycled away, Sho said, "I want to come back to Matsumoto and go to the game room with Yuki again. Can we do that, Dad?"

"Some day, maybe."

We turned our bikes away from Matsumoto for a mostly flat three-and-a-half-hour ride to Narai. In contrast to yesterday's lightly trafficked, dramatic mountain climb, today's route along Highway 19 was full of passing trucks and lined with miles of chain stores, pachinko parlors, love hotels, and car dealerships. The unsightly commercial sprawl slowly waned as we left the outskirts of Matsumoto, and we were soon surrounded by rivers and forests, but the heavy traffic rarely let up.

As we rounded a bend, I noticed a collection of graves clustered in a hillside at the edge of a copse of trees and decided to pull over. Some of the headstones were marble and covered with white inscriptions shining in the bright sun. Others, shrouded in the trees' shade, were made of gray stone and seemed older. I took a few pictures and stared for a moment, overcome by sadness. Not just sadness, but that same weird feeling that always rushed through me when I thought too much about death.

"What's wrong, Daddy?"

"I just feel sad sometimes when I pass a graveyard," I said, pulling him close.

Perhaps I already sensed that we would not see Yuki again. The following year I received a letter from his mother saying that he had managed to find a job he enjoyed, but had finally succumbed to liver disease.

Standing before the headstones, I had a flashback to visiting Eiko's mother's grave in Tokyo, before the start of this trip. I followed behind Sho and Saya as they darted under the ornate wooden gate that marked the entrance to a local Buddhist temple near my father-in-law's home in suburban Tokyo. The towering eves of the temple's two-story main hall loomed ahead, but we followed a short path off to its left, toward the graves. It was a warm day, and rays of sunlight sparkled off a dense collection of glossy granite headstones. They were arranged in neat rows, each with a narrow rectangular monument reaching over six feet in the air and rising out of two stacked square slabs that formed the base of the grave. The bottom square was slightly larger than the second. "It looks like a bunch of mini Empire State Buildings," Sho observed.

Seeing that he was distracted, Saya made a quick dash to grab one of the empty tan communal buckets next to a faucet at the cemetery entrance. "I fill it!" she said, grabbing the bucket and staring back at Sho with a triumphant look.

Sho recognized the power move by his two-year-old sister and quickly grabbed a long handled scrub brush and water scoop. "Well, I get to do the washing!" After a pause, he added, "And light the incense!"

Before Saya could respond, Eiko stepped between the siblings. While helping Saya fill the bucket half way with water, she looked at Sho and said, "We'll all take turns washing the headstone. And you will both get a chance to put in a few sticks of incense. Not only that, I've got a bouquet of flowers. The grave has two built-in vases, so you can each put in half the flowers."

"Yay!" Saya attempted to waddle away, dragging the bucket with both hands. Eiko leaned down to help her carry it, and Sho joined alongside, tapping the water scoop on his thigh as they walked past rows of graves. I pushed my father-in-law in a wheelchair. Eiko's eighteen-year-old niece walked beside us, followed closely by Eiko's two brothers and her sister-in-law.

"I'm sure Okaa-san loves this attention," Eiko's father said with a big smile. He wore dress pants and a short-sleeved collared shirt and carried incense and matches in his lap. "Nine of us coming to visit her grave. And she's especially enjoying those two making such a fuss over her."

Eiko's mom, whom we referred to as Okaa-san, "mother" in Japanese, had died of cancer fourteen years earlier.

"I wish Sho and Saya had the chance to know her," I said, glancing down at my father-in-law. Eighty years old, hair gray and back bent, he held onto the wheelchair armrests with frail hands as I pushed him carefully along the bumpy path.

He was much changed from the first time we'd met. In his mid-sixties then, he was a superb golfer and still worked as a senior corporate executive when I came to his home to meet my girlfriend's family for the first time. During the summer of 1993, I worked in Tokyo between my first and second years of graduate school. Eiko was living in New York City as a summer intern at the United Nations. We had met and started dating ten months earlier while studying at the Fletcher School of Law and Diplomacy at Tufts University in Boston. It was her mom's idea to have me over for dinner. I felt nervous as I stood in front of the door to their home in Tokyo, taking a deep calming breath before ringing the doorbell.

Eiko's mother, wearing an apron over her dress, answered the door with a warm smile on her face. Although it was our first meeting, I could see in her eyes that she already knew a lot about me.

"*Irasshai. Dozo, haitte kudasai.* Welcome! Please come in," she said. Eiko's family—her two brothers, Aki and Hide, Aki's wife Akemi, and their two-year-old daughter Arisa—were gathered around a dining table. The adults greeted me politely in Japanese. Eiko's father stood at the head of the table, back straight. I could feel him assessing me, his daughter's new boyfriend, and I suspected that he didn't approve.

He wore a suit and tie, and I immediately regretted my decision to put on an open collar, multi-colored striped short-sleeved shirt and jeans. Eiko's mother abandoned me for the kitchen to continue preparing dinner, and I sat next to my girlfriend's father. The rest of the family found their seats, leaving the one closest to the kitchen free.

"*Beeru nomimasu ka?* Do you want a beer?" Eiko's dad asked in formal Japanese.

"Yes, please. Thank you. That would be great. I like beer. Thanks a lot."

He gave me a blank look, and I thought to myself, "Quit trying so hard." Aki poured my beer and then filled his father's glass before his own. We spent the rest of the evening talking about America, Japan, politics, sports, etc. I could speak Japanese well enough to engage in a conversation, but I had a limited vocabulary, mangled many grammatical structures, and often mistakenly used familiar forms of verbs, instead of the more polite forms that would be expected of a young man speaking to an elder. By the end of the evening, the table was littered with the pitiful remains of my poorly constructed observations and attempts at engaging Japanese dialogue.

Eiko's mother flitted back and forth between the table and kitchen throughout the meal, bringing out food, clearing away dishes and ensuring that everyone was well taken care of. Several times, I caught her stealing glances at me from the kitchen with a knowing smile on her face.

Sixteen years later, we converged on her grave. Eiko helped her father unwrap the incense, while Aki divided the thin sticks into equal portions. Sho, Saya and I dipped scrub brushes into the bucket of water and cleaned off the surface of the headstone. Then I lifted up each child, one at a time, to dump a scoopful of water over the top. Dozens of clear rivulets streamed down the face of the stone.

Once the grave was clean, we lit sticks of incense to place in a small rectangular stone box sitting on top of the base. Taking turns, we followed the order of family seniority. Eiko's father went first. He pulled himself out of the wheelchair— his oldest son holding the handles so it wouldn't roll away— and stood unsteadily before his wife's tombstone. Holding his hands together in front of his face, he closed his eyes and bowed his head for perhaps five seconds. When he opened his eyes, I saw a tender look of love and contemplation and loss. Then he sank back into his wheelchair.

Aki, the eldest son, went next, performing the same ritual. He was followed by the second brother, Hide, then Eiko, the youngest of the three siblings. Akemi, Aki's wife, went next. Then it was my turn.

Standing before the grave, I pressed my palms together at my chin, tilted my head down slightly and closed my eyes, sending thoughts into the ether. "Thanks for being so sweet to me. I'm sorry I didn't have the chance to get to know you better."

Although I only met Eiko's mother a few times before she died, I felt a strong connection to her. She had worked in a toothpaste factory as a child during World War II, survived the horrific fire bombing of Tokyo, and come of age in the post-war period, when Japan was impoverished and occupied by U.S. forces. Unable to attend college, she nonetheless loved to learn and became adept at *ikebana,* flower arrangement. She also taught cooking classes.

She passed on to Eiko a sense of self-worth and a fierce determination to make a difference in the world. Eiko excelled in school and decided as a teenager that she would work for the United Nations. She pursued that goal with single-minded purpose and, after attending college in Tokyo, studied international relations at Tufts. Immediately after school, she passed the United Nations' competitive exam and received a contract for a professional position working in the UN Secretariat in New York City. I sometimes pictured Eiko's mother as a girl in 1945 toiling away in a factory in wartime Japan. She would not have been able to imagine that, decades later, her daughter would have such opportunities.

When we first met, I was intrigued by Eiko's mix of independence and idealism. As I stood, head bowed and eyes closed before the grave, I realized how much her mother must have cultivated this. A child of war who grew up in the midst of anguish, fear and deprivation, she instilled in her daughter a sense of purpose and appreciation for life as a gift to be cherished.

Now, on our bikes after leaving behind the forest graveyard, Sho and I began to ride beside a river through the Kiso Valley. I didn't know it at the time, but we were following a course that had served as a trade route through this mountainous part of central Japan for over 1300 years. During the reign of the shoguns of the Tokugawa family from 1603 to 1868, known as the Edo Period, this route was part of an official transportation network between Edo (the old name for Tokyo) and the ancient capital of Kyoto. The shogunate took many precautions to maintain its crushing grip on power, including a requirement that travelers remain on foot. As a result, a number of "post towns" with services for weary wayfarers emerged every few miles. The richest of these post towns in the Kiso Valley was Narai, the halfway point of the nearly three hundred-mile journey between Edo and Kyoto. The cluster of traditional wooden buildings set among stone paths was preserved to look as it did in the Edo Period, and

Narai is now a pleasant tourist destination surrounded by the stunning mountains of the Japan Alps.

The historical village's main street was nearly deserted, as Sho and I arrived around 4:30 on a Thursday afternoon. We wanted to stay in a *minshuku* Japanese inn, but the first two we visited were closed. We eventually secured a room as the only guests in an inn run by a seventy-seven-year-old woman named Mrs. Nagai.

"We're on a charity bike ride through Japan. How much for a room for the two of us?" I asked.

She looked down at Sho with a smile and said, "Five thousand yen." About fifty dollars.

That was an excellent price. "Sounds good. We'll take it."

Since we had arrived late, it wasn't reasonable to expect a prepared meal, as is commonly served at a *minshuku*. "I can't offer you a proper dinner, but I could make you both ramen noodles, if you'd like," Mrs. Nagai offered.

"Oh, don't go to the trouble," I said. "We'll just pick up dinner at a restaurant in town." She looked at me skeptically but kept her thoughts to herself.

Sho and I unloaded our saddlebags, stashed them in our room, then took a walk down the empty main street looking for a place to eat. As we left the inn, I noticed an old man, presumably Mrs. Nagai's husband, pull the window drapes open an inch to peek out at us. When I glanced his way, he quickly let the drapes fall back. We passed small shops and a few restaurants, all of which doubled as people's homes, and all of which were shuttered. We wandered around for about forty-five minutes alone in the dark night, the rumbling in our stomachs growing ever more insistent.

Finally returning to our inn, I asked Mrs. Nagai to make us some ramen after all. Sho and I kneeled by a low table on tatami mats in a small dining area. After a few minutes, our hostess entered the room and placed two steaming bowls before us.

She bowed and then said, "Sorry, but I misquoted the price for a room. It's actually seven thousand yen."

I considered protesting this bait-and-switch addition of twenty dollars to the room price, assuming that she was taking advantage of us. But I decided to let it slide. I suspected that her husband who had peeked out at us earlier—and was now nowhere to be seen—had chewed her out for giving us such a good price.

"That's okay," I said, and I saw relief in her eyes. "The noodles are delicious."

Before going to bed, Sho and I stole out into the darkness, flashlights in hand, to the edge of the river for some night fishing. Moonlight reflected off the dark rippling water that rushed by with relentless power. Like desperate merchants hawking their wares, thousands of insects called out from the surrounding darkness in a cacophony of chirps, scratches and twangs.

We settled down on a large rock beside the river, and Sho held out the flimsy collapsible fishing rod. "Sho, since we don't have bait or a lure, I doubt we'll catch anything."

"That's okay. I'll use my wits to outsmart the fish."

I cast the flashlight's beam onto the end of his line. The small shiny hook was bobbing on top of the undulating water. I teased, "Maybe a fish will die and accidentally float onto your hook."

"Maybe you'll teach me to fish, like a real dad."

"Ouch. That was a low blow," I said, whacking his head playfully.

We didn't catch a fish and soon were back at the inn. Sho and I bathed in hot relaxing water in an empty communal bath, then rolled out futons on the floor of our large tatami-mat room. It was a warm night, and Mrs. Nagai had opened the window to allow a pleasant draft. But I closed it when I noticed tiny black bugs drifting into the room. A small rotating fan provided enough relief from the oppressive summer warmth to allow us to fall asleep. As I drifted off, I listened in vain for any sounds of human activity in this empty town.

Sho and I started off the next day with a breakfast prepared by Mrs. Nagai—rice, miso soup, sautéed vegetables and grilled fish. We kneeled on thin pads, eating at a low table in the family room. A large TV was perched in an alcove nearby, providing an unwelcome distraction from the excellent meal. I don't like to watch TV while eating and would have turned it off, but Mrs. Nagai had changed the channel to a cartoon and made a point of inviting Sho to watch it. Sho didn't mind, no doubt preferring the kids' program to my rambling about today's route.

After saying goodbye to Mrs. Nagai, we got in another short fishing session by the powerful mountain river. No fish floated onto Sho's hook, but he seemed to relish the

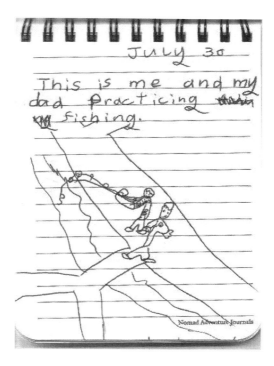

experience simply of squatting by the river, staring and waiting and hoping.

Today's destination was Takayama, which means "tall
mountain." We would soon learn first-hand why it got that
name. The first mountain we cycled up was full of switch
backs with ten percent grade slopes. It took us an hour and a
half to get to the summit. The experience was a repeat of our
ride over Sarugababa Pass two days earlier: burning quads,
numb hands, brief rest breaks every fifteen minutes to keep
from bonking, and breathtaking views. Once again, I found
myself repeating the helpful mantra "I *am* Climbing" to counter periodic waves of doubt that we would ever make it over
the mountain.

Sho pedaled hard up the steep sections until his legs gave
out. Then he rested for a bit while I did all the work, rejoining
me when his legs had recovered. We made light of the ordeal
by playing the "Fortunately/ Unfortunately" game.

Me: "Fortunately, we have the privilege of riding through
an incredibly beautiful part of Japan."

Sho: "Unfortunately, it's full of crazy steep mountains!"

Me: "Fortunately, we've ridden up mountains before and
know that we can make it to the top."

Sho: "Unfortunately, I'm going to stop pedaling for a
while, and let you do all the work."

Shortly after making it over and down the other side of
the first mountain, we did it all over again on a two-hour
climb crawling straight up to another pass, with equally steep
switchbacks. As we neared the summit, we came upon a family of wild Japanese macaques—also known as snow monkeys—perched a few dozen yards away on the guard rail,
nibbling leaves from overhanging trees. The group immediately turned its attention to us. A few jumped into nearby
trees and peered out while holding onto the branches. Others
crouched and looked ready to spring away at the first sign of
trouble. Sho and I immediately stopped our bikes and stood

still. I tried to calm my breathing, which was still coming in audible exhalations from the steep climb.

The largest macaque in the group stared at us and stood up on its hind legs. I heard several calls and the rustling of tree branches further down the mountain.

"I counted twelve of them, but it sounds like there are a lot more hiding in the trees," Sho said.

The macaque staring us down looked like it weighed perhaps thirty pounds and stood over two feet tall. Since it was perched on a fence, its head was nearly even with mine. Its long gourd-shaped face was pink, but the rest of its body was covered in thick brown hair. I could make out a stumpy tail.

"Is the big one challenging us?" Sho asked.

"I'm not sure, but let's be careful. I suspect he's the alpha male, and I don't want him to attack us."

"If he did, I'd punch him like boom, boom, boom!"

"That's a bad idea, Sho. I think they won't bother us if we don't bother them."

"But just in case, why don't we whack them with a big stick?"

"Sho, stop. We're not going to attack the monkeys. I remember reading about these guys," I said, digging out my guidebook and finding the section. "The book says that Japanese macaques live farther north than any other primate except for humans and are well adapted to cold climates. A group living in Nagano is famous for hanging out in the warm waters of the Jigokudani outdoor hot-spring."

"How cool would that be to go into an *onsen* with a bunch of monkeys!" Sho said excitedly.

"It also says that the monkeys have lost their fear of humans. They have even developed a taste for eating young human boys for a snack."

"It doesn't say that!" Sho protested then looked me in the eyes just to make sure.

One of the monkeys began scratching its rear end, and Sho did the same.

Finally, Sho and I slipped by, carefully pushing our bikes a respectable distance away on the far side of the road.

The view from the top of the mountain was inspiring. Tree-covered peaks stretched into the distance all around us, frosted by streaks of unmoving misty clouds. The rush of a river far below complemented the trill of hidden birds. It was a fitting reward for our hard work, and I closed my eyes and listened.

"Dad, what's your favorite dance?"

"Hold on, Sho. Let's stand here quietly for a minute and listen to the sounds from the top of this mountain."

Sho lasted about ten seconds before he started to make squeaking noises.

"I'm serious, buddy. I really want to enjoy this peaceful scene, just for a few minutes."

He nodded but had a mischievous glint in his eye. Seconds later, he made a few annoying chirping sounds and immediately said, "That wasn't me. It was a bird."

I shook my head and mumbled, "This is the price of coming here with an eight-year-old."

I had planned to reach Takayama today, but when we encountered the beginning of a third mountain climb at 6 p.m., I knew we wouldn't make it. I had mistakenly thought we had only two serious climbs today and would cruise downhill into Takayama in the last hour of daylight. Instead, once again we were struggling up, up, up. We had eaten most of our food and had little time left before the enveloping darkness would make the riding unsafe.

A local farmer had told me that there was a campsite ahead, but I couldn't find it before shadows started to close in around us. We continued to crawl slowly up the steep, narrow mountain road. I didn't want to risk getting caught halfway up a mountain in the dark and finally decided to turn back and return to a small village we had passed through seven miles earlier at the base of the mountain.

If there is one thing an adventure cyclist hates, it is riding over the same stretch of road twice. As I told Sho about this decision, he commented, "Usually, I'm a pain in the butt. But today, you were."

As we returned to the village, daylight already gone, we set up our tent on the asphalt by an outdoor bathroom populated by some impressive and intimidating insects. The location wasn't ideal, but it was better than sleeping by the narrow road on a mountainside. We munched through our meager snacks—peanuts and a few Soy Joy bars—and fell asleep with our stomachs still rumbling from hunger. Our bodies were worn out from nine hours of hard riding. But we were safe.

A heavy downpour soaked our tent all night, and I awoke the next morning under drops of water that had leaked through the rain cover. A pool several inches deep had

formed, and Sho giggled as he punched the top of the tent from the inside, dumping water off the edge.

"I guess we got a little more than we bargained for, huh?" I said as we broke down the soggy tent and loaded gear onto our bikes.

"Yep. So where are we going to eat breakfast?"

"The first place we find." My body felt weak at first, but soon grew used to climbing on an empty stomach as we rode back up the mountain, covering the same seven miles for the third time. When we reached the end of the climb, a beautiful, long descent into a tree-covered valley lay before us. A sign for a campsite indicated that it was two miles ahead. I paused to catch my breath and shook my head.

"Sho, this is about a half mile from where we turned around last night. We gave up just before we reached the top, and we had only a two-mile ride downhill to the campsite."

"I hope you learned your lesson," he said sternly.

We finally left the mountains and after an hour and a half of riding started to see signs of civilization. Suddenly Sho

yelled out, "There!" and pointed to a roadside restaurant. We were seated and eating in minutes.

After we returned to the road, bellies full, we happened upon a sumo festival in a small town. The festivities included a sumo tournament for elementary school age boys and a demonstration by a group of impressively large adult wrestlers.

A steady rain had begun to fall, but the sumo ring was protected by a large roof, and tents had been set up for spectators surrounding the ring. Sho was enthralled and asked if we could return next year, so that he could compete in the tournament. After the kids' competition was over, an announcer invited spectators to have a go against one of the adult wrestlers. Sho immediately volunteered, and the behemoth he was paired with toyed with him playfully. After lifting Sho in the air, the wrestler set him down gently and let my sixty-five-pound boy shove him out of the ring.

When Sho returned to my side, the announcer urged me to give it a try, too. "Why not?" I thought and followed instructions to disrobe down to only my bicycle shorts.

The muscle-bound sumo wrestler squared off in front of me, a bull moose of a man wearing only a tightly wound loin cloth and a menacing smirk. His oiled black hair was pulled back tightly and fastened into a topknot, reminiscent of a lost era when Samurai warriors held sway in Japan. His bulging shoulder and neck muscles fused together in an intimidating mass, and his torso reminded me of a sturdy oak tree. He was a remarkable specimen, a laughingly unfair opponent for a slender, middle-aged white guy with a farmer's tan.

I squatted down in the center of the sumo ring, preparing for battle and feeling silly in only a pair of bike shorts. Wriggling my bare toes into the sumo ring's gritty sand, I glanced briefly over my opponent's shoulder, beyond several dozen expectant onlookers, and focused on the pounding rain that was carving divots in the mud just outside the covered ring. The rain's ominous thudding seemed to grow louder, and a little voice inside my head whispered, "This is not a good idea. You are going to get injured, and you still have hundreds of miles to ride." But it was too late. I was already committed in front of the many excited faces of people who had come to watch the Sumo festival. Surrounding the outdoor ring, they huddled under dripping umbrellas and cheered for me to put on a show.

Sho stood off to the side, and I glanced over at him with a wan smile. He waved back with enthusiasm, still giddy from having just "won" his match. Now that I was in the ring, I sensed something was wrong. They let kids win for fun, but I could tell from the intensity of my opponent's eyes that the rules for adults were not so forgiving.

The voice in my head spoke up again, "Okay, remember, this is just for fun. Don't try hard. Just let him shove you out of the ring. Don't struggle, and you'll walk out of here uninjured."

Down to a trim 155 pounds, I was probably half my opponent's weight. As we squared off, squatting down and setting both fists to the sand so that our faces were only inches apart,

I whispered urgently in Japanese, "Sorry, but I am cycling across Japan with my son. Please don't injure me." I flashed a hopeful smile, but unnervingly, he did not reply or smile back. Instead he stared me down with a competitive intensity.

I puzzled over his non-response for a brief moment and realized two things simultaneously. First, it was probably a violation of the ancient rules of Sumo to talk to your opponent in the ring. But, I rationalized, he understands that I'm just a foreigner who wouldn't know any better. He's probably just following the rules himself and has to ignore me. But the second realization made my stomach seize up. As I reviewed the grammatical construction I had used, I realized I made a costly mistake. I had meant to say, "Please don't injure me", but in my panicked state, I'd said in Japanese, "Please don't injure yourself."

I had just made this hulk of a guy, who could snap me in half, think that I was some kind of wise guy who needed to be taught a lesson.

In front of my son.

Great.

Time slowed down as I lowered my shoulder and slammed it into his massive chest. Unencumbered by my opponent's thick muscles and fat, I quickly slipped my left arm across his body and secured a tight hold on his left elbow. Just as quickly, I reached under with my right hand to grip his loin cloth. I suddenly felt a jolt of confidence. As I pressed into the wrestler, I started to imagine that I might actually have a chance against this guy. I fantasized that the burly sumo wrestler had expected a soft, slow opponent but was shocked by my agility, strength and skill.

The little voice in my head yelled frantically, like a crooked ringside trainer, "Take a fall, take a fall!" But the ancient adrenalin rush of combat had taken over. I didn't care how big this guy was. He was mine. I had the element of surprise, as he had no way of knowing that I had been a champion wrestler. Of course, that was over twenty years ago. In the

Middle Tennessee high school region. And in the 145-pound weight class. But the muscle memory of the techniques came back to me immediately, and I felt the exciting sensation of having my opponent just where I wanted him. I imagined his unforgiving eyes now wide with surprise as I gave him more than he bargained for. All I needed was a little tighter grip and slightly better angle, and I would be able to shift his center of gravity, sending him sprawling to the ground. I strained with all my strength, feeling his massive weight grinding away at my lower back and legs. Just a little more, and he would be mine. My right foot was anchored in the hard sand, remarkably steadfast under much of his weight, ready to shift with a quick move to throw him off balance. Just one more second, and I would have him . . .

I remember a few things about what happened next. I remember the remarkable speed of his move. I remember how surprised I was to be slammed brutally hard to the ground. I remember the sickening feeling of my right big toe snapping

as he twisted me around it. He spun my body two full circles on the gritty sumo ring floor, ripping skin off the side of my legs and arm. And then I came to a stop, looking up at those intense eyes staring down with utter dominance.

I limped to the edge of the ring, bowed to my opponent and looked for Sho. The announcer intercepted me, microphone extended, and asked cheerily, "So, how was it?"

"Well, my son and I rode our bikes over two mountains yesterday. If I hadn't been worn out from all the riding, I think I would have taken him," I joked. Then I added, "I think I need to sit down."

I slithered out of the tent into the pounding rain, letting it wash the sand from my body.

"Your leg is bleeding," a passerby helpfully observed. "And your elbow." My right big toe was throbbing and stuck out at an unnatural angle. I worried that I would go into shock.

Sho came up to me, his jacket hood pulled up, rain dripping from its brim. "Are you okay, Daddy?"

"Sure, just need to recover a little." I tried unsuccessfully to exude confidence in front of my son. Accidentally twisting my broken toe as I lowered myself unsteadily to the wet ground, I fought off a wave of nausea.

Sho stood close and screwed up his face, as if he were having difficulty figuring something out. "Daddy, you're older than the sumo wrestler, right?"

"Yep," I answered, wiping blood from my elbow.

"Then why did you lose?"

"The older guy doesn't always win." I was now lying down prone with my eyes half closed, enjoying the raindrops slapping my face.

Sho accepted the answer but seemed to look at me differently, as if I had become a little more complicated and a little less impressive. He stared into the distance for a moment, then offered with an optimistic smile, "Well Dad. You got your butt kicked, but at least you tried, right?"

I squeezed open one eye and looked up at him, "You just figured out another one of life's little lessons. Just let me explain this one to Mommy, okay?"

And then I tried to figure out how in the world I was going to ride the next 500 miles with a broken toe.

Chapter 29

More Than We Bargained For, Part Two

I WAS DETERMINED NOT TO LET A BROKEN TOE DERAIL THE trip. After drying off and spending a few hours recovering in a nearby noodle shop, I limped over to the bikes, Sho by my side. The rain had stopped and the clouds were yielding to a bright blue sky. Sunlight warmed my neck as I lowered myself into a seated position on the ground and held out my injured foot. I snapped off a piece of a wooden disposable chopstick I had taken from the noodle shop and began to tape it to my swollen toe in a makeshift splint.

"Are you sure that's a good idea?" Sho asked, hovering over me.

"I think it's important to use a splint to keep the toe stabilized so that the bone will heal in the proper position."

"Is a chopstick the best thing to use?"

"No, I'm sure that's not what a doctor would choose. Where I grew up, we'd call this a 'poor man's splint.' I just don't feel like spending time in an emergency room. And this should work," I said with more aggression than necessary in my voice. There was no reason to take it out on Sho, but I was grumpy at having to deal with a broken toe and upset about the whole sumo ring debacle.

My bike shoe had three Velcro straps across the top, which I kept loose as I gingerly slid my foot inside. I groaned in pain as I squeezed my toe into the narrow end of the rigid shoe. Pulling one of the Velcro straps tightly across the top of my foot to hold the shoe in place, I let the bottom two straps lie across loosely so that my toe would not be squeezed any further. I stood up and snapped the bike cleat into the pedal, biting my lip in response to the initial twisting motion. But once my shoe was locked in place, the pain mostly subsided. Bike cleats are designed with a hard flat sole that distributes the weight and keeps the foot from moving around. This kept my big toe from being jostled, and I was able to pedal without too much suffering.

We rode an hour and a half into Takayama. As we neared the town, Sho spotted a sign for an *onsen* and shouted out, "Yippee! Finally, a bath. Sometimes you're so happy, you cry."

We got a room in a hotel and headed to the communal *onsen* to enjoy a long, hot soak. It had been two days since our last bath, and we really needed one. As I undressed outside the *onsen*, I removed the tape from my broken toe and found that the chopstick had dug into the webbing between my toes. The raw skin stung as I dipped my foot into the steaming water, and I let out a yelp.

Sho was standing behind me and asked, "Is the water too hot, Daddy?"

"Nope. I'm just suffering the side effects of a poor man's splint." I decided going forward to just wrap the toe with tape without the chopstick. If the bone grew back crooked, so be it.

After the bath, I relished the feeling of slipping into a comfortable bed, clean and dry. I taped up my big toe, and placed Band-Aids on my ankle and elbow.

Sho and I spent the next morning touring Takayama. A steady rain fell, and we wore ponchos as we explored narrow streets lined with old, traditional wooden homes and buildings, some of which dated back to the 1600's. This had been a wealthy merchant town for centuries because of its access to plentiful timber in the surrounding mountains.

Strolling down the well-preserved traditional shops on Sannomachi Street, I noticed a sake brewery. Takayama is known for its excellent local sake, and the breweries are easily identified by the *sugidama*, small cedar balls that hang over their entrances. Once you know what to look for, they are as obvious as barber poles.

"I know it's still morning, but I doubt I'll get another chance to sample local sake from Takayama," I said, walking toward the entrance.

But Sho pulled me back and said, "That sounds boring. Can we *pleeease* go to the Lion Dance place instead?" He looked up at me with pleading eyes. He was referring to Shishi Kaikan, the Lion Dance Ceremony Exhibition Hall, which housed lion masks, mechanical puppets and other items used in local festivals.

I sighed and felt sorry for myself. A childish voice in my head complained, "Sho always gets to do what *he* wants to, and I never get to what *I* want to do!" Which reminded me of something Saya might say . . . which reminded me of how much I missed her and Eiko . . . which reminded me that I was the one who wanted to go on this trip with my eight-year-old son, not alone . . . which reminded me that I was the daddy now . . . which meant, no whining.

I patted his back and said, "I shouldn't drink alcohol now anyway. We have some serious riding ahead of us."

The highlight of our visit to Shishi Kaikan came when Sho received a piece of parchment with the word "peace" written in English and Japanese by a large mechanical doll controlled by a hidden puppeteer. Sho folded the sheet proudly and stuffed it into a saddlebag.

"Maybe we should show this to the next sumo wrestler we meet so he won't hurt you," he suggested.

"Har dee har har."

We rolled out of Takayama in the early afternoon with plans to cycle fifty miles to the town of Shirakawa Go. Covering that distance would not have been too challenging on flat roads, but two mountains stood in the way. Having learned a lesson from our failed attempt to make it from Narai to Takayama in one day, I stocked up on food so that we would have plenty of calories available in case we got stuck in the mountains again.

Spitting rain and strong winds slammed against us, as we left the last signs of civilization and headed into the wild. Route 75 looked like a major road on the map, but in reality was a deserted, narrow mountain lane dotted with potholes and sometimes no wider than a single car's width. In two and a half hours, a total of five cars passed us. We rode through a few lightly populated farming communities, but we saw almost no one as we traveled up one side of a mountain and down the other amidst heavy raindrops thumping against the forest's thick canopy.

As we carefully descended the narrow pot-holed road, a steep drop off just to our right, Sho complained, "Where is everybody? I'm starting to actually miss being passed by cars."

"Be careful what you wish for."

"Daddy, let me tell you all the reasons that Route 75 sucks. The road is too narrow, too steep, too wet, and has too many potholes. There are no stores with food, and no one to hear us yell for help!"

"Well, unlike you, I'm enjoying this quiet route. The climbs are challenging, but we've already proven that we can handle them. And the forest is beautiful. Don't you love the sound of the mountain river below and the animals calling out in the trees all around us?"

"Maybe. But all the stuff I listed adds up to be way more suckish than the good stuff."

Route 75 ended in a T-junction at Highway 360, which would lead us directly to Shirakawa Go, a well-known tourist destination. I expected some fairly heavy traffic along this section and a few rest stops with food. However, the town at the junction was spookily empty, as if everyone had fled all at once. We rolled slowly past a few shops, all of which were shuttered. An erratic breeze shoved an old tin can across an empty parking lot in front of a boarded up store. I suddenly recalled images from the movies "Omega Man" and "28 Days Later," imagining that a group of crazed humanoids might emerge from behind one of the darkened buildings at any minute.

"What happened here?" Sho asked, clearly spooked as well.

"No idea, but my guess is that this used to be the main route to Shirakawa Go and this town serviced travelers passing through. But people must have stopped coming this way for some reason. Maybe an Interstate was built that took away all the traffic?"

"Well, I don't like the feeling here."

"Neither do I. But we have a dilemma. It's already five, and there is a big mountain between Shirakawa Go and us. We've got about two hours of light left, which is cutting it pretty close. We could set up our tent somewhere around here . . ."

Sho cut me off, no doubt with visions of zombies in his head. "I think we can make it over the mountain. We've already done one today. What's one more?"

I knew it was foolhardy, but for some reason, I also felt like going for it. Perhaps I was becoming addicted to the adrenalin rush that came with pounding up the steep inclines, but I wasn't ready to stop cycling for the day. It was as if the mountain was calling me, and I could not resist its siren song.

"Let's do this thing," I said, feeling particularly masculine, as we pedaled away from the eerie ghost town to tackle yet another peak. The rain had tapered off, and we were enjoying the cloudy, pleasant weather. We cycled past a roadside sign that announced the temperature in orange florescent digits: sixty-eight degrees. Perfect climbing weather.

The road was exactly what we expected: steep, narrow, and full of switchbacks and ten percent grade climbs. I noticed my legs tiring more quickly than I expected, no doubt exhausted from the previous four hours of mountain riding. And pressing down heavily, then pulling up hard on the pedals to maintain momentum up the steep climbs shifted weight to the ball of my foot and irritated my swollen big toe, which throbbed with each pedal stroke.

I shrugged off the discomfort and lost myself in the effort. "I *am* Climbing."

Sho and I struggled to keep our heavily laden bikes moving up the ridiculously steep mountain road. A sheer drop off on our left served to concentrate the mind, and the elusive mountain pass taunted us from somewhere above.

We passed through one small village on the way up, and I saw a young teenage girl hanging up clothes by an open window. I came to my senses for a moment, recognizing that we needed to escape the dangerous allure of the mountain and just stop for the night. Continuing on would repeat the same hubristic mistake I had made in the sumo ring. Why was it so hard for me to admit when I was outmatched?

"Excuse me," I said to the girl. "Do you know of any campsites or other places to stay between here and the top of the mountain?"

She retreated quickly and returned with her mother, who looked at me suspiciously and said flatly, "There is absolutely no place to stay between here and the top."

"Hmm. That's a problem," I answered. "I'm not sure if my son and I can make it over the mountain and all the way to Shirakawa Go before it gets too dark to ride." Hint, hint. For some reason, I couldn't bring myself to ask bluntly if we could sleep in her yard. There wasn't an obvious place to set up a tent, and I could tell that she wasn't interested in hosting a bearded weirdo who was dragging his poor son on a bicycle up a mountain at dusk.

"I'm sorry," she said and waited politely for us to move on.

Sho and I rolled away and did not see another person, house or passing car for the rest of the day. As the sun began to drop behind the tree line, and shadows began consuming the light around us, we pushed our weary legs harder and harder up into the craggy heights. The road was so narrow, and the drop off so intimidating, that Sho pleaded with me to ride all the way to the right, next to the sheer mountainside. It meant riding in the oncoming traffic lane, but since there was absolutely no traffic, why not?

As the pass stayed frustratingly out of reach, I recognized that we were going to have to sleep exposed on the mountain tonight. The only option was to set up our tent on one of the turnouts located every mile or so along the road. But this seemed unacceptably dangerous. What if a car pulled into the turnout in the middle of the night and didn't see our tent in time?

Every so often, I tried to keep up Sho's spirits by saying through heavy breaths, "Not too much further," and "Look how close the summit is!" I didn't say it out loud, but the top seemed like it was still far away. After a while, Sho was completely spent and could no longer pedal. He had been a tremendous help for the first hour and a half of steep climbing but had used up all his reserves in the extreme effort. He munched on snacks and finally asked to walk for a bit, as I rode along slowly beside him. We were running out of daylight as he climbed back on his bike. I felt as if I already had used up all my energy for the day and had nothing left to propel us up toward the elusive summit.

After two hours of chugging straight up this mountain and four hours of hard riding before that, I could hardly manage to keep turning over the pedals. Sho sat exhausted on his bike, apologizing for not being able to help anymore.

"Don't worry, buckaroo. You got us so close to the top, and I'm going to get us through this last little bit," I said between heavy breaths, knowing that I was lying. The shadows were growing longer alarmingly fast. It was already too late. The mountain had won.

Chapter 30

Dancing the Night Away

AS THE FINAL GLOW OF DAYLIGHT BEGAN TO FADE, I HOPED there weren't bears in the area and started looking for a turn-out where we could set up the tent. The road offered none, and I continued to pedal at an impossibly slow crawl up brutally steep switchbacks. By jerking the front wheel back and forth I was just able to keep the bikes upright while moving at close to zero miles per hour. My head was bowed, and sweat blurred my vision. My bike's frame creaked with a metallic groan as I cranked the handlebars hard in syncopation with each heavy pedal stroke.

Sho said something from behind, but I was too exhausted to catch it.

"What?" I grunted, still staring down a foot in front of my bike and struggling to keep from falling over.

"Daddy, I see something!"

I glanced up and saw just ahead a large clearing to the left of the road. A small shack with a large orange A-frame roof peeked through the trees. Near it stood a sign announcing our arrival at the mountain pass!

Sho and I jumped off the bikes and began whooping and hollering. "We made it to the top!" I yelled, giving him a high five.

"Yeah baby, yeah baby!" Sho sang while doing a funny dance.

The shack was unlocked and had a wooden cot for two built into one wall, a table, and even a few hangers we could use to dry off our sweat-soaked clothes. We moved our gear into the hut, now needing flashlights to see, and spread out our provisions on the table. Munching on our rations inside the comfortable enclosure, we congratulated ourselves on completing our toughest ride yet.

"I always knew we'd make it," Sho said while chewing on a rice ball.

An hour later my leg muscles twitched from exhaustion as I lay on the hard wooden bed. Sho was snuggled up close with an arm draped across my chest, a contented smile on his face. We drifted into unconsciousness while the sounds of the mountain whispered softly outside.

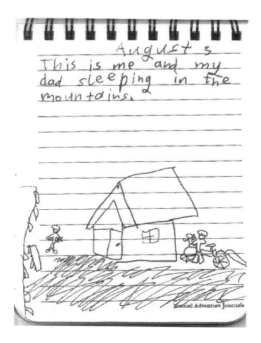

I was awakened at 5:45 a.m. by the bright morning sun bathing the mountaintop in a warm glow. While Sho snoozed, I stepped out of the hiker's hut into a bucolic scene filled with the sound of birds' morning song and the gentle rustling of wind through the verdant forest. The pre-dawn gray churned with bright orange hues, as the sun's rays began to spread across the surrounding mountain chain.

Sho woke up soon thereafter. As we were packing our bags onto the bikes, an elderly forest ranger pulled up in a truck near the hut and stepped out. He wore a green uniform and hiking boots.

"Good morning," he said with a polite nod of his head, his thin gray hair rustling in the wind.

"Good morning!" I responded, wondering if we might be in trouble for sleeping in the hut. I quickly explained, "We cycled up the mountain yesterday heading to Shirakawa Go and ran out of daylight. Was it okay that we slept in the hut?"

"Absolutely. It's for people just like you who need shelter. That's why we leave it unlocked. I hope you were comfortable."

"Very much so."

"Your son rode all the way up the mountain too?"

I nodded, and he looked at Sho with a mixture of admiration and incredulity. "Strong kid. Well, be careful on your descent. There have been rock slides that way, and the road is even narrower than the side you rode up."

On the trip down the other side of the mountain, I did my best to avoid debris from the rockslides, but my bike's back tire began to hiss fifteen minutes into the descent. I pulled the bikes to a stop and unloaded the gear. I patched the hole and checked for any remaining sharp objects in the tire before inserting the tube and loading the saddlebags back onto the bikes. Sho sat patiently on a small clump of grass nearby, playing his Nintendo DS.

Once under way again, we took it slowly down the narrow, winding debris-strewn road, staying well away from the precipitous drop-off. Only a three-foot guardrail protected us from falling thousands of feet, and we would have hurled our-selves right over it if I'd lost control. With numb fingers and burning forearms, I squeezed the brakes hard, determined to make it down safely.

As we neared the village of Shirakawa Go, we started to see distinctive farm houses with thickly thatched A-frame roofs. The style, known as *gasshō-zukuri,* means "clasped-hands" and was designed to withstand the heavy snow that falls on this part of Japan every winter. The roofs were steeply pitched and made of brown thatch that looked to be several feet thick. In contrast to yesterday's rain and mild tempera-tures, today was sunny and 90 degrees, and I had difficulty picturing the surrounding green fields covered in snow.

Our steep mountain road ended abruptly, and we were suddenly in the midst of hundreds of camera-toting tourists tramping back and forth through the main street of a small village. They all must have come from another route, because not a single car had passed us on our descent from the moun-tain pass. Several tourists uttered in surprise, "*Sugei!* Cool!"— and turned their cameras away from the houses to take pictures of our bikes as we rolled by.

"Where are we again?" Sho asked.

"Shirakawa Go. It's a village with about 1,500 people that was designated a World Heritage Site." I pulled out my guide book and read out loud, "Located in a mountainous region that was cut off from the rest of the world for a long period of time, these villages with their Gassho-style houses subsisted on the cultivation of mulberry trees and the rearing of silk-worms. The large houses with their steeply pitched thatched roofs are the only examples of their kind in Japan."

Sho and I spent the afternoon wandering through the small town, visiting a few of the traditional houses that were open to the public. Everyone I saw seemed to be either a tour-ist or an employee of a gift shop.

We decided to sleep in a small *ryokan* inn, where we were served a delicious traditional Japanese dinner. We sat on pads in a tatami mat room full of other visitors wearing comfortable *yukata* robes and surrounded by dishes of beautifully prepared food.

Our server, a gray-haired man wearing a short-sleeved white cotton shirt and tan pants, came over to our table and kneeled beside us.

"Welcome. It's an honor to have you stay here," he said with a bow. "The owner of the inn told me about your ride across Japan. It sounds amazing."

I nodded my head and said, "Thank you. The food is delicious."

"I'm glad you like it. I overheard you call your son Sho. Do you know that is the name of the river that runs through this town?"

"I didn't know that!" Sho said excitedly.

The man smiled and asked, "What character do you use to write your name?"

"*Hishou no shou*, to fly or soar."

"Oh that's an excellent character. The river is pronounced the same as your name, but is spelled with a different character that means 'manor'– not as impressive as yours."

Sho smiled at the compliment, and the man continued, "I want to hear more about your journey."

Sho and I happily shared stories of our ride so far and explained that we'd designed the route so that we could see as many of Japan's World Heritage Sites as possible.

"I hope this place remains a World Heritage Site," he said in a conspiratorial whisper.

"What do you mean?" I asked.

"The villages in Shirakawa Go and Gokayama were named World Heritage Sites in 1995," he explained. "This area was already a tourist destination back then because of the unique *gassho-zukuri* homes, but once it was recognized by the UN, many more tourists started showing up. A lot more money started pouring in, which was great for the local businesses. But the constant flow of tourists has damaged some of the traditional homes, and a few have been converted to gift shops with big parking lots.

"The purpose behind the UN's World Heritage Site designation is to preserve and protect a place's cultural heritage or an endangered wilderness area. Turning it into a tourist trap is definitely not what they want, and there are rumors that the UN may take away the designation. Also, even though we like the extra money, some locals fear that the old, simpler way of living is simply disappearing."

"What do you think is better—improving the economy or preserving the old way of living?" I asked.

"I want both."

The server left us to our meal, and Sho and I returned our focus to the delicious food.

"This is a big contrast to our Spartan mountain experience last night," I said, looking at the variety of dishes laid out before us.

Sho nodded enthusiastically and said, "Yeah, big time! Do we have to ride up another mountain tomorrow?"

"No. We've got a mostly flat fifty-three-mile trip to Gujo Hachiman, a small town famous for holding traditional street dances in a different part of town every night of the summer."

"Can we dance too?"

"I think anyone is welcome to join in. Let's plan on it!"

As we set off the next morning, the sun's hot glare was already beating down on us. The ride started with a thirty-minute steady climb up a meandering road that ran alongside the Sho River leading up to a large dam.

"I thought you said today's ride was flat," Sho complained.

"I said *mostly* flat. It should be slightly down hill once we get to the lake on the other side of the dam."

Soon we were coasting easily beside the man-made Lake Miboro, whose waters shimmered in the bright sun. When the dam was built in the late 1950's as part of a 215-megawatt hydroelectric power station, four villages with 230 homes were submerged by the new lake. Before evacuating their homes, villagers dug up two cherry blossom trees and transplanted them to Shirakawa Go. Every spring when the blossoms emerge for a week or two, then fall to the ground, it is said that each falling petal represents a tear for the mourning villagers who lost their homes.

The flat route was a nice treat after a week of mountain climbing, but we suffered in the 95-degree temperature. Sho and I pulled in to Gujo Hachiman at 3 p.m., dripping sweat and ready to get away from the pounding sun. We asked directions to the neighborhood that would host the evening's dancing, then navigated through the pleasant village, crossing over stone bridges and riding through narrow alleyways.

People were already putting up lanterns in preparation for the evening's festivities, and we found a nearby Japanese inn that had a room available. As we entered the lobby, a large Golden Retriever peered at us from behind the front desk, feet perched on a chair and head cocked expectantly in our direction. Sho offered a friendly bark, and the dog sauntered off to retrieve a human.

After checking in, we immediately changed into the soft *yukata* robes and slippers provided by the inn, and cleaned off our sweaty grime in the *onsen*. I slipped into a separate tub full of cold water, and my sweat immediately changed to goose bumps, but I didn't mind. It felt great finally to cool off.

We spent the end of the afternoon exploring the town, which boasted an imposing castle standing guard on a tree-covered hill looming over the village. For centuries, it represented the unyielding power of the Tokugawa government, but now it served only as a tourist attraction and, lit up by spotlights, a pleasant evening sight. A powerful river passed through the town, and we ate soy-flavored crackers and pumpkin ice cream on the way to the water's edge. Sho tossed stones into the rushing current and asked, "Daddy, how long would I survive if I fell into the river?"

"Not long, buddy. And let's not find out."

As daylight faded, the streets took on a festive atmosphere, and streams of people started to converge on our neighborhood. Most wore colorful *yukata* robes and many walked in *geta,* traditional Japanese wooden clogs that produced a satisfying hollow echo against the stone streets.

Although the sun had disappeared behind the hillside an hour earlier, the heat and humidity remained oppressive. My skin glistened with sweat. Sho ran energetically back and forth in front of street vendors who sold cheap food and enticed passersby with various games that cost one hundred yen a pop. Sho's favorite required the player to attempt to scoop up plastic fish out of a cylindrical plastic tub of flowing water using a small paper net that immediately started to disintegrate after getting wet. If you didn't move quickly enough, the fish dropped through the soggy scoop and you were left empty handed.

Sho failed on his first try, but the kindhearted elderly woman administering the game handed him another scoop for free and said, "Here, try again, but dip it in and out really fast." He netted a red plastic fish and proudly showed it off to the smiling woman.

Then the dancing began. A large float dominated the main street, from which a band blasted out a rhythmic traditional tune over loud speakers. A balding, elderly man played the flute. An older woman strummed a long-necked guitar-like instrument, a *shamisen*. A younger man beat on a *taiko* drum. And the lead singer belted out lyrics while holding a microphone. All of them wore colorful cotton *yukata* robes. A long line of dancers snaked the length of the street, steadily making their way around in a block-long oval. Local organizers helped to keep order as the procession of hundreds of dancers repeated over and over the same collection of leg and hand movements to the beat of the blaring music. Everyone was encouraged to dance, and after watching for a few minutes, Sho and I dove into the mix.

Just as we mastered the first series of moves, the music changed and the dancers commenced an entirely new dance. We struggled to mimic our neighbors and, once again, just as we finally started to get the dance down, the music changed and we had to learn a new set of moves. Someone stepped on my injured toe, and I let out a yelp. Sho didn't recognize that I was in pain and copied me with an enthusiastic, "Eeyow! This is fun!"

No one seemed to mind our lack of skill, and some local teenagers wearing blue and red *yukata* robes and bandanas wrapped around their foreheads took a charitable interest in teaching us the moves. They bounded beside us with playful smiles, patiently counting, "One, two, three, four, one, two, three, four . . . " as they showed us the dance. They could not have been more gracious, but I was very self-conscious, especially when I realized that Sho was picking up the movements more quickly than I.

The dance finally ended at 10:30 p.m., and while Sho hung out for a few minutes with our new friends, I helped a group of young men push the heavy float on its rollers into a parking lot at the end of the street to be stored away until next time. People drifted away, and the street that so recently was filled with raucous dance music was now filled with the sounds of night bugs.

Chapter 31
Kyoto Fireworks Fiasco

WE LEFT GUJO HACHIMAN THE NEXT MORNING FOR AN EASY twenty-five-mile ride to Seki City on Route 156. There was more traffic than I was used to, after spending so much time on deserted mountain roads. I appreciated the general downward slope, as we steadily descended the eastern spine of the Japan Alps toward the sea. We rode beside a broad river populated by black cormorants, their long wings outstretched as they glided over the roiling rapids hunting for fish. Competing for the same catch were fisherman wearing waterproof overalls standing thigh deep in the current, their long poles stretched out over the glistening water.

As we zipped along easily, relief washed over me. We had just completed a week of ridiculously hard mountain riding and were still going strong.

I yelled back at Sho over the wind, "You know what? If we can ride over the Japan Alps, we can definitely make it the rest of the way to Cape Sata!"

"Yeah baby!" After a while, Sho asked, "Where are we headed today?"

"Seki-shi."

"Sexy?" Sho said with surprise. "They named a city 'Sexy'?"

"No, Seki City. In Japanese, 'shi' means city. So it's called Seki-shi. This is where the company Shimano is headquartered. They made the gears for my Trek 520 bike."

Sho said, "I think they should make the city change its name to something less embarrassing."

A smiling, slender middle-aged man wearing a white floppy hat, beige shorts and a light blue short-sleeved shirt stood astride a red moped on the roadside as we entered the outskirts of Seki City. He flagged us down and shook my hand enthusiastically.

"Nice to meet you in person! I hope you aren't too worn out from cycling here. A local newspaper reporter is waiting at my home to talk with you and Sho. Please follow me."

His name was Kengo Kameyama, and he would be our host in Seki City. His son, the Director of the Japan National Tourism Organization's New York City office, had set up the connection. Mr. Kameyama rumbled ahead at a modest pace on his moped, and we followed him on a fifteen-minute ride to his house. We met his wife and incredibly cute granddaughter, a little girl about Saya's age who clung tightly to a stuffed animal elephant. Seeing her reminded me how much I missed my own two-year-old.

The reporter spent two hours interviewing us about the ride. She was particularly interested in Sho's perspective. "Why did you want to cycle across Japan," she asked him, pen poised above a white pad of paper.

"Because Japan has such great game rooms!"

"Any other reason?"

I looked at him expectantly, hoping he might talk about being proud to make such a long trip or to mention our work with the United Nations.

But Sho just said, "Nope."

After we finished the interview, Mr. Kameyama drove Sho and me to a large *onsen*, where we washed away our cares in a series of steaming, bubbling tubs that offered views of the surrounding forests. Afterward, we melted into massage chairs in the waiting lounge. I grimaced as my sore muscles were hammered, squeezed, rolled and crushed into submission. I tried to pay for the baths, but Mr. Kameyama shooed me away good-naturedly.

Although dinner was waiting for us at his home, Mr. Kameyama consented to Sho's request to stop by a nearby game room on the way back, where we spent forty-five minutes in computer-generated fantasyland.

While watching Sho play a game, I suddenly became light-headed and didn't feel well. One of the consequences of riding a bike for many hours, day after day, is a metabolism that demands constant sustenance. I hadn't eaten for several hours, distracted by the newspaper interview and the baths. I excused myself and found a "Mr. Donut" store across from the game room. After munching down three pumpkin flavored donuts, I felt much better.

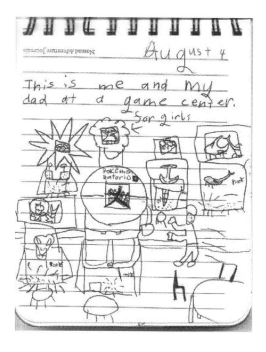

On the drive home, Mr. Kameyama pointed out a number of shuttered businesses in downtown Seki City. "The economy in Japan has been weak for nearly two decades, and small towns throughout the country are suffering."

We returned home to find that Mrs. Kameyama had prepared an impressive meal of sashimi, fried chicken, cooked vegetables and sukiyaki. The donuts in no way diminished my appetite, and Sho and I ate and ate and ate, staying up late to relish the delicious food and wonderful company.

I was awakened at 5:00 a.m. the next morning by the sound of screams just outside my window. Sitting up abruptly on my futon and jerking my head toward the piercing sound, I quickly realized that the jarring noise was coming from dozens, perhaps hundreds, of crickets congregating in the Kameyama's front yard. It would be impossible to return to sleep, so I pulled out my journal and wrote for a couple of hours while sitting cross-legged and hunched over. Sho lay beside me blissfully unconscious, and I marveled at his ability to sleep through the racket.

Mrs. Kameyama treated us to a sumptuous breakfast before we loaded gear on our bikes for the fifty-six-mile ride to the city of Hikone. A reporter from another regional newspaper stopped by to interview us and took pictures before we rode off. As we were posing, Sho whispered to me, "A lot of people are making a fuss over us, but I don't feel special."

"Well, you are doing something quite unusual," I said while holding a smile for the camera. "But I'm glad you're not letting the attention go to your head. I'm not interested in dragging a prima donna across Japan."

He kicked my foot playfully and accidentally hit my broken toe. I grimaced and yelped, and the journalist said, "Hold on. Let's take that picture again."

A drenching downpour soaked us as we left Seki City. But since the temperatures had reached the high eighties, we didn't bother with any rain gear. Unlike how I felt during our wet, shivering rides in Hokkaidō, I now enjoyed being cooled off by the rain. Eventually the skies cleared, and the hot wind dried us off as we cycled.

We took a break at a convenience store in the town of Ōgaki. I said, "Sho, have you ever heard of Matsuo Bashō."

"Who was he?"

"He was a famous haiku poet. In the late 1600's, he wrote about his travels all over Japan on foot. And the town we're in right now was his final destination on the last trip he took before he died. Almost every Japanese person will recognize his most famous poem, which goes:

Furu ike ya
kawazu tobikomu
mizu no oto.

Say that to a Japanese person, and they'll immediately say, 'Bashō!'"

Sho asked, "What does that mean?"

I translated for him:

An ancient pond
a frog jumps in
the splash of water.

Sho said, "What's the big deal about a frog jumping into an old pond?"

"A lot has been written about the meaning of this poem, and I don't think I can do justice to it. But basically, I think Bashō felt a deep connection and sense of peace when he was out in nature. He would say that even the most mundane of things, like a frog jumping into a pond, offers the careful observer a hint of the mysteries of the universe."

Sho was staring at me with his mouth agape. "What?"

"When you go to college, take some philosophy and poetry classes. Then give me a call, and we'll talk more about that poem. Here's another interesting fact: Bashō wasn't even his real name. It's a type of banana tree he liked so much he decided to use it as his pen name. And he loved to travel and explore, just like what we are doing."

Sho humored me by nodding and pretending to be interested in my musings, but I could tell that he had tuned me out.

As we pedaled out of town, I thought more about the kinship I felt for Bashō. He started on the first of his journeys when he was forty years old, the same age I was when Sho and I decided to cycle across Japan. And he sought inspiration in nature, in "the billow-crested sea"; "the fumes of early-ripening rice"; "a cricket singing underneath the dark cavity of an old helmet." My journal was filled with attempts at describing the beautiful natural scenes I witnessed, but the words always seemed inadequate. Bashō struggled too: "My pen strove in vain to equal this superb creation of divine artifice." He was dead at age fifty, reminding me that if there is something you want to do, the time is now.

Sho and I rode through ever-increasing urban sprawl and were hemmed in by a constant rush of traffic that kept our bikes on a tight line along the narrow shoulder. With less than a yard between the cars' side mirrors and us, I tried to stay simultaneously relaxed and intensely focused. Sho made a game out of trying to read out loud every license plate he saw. It required him to talk rapidly non-stop, and after a while he gave up, saying, "Holy crap, this is impossible!"

By mid-afternoon, we came upon a line of stopped cars and trucks that stretched for several miles.

"Do you know what this is?" I asked, as we carefully rolled by the unmoving vehicles.

"A traffic jam?"

"Exactly. Not only that. It's the first major traffic jam we have encountered in forty-two days of riding. We're headed in the direction of both Osaka and Kyoto. I think we're in for an experience that is the exact opposite of the lonely Japan Alps."

We reached Hikone at the end of the afternoon. The city is home to a Bridgestone tire manufacturing plant and several headquarters of local corporations. Its roads have been crowded for many centuries with various forms of traffic traversing an ancient trade route. Hikone's claim to fame is a nearly 400-year old castle that was designated a National Treasure. Sho and I made plans to visit it first thing in the morning.

I found a business hotel that looked inexpensive. As we entered the simple lobby, Sho asked, "Why don't we just sleep in our tent?"

"Normally that's what we would do. But it's just too hot now. If we tried to stay in our tent tonight, we would lie there steadily getting soaked with sweat, miserable and unable to fall asleep."

I approached the hotel clerk perched behind a desk. He gave me a bored look as I asked for a single room.

"There are two of you," he responded. "I have a double for ten thousand yen."

"We don't need a double," I said. "We're cycling across Japan and usually sleep in a tent, so a single bed will feel like luxury to us. How much for a single?"

He paused as if considering whether to argue with me. I suspected that we were breaking the hotel's one person/one bed policy. Finally, he shrugged and said, "Six thousand yen."

"We'll take it!"

It was already muggy and in the low nineties as Sho and I cycled away from our hotel the next morning to visit Hikone Castle. The keep rises dramatically above the town, its black decorated arches set off at sharp angles and contrasting beautifully with the castle's white walls.

"It kinda reminds me of the castle in Tokyo Disneyland," Sho said.

"Don't let any of the staff overhear you say that—you might get us kicked out of here," I teased. "Back in the Edo Period, this place was all about maintaining power. Unlike Disneyland, which is all about making money."

"And now this place is all about looking cool," Sho said. "Which it totally does."

Dripping with sweat in the uncomfortable heat, we spent an hour and a half exploring the castle grounds and debating the various ways an attacking army might succeed in taking the castle. As I stared out over the ledge of a mighty stone wall a few yards away from an ice cream stand, one of Bashō's poems came to mind:

A thicket of summer grass
Is all that remains
Of the dreams and ambitions
Of ancient warriors

On the previous day's ride, we had passed through Sekigahara, a town famous in Japan as the scene of a decisive battle in 1600 that marked the end of a century of civil war. The victory cemented Tokugawa Ieyasu's rise to power and ushered in the Edo Period, over 250 years of a brutally effective totalitarian government. Numerous TV shows in Japan are set in this period of the country's history. Analogous to romanticized Westerns in the U.S., they are known as "*Jidai Geki*" (period drama) and invariably feature Samurai warriors engaged in utterly unrealistic sword fighting.

The construction of Hikone Castle began shortly after Tokugawa Ieyasu's victory in Sekigahara. Completed in 1622, it served as the center of power for a loyal regional clan throughout the Edo Period. But by the late 1800's, Japan embarked on a furious modernization effort that dismantled the previous political system. In the 1870's, Hikone Castle, along with many other Edo era castles, was slated to be destroyed. It took the intercession of the emperor—who saw the stunning keep while touring the area—to prevent its destruction.

When the Edo Period came to an end, sword-bearing Samurai warriors trained in the harsh discipline of self-sacrifice and loyalty to their lords were replaced with gun-toting soldiers indoctrinated with a sense of national pride. Japan would prove remarkably adept at copying Western war-making technology, and unlike almost every other country in Asia, it was never colonized by a European power. However, Japan's military prowess would metastasize in the twentieth century with disastrous consequences.

We left Hikone Castle in the late morning and cycled toward Japan's ancient capital of Kyoto. We had to drink frequently in order to keep from becoming dehydrated in the oppressive heat. Hugging the coastline of Lake Biwako, we enjoyed beautiful views of the massive lake, which was nearly 120 miles in circumference.

Sho said, "It feels like we're riding beside the ocean."

As before, a constant stream of traffic kept us hemmed in on the narrow road. When we reached the impressive Biwako Ohashi Bridge, I was relieved to use the pedestrian path to keep us safe from the vehicles zooming by. We crossed over the towering bridge and made our way to Hama Ohtsu, a town on the southwest corner of Lake Biwako, then turned west for the long climb over the hills surrounding Kyoto.

The streets of Hama Ohtsu were filled with people strolling around in festive kimonos. We deduced that there must be a summer festival going on. As we rode out of town, we passed a line of cars caught in an incredible traffic jam coming towards us that didn't stop until we reached Kyoto an hour later. We asked a passerby what was going on, and he explained that there was a major fireworks display starting at 7:30 p.m.

I said, "Let's find a place to sleep, then figure out how to get back to Hama Ohtsu in time to watch the fireworks."

Kyoto is surrounded by steep hills, but after our mountain climbing in the Japan Alps the previous week, we were hardly fazed by the effort. After checking into a downtown hotel, we quickly showered and rushed out to catch a train going back the way we'd come. On the 30-minute ride to Hama Ohtsu, we excitedly anticipated the awesome fireworks display we were going to witness.

"Remember the fireworks at Kashiwazaki?" Sho said. "I bet these are going to be ten times better!"

As we neared our destination, loud booms reverberated outside, and we joined others inside the train straining to catch glimpses of the fireworks display through the windows. The train came to a stop, and we piled out onto the platform, merging into a confused crowd of people being herded by dozens of police officers shouting orders through megaphones. Each time we approached a marked exit, we found it blocked by the police. Crowded pools of people surged around in confusion. Flashes of light and explosions nearby teased us with the knowledge that we were missing all the action. After fifteen minutes of fruitless attempts simply to get out of the train station, I approached a police officer guarding a barricade that blocked a staircase to the street below.

"I'm sorry to bother you," I said, keeping Sho close as people jostled by us. "My son and I would like to see the fireworks, but we can't seem to get out of the station."

He gave us a sympathetic look and said, "The fireworks are almost over. We're getting ready for everybody to come back into the station."

"My son really wants to catch at least a little bit of the show. Is any exit open?"

The police officer looked from side to side nervously and said, "I'm not supposed to do this, but I'll let you jump the barricade and go down the stairs. Just be careful. It's about to get dangerous around here."

We thanked him and hurried down a street to a nearby intersection full of onlookers. Buildings obstructed our view, so we could only see the explosions high in the air.

I lifted Sho onto my shoulders, but he complained, "Daddy, I still can't see. Let's go to the lake."

The shore was about a half mile away, and we started weaving through the increasingly dense crowds. I quickly began to have a bad feeling about this situation. "Sho, I think we should start heading back toward the train station," I said nervously.

"Aw, come on, Daddy."

I ignored his protests and started to retrace my steps, apologizing as I pushed through the thick throngs. The show came to a sudden end, and for a brief moment all was quiet and calm. Then the mass of people surrounding us started to turn toward the station. Police officers started yelling directions all around us. I looked back toward the lake and saw a flood of humanity heading our way.

"Buddy, it's about to become insanely crowded," I said, setting Sho down, grabbing his hand and pushing forward as quickly as possible.

Sho and I made it back to the station and raced up a staircase. Many others ran alongside us, like survivors fleeing a natural disaster. As we rushed along a crowded corridor leading to a set of turnstiles, we rounded a corner to find a line of police officers pulling up a barricade.

"Everyone stop!" they ordered through megaphones. A mass of people closed in on us from behind, and we were soon trapped in a sea of thousands of nervous revelers. The summer night's heat and humidity were oppressive and made worse by the press of people. I imagined dangerous scenarios of the panicked crowd trampling us or crushing us against the barricades.

As we waited, Sho said he was thirsty. I glanced down at the bottle of water in my hand and noted that it was one third full.

"Sho, I have no idea how long we're going to be stuck here, so let's make this last. Just take a small sip."

The corridor filled with ever increasing numbers of people trapped behind us. No doubt a throng of thousands stretched down the staircase and into the streets. Another large group of people were barricaded in front of an entrance to our left. Each group eyed the other, and I wondered which one the police would let through first. The authorities held us there for about twenty minutes until another huge block of people amassed in front of us at the turnstiles had shuffled onto the waiting trains below. Then the police gave our group the go-ahead. Sho and I pushed forward in a slow shuffle, squeezed in all directions. At one point, he began to get pulled away from me by the crowd, and I yanked him back with both hands. He glanced at me nervously, and I counseled, "Don't fight it. Just follow the flow of the crowd, and no matter what, don't let go of my hand."

We were soon caught in a crushing standstill at the turnstiles that led down to the train tracks. I had purchased return tickets when we left Kyoto and imagined what a nightmare it would have been to attempt to buy tickets at a counter in this crowd. We waited another twenty minutes before squeezing our way down to the train platform, hands tightly clasped. When our train arrived, we were crammed into a car with barely enough space to turn from side to side. Luckily, Sho and I were the last to enter and could lean against the door, instead of swaying back and forth in the thick crowd.

As the train began to slowly roll away, I noticed two girls standing to my left. They looked to be about fourteen years old. Their faces were streaming with sweat as they faced one another with stoic expressions. And then I noticed the middle-aged man pressed behind one of the girls. It was hard to tell in the crush, but after a second look, I could see his hand reaching under the girl's skirt. I had heard that molesters are common on the crowded trains in Japan, but I had never seen one. The problem was so widespread that many subway lines in Tokyo offer women's only cars. Based on various conversations with my Japanese friends, I suspected that nearly every girl who grows up in a major city in Japan is molested on the train at some point. For many, it is a regular occurrence that starts as early as elementary school.

The girl sighed with what seemed to be resignation and looked down blushing. She was either too intimidated or embarrassed to call him out, and her arms were pinned in front of her anyway, making it difficult to stop him. I didn't feel like making a scene myself, especially with Sho there, but I did want to help the girl.

Speaking loudly enough for the molester to hear, I said to Sho, "That girl looks like she's sweating a lot in this heat. Why don't you offer her some of your water?"

"Who?" Sho asked.

I pointed to the girl, who glanced up at me with a surprised look. Sho held out his bottle. "Would you like some?"

With our attention shifting to the girl, I saw the man retract his hand.

"Oh, no thanks," she said with a polite nod of her head. "I don't need any."

"Just let us know if you get thirsty. We're happy to help you," I said with a smile, then looked meaningfully into the man's eyes. He gave me a baleful look before turning to the side to face away from her.

When we returned to our hotel room, Sho and I flopped down on the bed, exhausted. I looked at my watch and said, "Well, we were gone for a total of two hours and saw about ten minutes of fireworks."

"Yeah, Daddy. That was an epic fail."

"True. Let's call today the 'Kyoto Fireworks Fiasco.'"

Chapter 32

Something Evil
This Way Comes

KYOTO. IMPERIAL CAPITAL OF JAPAN FOR OVER 1,000 YEARS.
An ancient city endowed with sculpted gardens, awe-inspiring
temples, shrines, palaces, and theaters. A place of mysterious, hidden traditions. The menu for a visitor overflows with
options: visit the famous Kiyomizu-dera temple complex
with its beautiful wooden terrace and commanding views.
Stand in awe before Sanjusangendo's impressive collection of
1,001 golden Buddhist statues, each one unique. Ogle Heian
Jingu Shrine's bright orange hallways, massive structures and
sprawling courtyard. Take a contemplative stroll along the
wooded Philosopher's Path. Seek inner peace at Ginkakuji
Temple of the Silver Pavilion, with its sublime hiking trails
and stunning sand sculptures.

I had decided to take the day off from cycling so that we
could explore Kyoto. And we spent the morning . . . bowling.

Seriously.

I just couldn't say no to Sho's puppy dog eyes as he fer-
vently asked for "just a little fun on a rest day." I decided that

after a month and a half of intense riding he deserved to get his way this time.

When we returned to our parked bikes after bowling, I found a bright yellow official police notice attached to my handlebars. I couldn't read all the characters, but I got the gist of the note: we were parked illegally. The bike racks outside the game center had been full, so I had locked our bicycles to a street sign in a nearby alleyway.

I crumpled the note and said to Sho, "Just a few days ago, we were at an alpine pass surrounded by monkeys and mountain mist. And now we're having trouble finding a place to park our bikes. It's surreal."

We set off to explore Kyoto. Our bikes felt ridiculously light without luggage, and we zipped easily among the city's impressive sights. The people were as interesting to observe as the buildings. We saw a pair of kimono-clad geishas tottering on distinctive wooden clogs down a stone sidewalk, each holding a colorful parasol tipped carefully to block the sun. Bright blue morning glory *kanzashi* ornaments were carefully pinned to each woman's hair. A geisha wears specific hair ornaments depending on the month. If we returned in September, these women would don purple Japanese bellflowers to signify the beginning of autumn. Their bright red lips contrasted with the white paint on their faces and stood out like blood on freshly fallen snow. The geishas disappeared into the crowd, which included conservatively dressed businessmen and groups of sauntering, texting teenagers dressed like hipsters from Brooklyn.

And foreigners—that is, non-Japanese—were everywhere. Over the past six weeks, I had become accustomed to being surrounded only by Japanese people, and Kyoto's lack of homogeneity was curiously jarring.

We nibbled on various snacks from street vendors. Sho's favorite was a refreshing cucumber on a stick that helped him cool off in the oppressive heat. On the way to Kiyomizu-dera Temple, we stopped to ask directions. A helpful stranger pointed the way, adding with a concerned look, "It's a steep climb to the temple, though. Might be a bit much to try on a bicycle, especially for a kid."

Sho said, "You have no idea where we've been!"

Later that night, we ate dinner in a boisterous *izakaya*, which included a bar and restaurant. Our table was next to the counter, and a young American sitting by himself a few feet away turned in his seat and struck up a conversation. He held a beer, and from his slurred speech I could tell that it was not his first. "Mind if I join you?"

"Sure, why not?" I said, indicating the empty chair between Sho and me.

We learned that he had moved to Kyoto after graduating from college in the U.S. and had been teaching English in Japan for five years.

"Do you and your kid live here?"

I told him about our trip, and he yelled out in Japanese, "Waiter. Get this man a drink right away!"

"I'm good," I said, waving away the waiter who approached us.

"Seriously, dude, you deserve a drink," the young man persisted. "I mean, who does something like that? Are you trying to break a record or something?"

I told him about our tree-planting fundraiser with the United Nations, and he started shaking his head.

"Environmentalism has failed, dude. When I was in college, I considered myself an environmentalist and went to marches, handed out literature and tried to convince people to stop driving SUV's. But after living in the real world for a while, I realized that there's no way to stop people from trashing the planet. I read Rachel Carson's *Silent Spring*. Okay, so the book eventually got DDT banned, and a bunch of birds lived who would have choked on chemicals . . ."

I interrupted, "The book did more than that. It marked the beginning of the environmental movement in the U.S.

It raised the consciousness of an entire generation to how thoughtlessly they had been polluting the planet."

He rolled his eyes and said, "No offense, man, but raising consciousness, like your cute tree-planting campaign, makes the holier-than-thou environmentalist feel good about himself. But it doesn't change reality. The reality is that people are motivated by self-interest. Make a slash and burn farmer choose between saving some trees and feeding his kids, and what choice do you think he'll make? How many environmentalists do you know who actually follow their arguments to their logical conclusion? If they did, they would have to give up driving, using electricity, eating sushi. It ain't gonna happen. In just the last hundred years, the number of humans has quadrupled. We're like a virus spreading across the planet. There are already seven billion resource-consuming, self-interested, procreating creatures crawling all over the place. It's unstoppable."

I shook my head. "That's a cynical way of looking at it. Giving in to despair or feeling guilty doesn't lead to anything of value. In my job back in the States, I invest in clean technology companies that are tapping into human creativity to solve environmental problems. The human race has demonstrated a remarkable ability to find innovative solutions to the most intractable problems."

"Yeah, like how to get laid."

Sho's eyes widened.

I said, "*Dude*, you're drunk."

He laughed and said, "Maybe. But you're hopelessly idealistic."

Early the next morning, while Sho slept, I left our hotel room to take a walk. The streets were mostly deserted, many shops still shuttered, as I made my way to a large city park a few blocks away. Clumps of trees were interspersed among grassy fields. Birds called to one another, and squirrels scampered up tree trunks as I strolled along, enjoying the peaceful scene. Occasionally, a jogger or dog-walker passed by.

Suddenly, off to my left, I heard music begin to blare from crackly speakers, then a garbled man's voice. I followed the noise and came upon a group of perhaps thirty elderly men and women dressed in sweat suits. They stood spread out on a field in a large circle around a ghetto blaster that was tuned to a national public radio station. The announcer welcomed everyone to *rajio taiso*, a government-sponsored morning radio calisthenics program that is aired across the country. He quickly put everyone to work. The large group followed along dutifully, performing exercises in syncopation with their compatriots in the park and around the nation.

When I returned to the hotel, Sho was just waking up. I told him about the radio exercise program and he said, "That's a cool idea. Do they do the same thing in the U.S.?"

"There are lots of exercise classes people can take at private gyms, but there isn't a national radio broadcast every morning. I like the idea, but somehow I don't think American culture would embrace it."

"Why not?"

"Many people in the U.S. don't like the government to tell them what to do, even when it's for their own good. Maybe if a private company came up with a program and paid for it to be aired at the same time every day across the U.S., people wouldn't mind. But if it's a program run by the government and paid for by taxes, I don't think it would fly. Who knows? Maybe no one has tried."

I later learned that the idea had originated back in the 1920's in the U.S. when the Metropolitan Life Insurance Company sponsored daily, fifteen-minute radio exercise programs. Japan adopted the approach but used it mainly to improve the conditioning of their soldiers. After the end of World War II, the program was re-introduced without the militaristic tone and with an emphasis on general physical fitness. MetLife's effort did not enjoy the same longevity.

After breakfast, I said, "Sho, today we're covering only twenty-eight miles to Nara, so we've got plenty of time to see a little more of Kyoto in the morning before we have to start riding."

"Let's play pool!" he said. "I saw a couple of tables in the game room when we were bowling."

"You gotta be kidding me," I said, but Sho's pleading look melted me for the second day in a row. "Okay. But when we get to Nara, the first place we're going is the Todai-ji Temple, not some random game room. Agree?"

"Agree!"

After billiards, we were preparing to ride to Nara when my phone rang.

"*Moshi moshi.* Hello," I said.

"*Moshi moshi!* It's Aki." This was Eiko's elder brother who lived in Tokyo with his wife Akemi and teenage daughter

August 9th

This is me and my dad playing pool.

Nomad Adventure Journals

Arisa. "Akemi and I are on a weekend trip to the Ise Peninsula and thought we might drive over to Nara to see you and Sho. It'll take us a few hours to get there, and we'll need to leave at the end of the afternoon, so it will be a short visit. But we wanted to see you in person."

"That sounds great!" I said. "The only issue is that we're still in Kyoto. If we leave right now, I think we'll arrive around 3:30 p.m."

"Then we'll have about ninety minutes together."

"Sounds like a plan."

We left Kyoto immediately and cycled along a busy road heading directly to Nara. There were quieter, more pleasant options, but I chose to take the quickest route in order to have as much time as possible with Aki and Akemi. As we rolled into the center of Nara, the two of them jumped out of their car and gave us a hearty welcome and an enthusiastic cheer. It felt so nice to see family.

After checking into a nearby hotel and locking up our bikes, Sho and I hopped into their car and headed to the deer-infested park at Tōdai-ji Temple. The Shinto religion reveres the Sika deer as the gods' messengers, and the pesky animals wander around freely, mingling with the tourists. Visitors can buy packets of pellets to feed them, but you have to be ready once you do. The minute you buy food, the deer converge on you, aggressively shoving and nipping. I was bitten on my waist, leaving a nice bruise, but Sho was too fast for the obnoxious creatures. He looked like the Pied Piper, running up the long path toward the temple trailed by a line of hungry deer eating the pellets he threw over his shoulder as he ran.

We didn't have enough time to visit the inside of Tōdai-ji Temple, so Sho and I vowed to return the next day on our own. Aki and Akemi drove us back to our hotel and gave us a reluctant farewell. A pang of loneliness washed over me as I watched them drive off, and I suddenly longed to see Eiko and Saya. I had been apart from my wife and daughter for six weeks, and it would be another three before we would be reunited. Matsuo Bashō put my emotions into words when he departed on one of his journeys: "I felt deeply in my heart both the sorrow of one that goes and the grief of one that remains."

That night, as I was reading to Sho in bed, my cell phone rang. I immediately knew who it was. From the first day of our trip, my father-in-law had called from Tokyo every other day without fail at precisely 9 p.m. The disapproval and disappointment I had sensed when we first met fifteen years earlier had been replaced in the intervening period by genuine affection. Our conversations were usually brief, and he always began with the same two questions: "Where are you now?" and "Is everything okay?" He had recently added: "How is your sumo wrestling injury?"

"It's fine," I lied. My toe still ached regularly, an annoying reminder of my poor judgment.

Then he asked, "Where are you headed tomorrow?"

"The temple town on the top of Mount Kōya. We're going to stay in a Buddhist monastery. It should be very cool."

He said grimly, "Well, you've got a big problem."

"What's that?"

"You're heading directly into the path of an oncoming typhoon."

Chapter 33

Climbing to Mt. Kōya

THE NEXT MORNING, A DRIVING RAIN FELL STEADILY OUT-
side, as Sho and I debated what to do. The typhoon was barreling along the eastern coast of Japan, and we decided to stay
a second night in Nara.

"You sure we can't just go for it, Daddy? We've ridden
through rain lots of times."

"Well, there's rain and then there's a typhoon. One gets
you wet. The other blows you off your bike and cracks open
your skull."

His eyes widened and I continued. "From what I understand of the typhoon's path, I think we can get away with a
day trip, though. Let's ride to Hōryū-ji, which is on our list of
World Heritage Sites to visit and is around nine miles from
here. It's an ancient temple complex built in the seventh and
eighth centuries—apparently, the pagoda is the oldest wooden
structure in Japan. We can ride there, have lunch and be back
in the early afternoon."

"There must be something wooden in Japan that is older,"
Sho said. "Like some doghouse or something."

"My guidebook may have said 'one of the oldest.'
Whatever."

We found our way to Hōryū-ji and arrived dripping but in good spirits. The temple buildings were laid out in a rectangular courtyard, and we walked the perimeter. Sho played "See how far I can jump" from the top of the temple's broad entry steps and "See how wet I can make my hair from this stream of water pouring off the temple roof." I appreciated the fact that we could enjoy most of the sights from the outside. We were so thoroughly soaked that I would have been embarrassed to track wet footprints on the immaculate wooden floors.

The ancient five-story pagoda stood over one hundred feet tall in the center of the courtyard. Rain poured off the tips of the eves of each of the five stories, forming mini waterfalls.

"There it is," I said to Sho. "The brochure explains that scientists dated the wood used to build the pagoda to the year 594."

"Looks good for something so old. Even better than you," Sho said laughing.

After we had our fill of temple touring, we dried off enough to eat lunch in a nearby noodle restaurant. Sho folded the thin, rectangular paper chopsticks holder into a tight triangle, and we played "football" on our table until the food arrived. This was one of Sho's favorite ways to pass time in a restaurant, and he became skilled at flicking the paper ball just to the edge of the table without it falling off, thus scoring a touchdown. His field goal kicking was also quite good, but could be a problem, as it was today when the ball flew into the laps of people sitting at an adjoining table. Thankfully, they handed the paper ball back with a smile, but I didn't want to press their patience. "Let's play the 'no field goal' version from now on," I suggested.

On our ride back to Nara, I accidentally entered a bypass that transformed our annoying, but acceptably busy road into an alarming and unacceptably dangerous highway. I realized my mistake about one hundred yards in.

I cursed under my breath, annoyed. After our experience on the expressway in Hakodate, I had promised myself that I wouldn't make the same mistake again. We came to a stop, waited for a break in the traffic zooming by, then turned our bikes around and walked against traffic as close to the guardrail as we could.

"That was not good, Daddy," Sho observed, once we were safely off the bypass.

The steady rain continued, but the typhoon's dangerous winds remained fifty miles to the east and headed toward Tokyo, so we decided to continue sight-seeing. We cycled back to the Tōdai-ji Temple to re-visit the deer Sho had courted the day before. The greedy, assertive beasts were pleased to see their generous friend return and chased Sho all over the temple grounds, gobbling up the pellets he dropped over his shoulder while running and giggling.

The Buddha inside Tōdai-ji Temple is a wonder to behold, a gargantuan statue that reaches forty-nine feet overhead and is barely contained by the cavernous temple. As we approached the main hall that holds it, I said to Sho, "The temple brochure says that the Great Buddha Hall was built in the year 745 and is still the world's largest wooden building. Isn't that cool? We saw one of Japan's oldest wooden structures this morning. And we're now looking at the world's largest bronze Buddha in the world's largest wooden building."

Sho was too distracted to hear me, though, and screamed, "Ahh! Another deer is coming for me!"

We escaped up the steps of the building, leaving the deer outside. Throngs of visitors surrounded me as I stared up at the Buddha's meditating form looming over us all. Its serene visage was mesmerizing, and I contemplated life's meaning for about a minute before Sho pulled me over. "Dad, check out this awesome thing I found."

One of the temple's attractions is a broad column with a relatively small square hole running through it. Those who can crawl through the tight space are said to enjoy good luck. Sho stood in line behind other kids and skinny adults, then made it through easily.

"Now I'm all set!" he rejoiced after passing this impressive Buddhist test. "You try it Dad!"

The opening was maybe two feet by two feet. "No thanks."

The rain had tapered off by the time we rode back to our hotel and we seemed in no further danger from the typhoon. As we changed out of our damp clothes, I glanced in the bathroom mirror and did not like what I saw. I hadn't shaved since we'd started riding and had grown a full, if not particularly impressive, set of whiskers. Early on, the beard and mustache represented a kind of letting go of my professional identity, a celebration of the adventurer's freedom. But the intrusive mess of hair tickled the sides of my mouth and made me look older than I felt. It was also becoming itchy in Japan's scorching summer heat. It was time to shave it off.

I used a small pair of scissors from my medical kit to whittle down the tangled fuzz. Soon it was short enough for me to apply shaving cream and start to work with a disposable razor I'd bought at a convenience store. Twenty minutes and several stinging cuts later, the nest was gone.

Sho had grown used to seeing me with a beard and mustache and gave a surprised shout when I emerged from the bathroom. After contemplating my new clean-shaven look, he concluded, "You look stupid and cool. Fifty percent stupid. Fifty percent cool."

"Um, thanks?"

The next morning, we said goodbye to the ancient city of Nara and rode south along an annoyingly busy route out of town. A shining silver BMW zoomed by, and I noticed a bright yellow smiley face sticker discreetly placed in the left corner of its rear bumper. What might have been an unremarkable sight back in the U.S.—a sticker affixed to a car—practically screamed out for attention here. This was the first bumper sticker that I had noticed since we started our ride. I suspected that the driver, whose face I had not seen, was a foreigner. It is simply unheard of in Japan to plaster your car with bumper stickers. What is it about the United States that makes so many people want to turn their cars into advertisements for their political, religious or random opinions?

Growing up in Nashville, I had often noted down amusing bumper stickers. My favorite read, "Eat More Possum." I wondered if the driver genuinely felt that the world would be a better place if people consumed this misunderstood (and misspelled) source of protein. I imagined him at dinner parties explaining with great passion, "It's not just road kill. I'm telling you, it's darn good meat." My other favorite bumper sticker read, "I'm the princess. Who the hell are you?" I laughed out loud, imagining the reaction people in Japan would have to that one.

"Everything okay, Daddy?" Sho asked from behind, raising his voice so that I could hear him over the wind and traffic.

"I was just thinking about funny bumper stickers," I yelled back over my shoulder.

"Oh, I can make up one! How about, "Would you rather be eaten by an anaconda or stung to death by a thousand bees?""

"Hmm. I'm not sure that would fit on a bumper."

And for the next hour, Sho came up with a stream of "would you rather" questions, each more ridiculous than the last. I was not allowed to equivocate in my responses. When I balked at whether I would prefer to eat a live bullfrog or a live chipmunk, Sho was unyielding. "Daddy, you have to choose. You can't not choose. It's not an option."

"Bullfrog," I responded with little enthusiasm.

"Yes, that's the right answer."

I breathed a sigh of relief when we finally turned off the crowded main route onto a much quieter road toward the town of Asuka Mura. A candidate to become a World Heritage Site, the quaint village of just over 6,000 residents boasts a pleasant Buddhist temple and some unusual ancient granite stones. No one knows the origin of the mysterious, colossal rock structures, which may have been burial sites or places for communal worship or the result of a group of early Japanese stone cutters looking to display their skills on something more ambitious than pottery. Sho, however, wasn't interested in uncovering the mysterious origin of the most famous of these stones, Ishibutai Kofun. As I stood by reading historians' theories, Sho scrambled to the top, easily ten feet up and used it as a launching pad for some impressive leaps onto the ground.

After we had our fill of the mysterious rocks, we toured the local temple and ate a leisurely lunch in town, not eager to resume riding in the oppressive summer heat. Finally, Sho and I mounted our bikes and headed south. Rice fields stretched around us. Mountains loomed in the distance. And one of those, Mt. Kōya, waited for us. Today's destination was a collection of over one hundred Buddhist temples in the heart of the Kii Mountain chain. The base for the Shingon Buddhist sect, the town of Kōya was founded almost 1,200 years ago by the monk Kūkai, after he returned from a spiritual journey to China. Many temples offer lodging for visitors, and Sho and I had a reservation at one.

But we had to get there first. I knew we should not have lingered in Asuka Mura until mid-afternoon, and I tried to keep up a quick pace. Unfortunately, the route was hilly from the start, and the muggy ninety-degree weather sapped our strength. We plodded along at a modest speed, and I began to fear the unpleasant and dangerous prospect of cycling up the narrow mountain road in the dark.

I was actually looking forward to another challenging ride up a mountain, confident that we could make the long, steep climb up Mt. Kōya, after our successful week of riding over the Japan Alps. The main question today: could we ride fast enough to arrive before nightfall?

We cycled over the rolling terrain for two hours before reaching the base of Mt. Kōya at five, where I nearly made a significant mistake. We came to an intersection with a sign that pointed us in a different direction from the route my GPS said we should take. Assuming that there must be two alternate routes, I ignored the sign and followed my GPS's instructions. After a few minutes, I realized that I'd just forgotten an important lesson from this trip: when in doubt, ask a local. So I did just that, pulling to a stop in front of an old man bent over pulling weeds out of a small garden in front of his home.

He smiled up at us, folds of sturdy aged skin looping around his deeply tanned face like a meandering moat. His overalls were dirt-stained and worn, and his wrinkled hands held firmly to a just plucked, wilting weed. Raising his eyebrows and ogling our connected bikes, he said, "Wow, look at that!"

"I'm sorry to bother you. Is the Mt. Kōya temple town this way?" The old man moved away from his garden, tossing the weed aside, and took a closer look at Sho's bicycle.

"Nope," he said, shaking his head. "You're headed up to one of the summits. There's nothing there but forest. The road is narrow, steep and has a lot of debris from rockslides on it. The temple town you want is back in the other direction."

I had entered "Kōya-san" in Japanese into my GPS, which confusingly is the name of both the Buddhist temple town and the collection of mountains in the area. I learned later that there is no single mountain called Mt. Kōya. Relieved at having caught the potentially devastating mistake, we turned back with a grateful thank you to the man who had just saved us from an unplanned overnight stay on an exposed mountaintop.

He gave Sho a smile and hearty "*Gambatte!* Good luck!" as we pulled away. After a moment, I glanced back to see him still staring after us.

The first hour of climbing through the forest covering Mt. Kōya's lower reaches was beautiful, but a bit disappointing. I had expected a challenge similar to the Japan Alps, but this was full of modest ascents followed by easy flat and downhill sections. I murmured to myself, "This will be a piece of cake," happily ticking away the miles at a solid clip. But at 6 p.m., with just over an hour of sunlight left, the mountain got serious. No more easy slopes and refreshing down hills. The real climbing had begun with regular doses of long, winding ten percent grades mixed in with the "easy" sections at six to eight percent inclines. We trudged up at a crawl, sweat dripping down to sizzle on the hot pavement. I pushed down hard on the pedals and struggled to maintain forward momentum up the steep, unforgiving, narrow road.

My body protested at having to work so hard at the end of a day of riding. Sho complained that he was ready to stop. And most annoying of all, cars constantly passed us from both directions, headed to and from the popular tourist destination. Unlike the deserted climbs through the Japan Alps, where we could swing out and back on the empty road to generate momentum, the traffic forced me to maintain a straight line squeezed to the far side of the road, allowing little room for error next to the sheer drop-off a few feet to our left. Only a low guardrail stood between the valley and us.

Another hour of hard pushing up, up, up, and we were still climbing. The sun's rays faded away behind the mountain's forest canopy, and darkness enveloped us. I turned on lights at the back and front of our bikes to ensure that the cars could see us. The traffic was dwindling, and we experienced long stretches of riding through oppressive darkness under the menacing fingers of the overhanging trees. My front light illuminated a constant stream of spooky shadows as I jerked the bike back and forth with each heavy pedal stroke up the incline. Eerie sounds emanated from the darkness and echoed across the black expanse just beyond the road's edge.

"Daddy, this is really spooky. I don't like it."

"I don't like it either, Sho. We'll get there soon." I was annoyed at my hubris in thinking we could make it to Mt. Kōya before dark. I seemed to overestimate my capabilities constantly. Despite his complaints, Sho didn't give up. What choice did he have? And despite being annoyed at my overconfidence, I knew that we had a safe place to stay waiting for us at the top. We just needed to get there.

Finally, after a brutal series of steep switchbacks, we rounded a corner and came upon a huge, brightly lit red Buddhist gate. Called *Daimon* ("big gate"), it glowed against the dark forest background and offered a hearty welcome to tired wanderers. We had made it to the temple town of Mt. Kōya! An hour after dark and completely spent, but we had made it.

I navigated through the compact mountain town to Rengejo-In, the temple where we had a reservation. Thankfully, they ushered us immediately into a tatami mat dining room. We sat cross-legged on cushions before a collection of delicious flavored tofu, *miso* soup, mountain vegetables, rice and hot tea. Famished from the exhausting ride, we greedily consumed the meal while still in our sweat-soaked cycling clothes.

Lounging in the temple's hot *onsen* bath afterward, our bellies full and memories of the spooky alpine ride already fading, I said to Sho, "I need to change."

"What do you mean," he asked, gently waving his arms through the steaming water.

"I keep underestimating our challenges, like today when I thought that we could get here before nightfall. I made you suffer as a result. I think I should be more humble and take fewer risks."

"That's okay, Daddy." He gave me a splash. "I like you the way you are."

Chapter 34

Disrupted Meditations

AT 5:55 IN THE MORNING, A MONK HIDDEN SOMEWHERE within the temple began to beat a gong in a slow, steady rhythm.

Bong . . . Bong . . . Bong . . .

The intense, enveloping tolling echoed through the quiet morning, sound waves bouncing off the meticulously crafted sand sculptures and manicured trees of the temple garden.

Bong . . . Bong . . . Bong . . .

The reverberations cascaded through me, shaking my bones and pulling me out of a deep, exhausted slumber. I rolled over on the futon to see Sho groggily smiling up from under the thick folds of his soft comforter.

Bong . . . Bong . . . Bong . . .

The sonorous noise drifted out of the mountain valley and dissipated among the surrounding peaks of Mt. Kōya.

"Ready for some chanting?" I asked Sho.

"Yep!" He pulled himself up from the futon, hopping around on one foot on the tatami mat as he pulled on his pants.

We shuffled quietly down the long, hard wood corridors, converging with other guests emerging groggily from their rooms to participate in the morning Buddhist ritual. We passed an opening leading to a beautiful garden in the center of the temple and felt the warm morning air rush over us, hinting at the heat to come. After navigating several turns through the large complex, we left our slippers at the entrance of the ceremony room and quietly found a place to sit on the tatami mats with about fifteen other guests. The room was dimly lit and adorned with Buddhist images and paraphernalia, the smell of incense wafting over us. Nine monks with shaved heads and flowing robes sat, legs folded easily beneath them, on mats in the front, each holding a book of *sutras*. Ryusho Soeda, head of the temple, sat in the middle and led the ceremony, his dark robes wrapped comfortably around his frame. I made a mental note to tell Eiko that men wear their robes left over right.

The chanting began immediately. Sho sat enthralled as the monks chanted with a deep, hypnotizing rhythm. Every so often, one would strike a gong or a clanging cymbal or bells. Sometimes one monk would start to drone out the beginning of a new section of the *sutra*, and the others would join him after a few seconds, their voices merging together powerfully. I closed my eyes and let the chanting take over. My thoughts drifted over the past month and a half of riding, and I marveled we had made it this far without any serious sickness, injury or mental breakdown. I opened my eyes and looked at Sho, who was sitting close to me, taking in the morning ritual. Since we began this trip, he had grown stronger and bigger, less apt to complain about minor inconveniences and patient enough to sit through forty minutes of Buddhist chanting. Although random strangers regularly told us that this trip was too hard for an eight-year-old, Sho seemed to be thriving.

When the monks finished, they filed quietly out of a side door, except Mr. Soeda, who turned toward the visitors in the room. His round, middle-aged face was serene, and he moved slowly and with purpose, exerting a calming presence over his hushed audience. He paused as he silently took in our faces and smiled gently. Accustomed to foreign guests, he spoke in heavily accented English, describing his religious beliefs and the story of Kūkai, the founder of Shingon Buddhism. Kūkai chose Mt. Kōya as the sect's headquarters over 1,200 years ago, following a voyage to China, where he studied with a well-known Buddhist master. Followers believe that Kūkai is still alive after all those years, meditating in a big stone cave underground and watching the world.

"Perhaps it must seem very strange or absurd for you that the one who lived almost 1,200 years before can keep meditation inside underground walls until today." Mr. Soeda smiled. "The reason why such an irrational belief could survive for so many years is that still today, many people can experience an encounter with Kūkai, mainly in the crisis of their life, physically or psychologically. Kūkai has been believed to send his supple body not only to believers, but also to unbelievers, to make them aware that they are watched by Kūkai. So these repeated experiences encountering Kūkai over time and space make this irrational belief –" here he paused for effect "– super rational."

"What a cool way to start the day!" Sho said, as we shuffled out of the ceremony hall.

"I'll get you up every day at 6 a.m. from now on."

"Maybe it's not *that* cool."

After breakfast, Sho and I hopped on our bikes, unburdened by our heavy gear, and explored the town of Kōya. We visited the massive Daimon gate that had welcomed us the night before. It was impressive but in daylight did not have the same mystery and power of the evening before, when its brilliantly lit, towering orange beams represented salvation from our exhausting bike ride up the mountain in the dark. We sat in the shade of the massive structure and called home. It was a pleasant relief to talk with Eiko and Saya, who rambled on about her latest exploits. "Mommy let me stand on the monkey bars!" I closed my eyes and smiled, picturing her tiny body in the playground. Finally, it was time to say goodbye, and we continued on to see Kōya's impressive mix of temples and tombs.

Many followers in the Shingon sect choose to be buried at Okunoin Cemetary, a sprawling collection of thousands of graves spread throughout the dense forests surrounding Kūkai's mausoleum on the outskirts of Kōya. Sho and I hiked along a burbling, flowing mountain stream, passing countless graves. The varied headstones were everywhere, competing with one another to proclaim the previous existence of the entombed. Some were nothing more than simple, modest stones marking the spot, while other gravesites were over-the-top. My favorite was a towering carved rocket ship pointing skyward and threatening to blast off.

"Wow, what is that, like twenty feet tall? This guy must have really loved outer space!" said Sho.

I learned later that many companies offer graves in Okunoin for former employees. The rocket ship headstone had been paid for by an aeronautics company.

No one knows exactly how many burial sites there are in Okunoin—estimates say about a half million—but Sho did his best to visit every one, running back and forth along the main pathways, then challenging me to find the most creative route through myriad trails that disappeared into the surrounding forest.

Throughout this ride across Japan, we'd passed many graveyards. Usually, they were modest collections of beautifully chiseled and meticulously cared-for headstones, nestled into a forest by the road or carved into the side of a hill. As we passed them, I made a habit of saying to myself, "That's where you're headed." This didn't stem from a macabre sense of despair, but reflected an attempt to provide some context for this crazy adventure. If I am only here for a while, I reasoned, I might as well do something out of the ordinary.

Our wandering around the graves of Okunoin over, it was time to go back to Rengejo-In for a meditation session. We returned to our temple lodging and re-entered the ceremony hall where we had observed the morning's chanting. Sho had enjoyed that experience and was eager for the next new adventure.

"Do you think I'll like it, Daddy?"

"I'm not sure, but please do your best not to make any noise."

This time, there were no gongs, no cymbals, no bells. There was only silent sitting on tatami mats in the darkened room, led by the mindful, passive, settled presence of Mr. Soeda, wrapped in the smell of incense and shared with a dozen others. I relaxed into a comfortable seated position, focused on my breathing, slowing it down until it was hard to tell whether I was inhaling or exhaling, and descended into a barely conscious state. At first, a stream of random thoughts and hidden worries intruded: the dull ache in my toe, images from yesterday's monster ride up the mountain, the spooky bike light casting strange forms into the black night as my legs screamed in protest, Sho's well-being, my priorities, a thousand years of history calling out for me to listen for a message that I couldn't seem to hear. The sprawling graves of Okunoin, aching muscles, anxiety over whether we would complete the ride on schedule, missing my wife and daughter . . .

But gradually the thoughts dissipated, evaporating into the stillness, until all that was left was my breath, still moving in and out, but barely perceptible. A kind of mental opening was occurring. A letting go. A mindfulness. A wonderful sinking into the eternity of the moment.

I felt a tug at my sleeve. "Dad!" Sho whispered. I ignored him, but the peaceful state that I had started to enter receded. "Dad!" he whispered again, and I could feel the collective annoyance in the room at this unwelcome intrusion into the magical silence. I opened my eyes.

"I'm going outside to play my DS, okay?"

I nodded, and he crawled across the tatami mat floor and slowly creaked open the wooden sliding doors. Then he creaked the doors closed again. Each sound he made reverberated like a bomb, and I winced at the rude intrusion on my fellow guests' meditations. Mr. Soeda sat impassively at the front, unbothered, unmoving and serene. The other guests, not nearly as practiced at meditation, shot me irritated looks.

That evening, Sho and I wore comfortable cotton *yukata* robes down to the dining hall, a large tatami mat room near the temple entrance that could easily hold over a hundred people. Unlike our first dinner, when we had dined alone, now we sat on the floor among twenty guests. Only one was Japanese, and he was seated by himself, separate from the group for some reason that was never explained to me. The rest were friendly tourists from Germany, Italy, Canada, the U.S. and France. They cooed appreciatively over the lovely lacquer trays full of *miso* soup, mountain vegetables, hot tea, rice, and a delicious flavored tofu dish.

Happily, the group was too well mannered to blame us for disrupting the meditation ceremony, and we all chatted politely about our experiences traveling around Japan.

After a while, Kiyomi Soeda entered the room. The eighty-nine-year-old matriarch of the temple wore a brightly colored kimono and exuded self-confidence and vigor. She looked much younger than her age and professed to have enjoyed excellent health throughout her life. "Only recently, I have begun to have difficulty hearing, and my legs feel weak at times," she lamented. We all munched our food in silence as she settled down comfortably in front of a microphone and told us her fascinating story.

Until around 1880, women were not permitted to live in Kōya, which was meant to be a Buddhist retreat for men only, far away from the temptations of society. Priests were not allowed to marry, and heads of temples chose their successors from among their disciples. This changed in the late 1800's, when it was decided that priests could marry, and their succession became hereditary.

Born to one of the priests in Kōya in 1920, Ms. Soeda was a restless girl and left the isolated mountaintop community in the late 1930's to study English at a university in Tokyo. When World War II began, she returned from Tokyo and her friends asked her suspiciously why she had "studied the language of the enemy." After the war, when knowledge of English was a useful skill, the same people praised her far-sighted wisdom.

In 1946, she married the head of Rengejo-In and moved into the temple, which was in a sorry state. The ceiling of the beautiful room we were sitting in had a leak they could not afford to repair, and the rain ruined the tatami mats.

"Where you are now, was a mud pit," she told Sho. "We had to lay down wooden slats to walk across this room. There wasn't enough food either, so we all grew sweet potatoes. Because of the lack of sun up here, they were stringy, skinny things that had little taste, but it was better than starving. When we ate rice porridge, I remember being able to count the number of grains in the bowl, it was so meager."

Sho looked down at his half-eaten bowl of rice. Perhaps feeling guilty for leaving so much, he took another bite.

She went on to tell us about Kūkai, going into more detail than her son had following this morning's chanting ceremony. She told us of Kūkai's decision to study esoteric Buddhism in China, of his prodigious intelligence, and of how he found a famous teacher in China and became his chosen successor after only a year and a half of study.

I noted the way many institutions, from politics to religion to business, ascribe phenomenal exploits to their leaders. Perhaps we all want to believe that our leaders are heroic. There are those fantastic stories of Samurai soldiers blocking bullets with their swords. There is also the story that the Emperor of Japan was a direct descendent of the goddess Amaterasu and thus a living god on earth. Militarists used this myth in the lead-up to Japan's horrific expansion through Asia. Not all quaint stories are benign.

Chapter 35

Awa Odori

SHO AND I AWOKE TO THE GONGS AGAIN THE NEXT DAY. Interested in another round of Buddhist chanting, we shuffled sleepily down the long temple corridors to the ceremony hall to observe the forty-minute ritual with about fifteen other guests. The chanting was just as mesmerizing as the day before, and Sho sat snuggled in my lap, enjoying the experience.

After stocking up on snacks in town, Sho and I started the long descent from Mt. Kōya toward the coast. Today's destination was Wakayama, about thirty-nine miles away. It was sunny and hot as we began to ride, sweat beading on top of my sunblock-slathered skin, but soon after we started the descent, a sudden downpour began. I stopped the bikes and pulled rain covers over our saddlebags. It was so warm that Sho and I didn't bother with jackets, rain pants or booties. I kept a careful, firm grip on the brakes as we made our way down the twists and turns of the wet alpine road, keeping close to the side to let cars pass every minute or two. The regular ordeal of managing the heavily laden bikes on long descents had taken a toll, and the tips of three fingers on my left hand had been numb for the past few weeks.

The squall was over soon, replaced by the pounding summer sun, its intense heat combining with the steady downhill wind to dry us off quickly. Small rivulets of rain water trailed down the road's edge, gurgling softly beside us for a few minutes before evaporating. Suddenly, I heard a sound coming from the rear wheel.

"You got a flat!" Sho announced, and I pulled over immediately.

"*We* got a flat," I corrected. "But at least it's not raining any more." I tried to keep a positive attitude despite the unwelcome delay.

There was a pullout just ahead with plenty of space to work on the bike. And the view was stunning: deep green forest-covered mountains stretching out into the distance, painted over by the shadows of dramatic cloud formations in the yawning sky. Sho took the delay in stride and started searching for interesting bugs in the brush, while I turned my back on the vista and went to work.

This was the tenth puncture of our ride, every one of which had occurred on my bike's rear tire, made vulnerable by the burden of my weight and the two heaviest saddlebags. Fifteen minutes later, the flat fixed, we continued our descent of Mt. Kōya. The heat steadily intensified, and soon we were baking in the oppressive, humid warmth. After reaching the base of the mountain, we turned west to ride along a river toward the coast and soon spotted an inviting rest stop. We pulled in, navigated around several monstrous tour busses and came to a stop in front of the bathrooms, dripping sweat that seemed to sizzle on the concrete. Sho begged for ice cream from a nearby vending machine, and I sent him off with enough money to get one for me too.

As I leaned our bikes against a wall, I felt a tickle on my right calf and looked down to see a black and yellow, long-legged spider clinging to my skin. It was about two inches in diameter. Sho and I had seen many spiders like this throughout our ride. Their intimidating size made them excellent subjects for Sho's photo collection, but I had no interest in finding out whether they were poisonous. I quickly, but gently, flicked the creature onto the sidewalk and watched it scramble away toward the women's rest room. When Sho returned, I pointed out my new friend.

"Daddy, he's awesome!" Sho exclaimed, and we spent the next ten minutes studying the spider and protecting it from being stepped on by visitors, most of whom didn't share our interest in him. Before continuing on, we made sure that the spider had made it safely up a wall.

"Daddy, he's going to peek in on the ladies!"

"I won't tell, if you won't."

The Kii Mountain range faded behind us as we made our way to the coastal town of Wakayama, arriving by four. I was interested in visiting its historic castle, but Sho convinced me to go bowling with him instead. We planned to catch a ferry early the next day, so it was unlikely that we would ever get the chance to see Wakayama's castle again.

"I think I'm being too nice to you, Sho. We keep skipping all the places I want to see so that you can bowl."

"That's not true!" he protested. "You get to decide where we ride every day. I just want to have a little fun every so often."

That night, I found a cheap single room in a business hotel near the ferry terminal. Just as in Hikone, the clerk tried to make us pay for a double room, but he acquiesced when I insisted on a single. I probably reinforced a stereotype that foreigners are pushy, but I was okay with that, and okay with saving fifty dollars.

Later that night, after Sho had taken a bath and written in his journal, I read to him in bed. One of the effects of cycling for many hours each day is the powerful need for a good night's rest. By nine, I was exhausted and started to fall asleep while reading out loud. Sho elbowed me several times, as I lost the text and slipped into groggy babbling. My body ached for sleep, but I had to stay awake. I got Sho to sleep by 9:30, then crawled silently out of the bed and settled behind the small desk in the narrow room. I turned on my laptop and spent the next hour and a half laboriously uploading pictures to TV Japan over a slow wireless connection. The news program was running another story on us and had requested pictures no later than that morning, but I had been unable to get an Internet connection in Mt. Kōya.

Once that was finished, I logged onto the United Nations Environment Programme's website. Sho and I had been asked to respond to questions about our trip submitted to the UN, and I worried that there would be a hundred e-mails from around the world waiting for us to respond. I needn't have worried. There was only one question, asking whether we were encouraging people to ride bikes even in bustling cities in developing countries, where it could be very dangerous for a cyclist. I answered that staying safe is the most important aspect of choosing where and when to ride.

The question reminded me of my experience training for this adventure with Sho. We had spent the previous year riding all over New York City and the northern suburbs of Westchester County. I had been surprised to find that I felt safer on the crowded streets of Manhattan than on the leafy roads of the suburbs. Drivers in Manhattan, while often aggressive, were accustomed to heavy vehicle and pedestrian traffic, and their speed was checked by traffic lights and traffic jams. You could safely cycle if you followed the rules, went at a reasonable pace, never suddenly swerved out into traffic, and watched for opening doors from parked cars. But the suburbs were filled with drivers on cell phones, cruising 60+ miles per hour on narrow roads, seemingly oblivious to pedestrians or cyclists. Manhattan was a cinch; the suburbs were scary.

After submitting my answer to the online question, I contemplated the next day. We'd be visiting Shikoku, one of Japan's major islands, often skipped by foreign tourists. We would start in Tokushima, an oceanside town I had yet to research. Exhausted, I crawled into bed, deciding I'd read about it on the ferry.

The next morning, as Sho and I found seats on the crowded ferry from Wakayama to Tokushima, I noticed an information desk. I approached a young uniformed woman sitting behind the counter. She gave me a weary nod. "May I help you?"

"Do you have any recommendations of places to stay in Tokushima? A small room with one bed is fine. Cheap is good."

"Are you joking?"

"No. My son and I are cycling across Japan and we choose where to sleep as we arrive in each new place."

She maintained an official façade, but I detected something more in her eyes. Astonishment? Disdain? "There is no way you are going to find a place to stay anywhere near Tokushima."

"We have a tent. How about a campsite?"

"I'm sure those are all booked up too. Unless you want to make a reservation for next year's celebration, I really can't help you. Sorry."

"What do you mean, 'next year's celebration'?"

"Of Awa Odori," she said, as if speaking to a child.

"I've never heard of it. What exactly is going on?"

She paused a moment, perhaps deciding whether I was making fun of her, then explained, "Tonight is the first night of Awa Odori. It's the largest dance festival in Japan and lasts three days. I would guess that about one million people from all over Japan should be arriving in town right about now, with reservations booked months in advance."

"Oh, I see. Thanks."

I returned to Sho, who was happily playing his DS. "Did you find us a place to stay?"

"Not exactly. Hold on, while I check out something in the guidebook." I began reading about Awa Odori, a dance festival over three hundred years old and known as the Mardi Gras of Japan. After a few minutes, I turned to Sho and said, "I've got a 'would you rather' game for you: would you rather have no place to sleep tonight but get to check out a massive dance party, or have a comfortable place to sleep but have to skip the party and ride for a couple hours?"

"That's easy," he said. "Party!"

Chapter 36

Temptation to Cheat

IT WAS EARLY AFTERNOON WHEN THE FERRY DOCKED AT Tokushima's busy port. Sho and I waited by our bicycles until all the cars had driven out of the ship's large hold, then we cycled toward the center of town. Signs of an impending party were everywhere. Strings of lights and multi-colored hanging lanterns decorated the wide, bustling streets of the modern downtown. We passed members of dance troops wearing identical outfits—often light cotton robes with matching designs. A few women wore large, distinctive straw hats that resembled oversized upside down tacos, with straps stretched tightly across the wearers' cheeks and chins.

I kept an eye out for a city park where we might surreptitiously free camp, but I found nothing suitable, and throngs of people were everywhere. Even if the police didn't move us off, it was unlikely that we would find a place to set up our tent away from the revelers. I worried that someone might steal our bikes while we slept and decided that I would stay awake all night on guard.

"I'm not so sure this was a good idea," I said to Sho.

"Come on, Dad. You're not that bad a dancer."

"You're a barrel of half-wit jokes. I'm just worried that we won't find a safe place to sleep tonight. Anyway, let's at least go to the heart of the action." I pulled our bikes to a stop, hoping to ask someone for directions. I approached a kind-looking woman walking with two young children dressed in colorful *yukata* robes.

"*Sumimasen.* I'm sorry to bother you," I said with a polite bow. "Do you know where the dance festival starts?"

"Yes, it's not far from here," she said, pointing down the road. "Keep going a few blocks through the next major inter-section. You'll see the police barricades set up on the left. Is this your first Awa Odori?"

"It is. In fact, I only found out about the festival this morn-ing. I'd never heard of it before."

"Well, you're in for a treat. Tokushima has a population of around 250,000, but this weekend there will be about one and a half million people here, all of them dancing. Have fun and be careful."

We resumed cycling, and as we neared the intersection, I saw a large Toyoko-Inn Hotel on the corner.

"I'm sure there's nothing available, but it can't hurt to check," I said to Sho as I locked up our bikes in front. The lobby was packed with people checking in, and Sho played his Nintendo DS beside me while we waited in line. Twenty minutes later, I reached the check-in counter and stood before a woman who seemed slightly frazzled but was still smiling. "Good day. What name is your reservation under?"

"Actually, I don't have one," I said, feeling foolish for even trying. "I'm sure all your rooms are booked, but I thought I might just check, in case you had a cancellation. A single bed is fine."

She made a few taps on a keyboard and said, "You're in luck. We have a single available for 6,500 yen. Will that do?"

"You're not joking, right?" This was too good to be true.

"Most people arrive in groups of two or more, so we have a few single rooms available. I hope you and your son enjoy the dancing."

I looked down at Sho and said, "Give me a high five, buddy!"

"See, I told you I was right. I never lose 'would you rather' games."

We left the hotel after dinner and joined a large crowd of people heading toward the Awa Odori parade route. The early evening sky was beginning to darken, but the town glowed with bright street lamps and hanging lanterns. Police officers directed us toward a sidewalk that was crammed with human beings of all ages. Many had settled along the roadside to get a good view of the parade of dancers that would soon pass. Sho and I squeezed through the throng of people and found a spot on the curb to sit and watch.

We soon heard drum beats and singing headed our way, and the spectators started to cheer. A line of perhaps thirty dancers dressed in white robes performed syncopated moves while slowly edging down the road. Behind them four young

men with white handkerchiefs wrapped around their heads and broad taiko drums strapped to their chests pounded out a rhythm while kicking their legs out side to side.

More and more dancers filed by, always in color-coordinated groups and always performing moves in synchrony with one another to the beat of drums. After about an hour, people along the road began to leave their viewing spots and join in. The dancers encouraged the spectators to join them, and soon the parade morphed into a street party. Sho and I dove into the fun, laughing and making up our own moves. A stranger grabbed my arm and pulled me into a circle of people dancing around a talented percussionist beating out a complicated but pleasing rhythm. Sho followed close behind. We spent the next few hours dancing the night away, joining groups of revelers who welcomed us with smiles and cheers.

At one point, we began dancing in front of a band that had set up two large speakers on the street. Surrounded by six band members playing drums and stringed instruments, a bearded elderly man belted out songs into a microphone he held. Around fifty people danced and moved as a group in a slow circle around the performers. Sho and I were sweating from the exertion in the warm summer evening, and a smiling kimono-clad woman handed us each a round fan.

As we thanked her, three shirtless white male Americans who looked college-age bounded into our midst. They bumped into the woman who had given us the fans and threw themselves into the throng of dancers, jostling people as if they were in a mosh pit. One of the boys grabbed the microphone from the singer and began yelling out drunken gibberish. The musicians continued playing, and the singer just laughed it off, patting the young man on his back and clapping at his ridiculous singing. The Japanese people who were shoved by the other two Americans attempted to maintain their balance and did not push back.

"Why are they being so rude?" Sho asked.

As they came spinning out of control back our way, one looked like he would barrel into Sho. I jumped forward and wrapped my arms protectively around my son, leaning my shoulder down so that it jammed into the college boy's sweaty ribs as he collided with me. As he fell back in surprise, I said in English, "Watch out for the kid."

The college boy jumped up with a crazy grin and said, "Hey, an American! What's up duuuuude!" He slammed my back hard and shouted, "This party is out of control!" Then he chased after his buddy, slamming him from behind and bumping into a few other dancers who laughed politely while struggling to remain upright.

I looked down at Sho and said, "I think it's time for us to head back to our hotel."

"Do we have to, Daddy? This is so much fun."

"Sorry, but it's getting late." I pulled him along, noticing that the two Americans had sandwiched a young woman and were grinding away.

We fell asleep seven stories above the raucous street scene, to the sounds of beating drums, music and the cheering of revelers, many of whom didn't return to their hotel rooms before sunrise.

We spent the next day cycling up the eastern coast of Shikoku and visited Naruto Bridge, where we looked down on swirling whirlpools formed by the clashing currents of the Pacific Ocean and the Seto Inland Sea. The massive suspension bridge included a protected walkway and well-placed glass floor panels, creating an awe-inspiring and revenue-generating tourist attraction.

We also made time to visit the marvelous Ritsurin Garden in the town of Takamatsu. Sho and I strolled for a couple of hours on footpaths through a peaceful chestnut grove and beside ponds full of lotus blossoms. We dropped bread from a stone bridge over a narrow stream to dozens of hungry koi that literally crawled over one another to get to the food. The constant static of cicadas filled the air, a sound that I will always associate with summer in Japan.

We cycled for another day on Route 11, which runs along the northern coast of the island of Shikoku. The traffic was relentless, and the unbroken line of chain stores beside the road made it hard for me to tell when we left one town and entered another.

At one point, Sho asked, "Daddy, which is better? A square or a circle?"

"Those are shapes, not relative concepts, so one isn't better than the other."

"You have to choose," he insisted.

"It depends on what you're interested in, or what shape you need at the time. A circle may be better when you need to fit something into a round hole. But a square may be preferable if you are designing a box, for example."

"Quit dilly-dallying! You have to choose. Which one is better?"

"Okay, a square," I said.

He shouted triumphantly, "Wrong! It's a circle, because it doesn't have any corners."

"I think you're just making up games I can't win," I said crossly. "I bet if I'd chosen a circle, you would have explained why a square is superior."

"Not true, Daddy. Don't be upset because you lost."

"I'm not upset!" I shouted.

Near the end of the afternoon, as we passed a sign welcoming us to the town of Toyohama, I decided to rest for the day. Seeing a group of three men chatting in a parking lot, I pulled to a stop and said in Japanese, "Excuse me. Sorry to bother you, but do you know of a campsite or hotel around here where we could sleep?"

One of the men stepped forward and said, "Not around here." He was middle-aged, had close-cropped hair, and wore glasses, tan pants and a blue short-sleeved shirt. I saw in his eyes a combination of mischievousness and intelligence. He looked more closely at Sho and our heavily laden bikes. "What are you two doing?"

"Cycling across Japan. We started in Cape Sōya and are on our way to Cape Sata. We wanted to visit Shikoku on the way."

The man said, "You're insane. How old is your son?"

Sho said, "I'm eight."

"Eight?! That's way too hard for an eight-year-old to try. What kind of father are you?"

The man turned to his friends and said, "You two are going to have to go ahead without me. I need to rescue this boy from his foolish father." The men gave us a wave and drove away in a car. Turning back to me, he said, "My name is Junji Itami. I run the community center in town—it's this building right here. I don't have beds, but you're welcome to sleep on the floor. Will that suit you?"

"Sure," I said. "We've got sleeping pads, so that would work fine."

"Good. Let's get your bikes inside, then I'll drive you to a bathhouse to clean up, and after that we'll eat dinner together."

Turning to Sho, he said, "I'm sorry you've got a crazy dad, but I'm here to help. Do you like baseball?"

Sho nodded.

"Great. After dinner, I'm taking you to a batting cage."

As we drove to the bathhouse, Mr. Itami said, "If it had just been you, I would have told you to sleep beside the road. But your kid melted my heart. How could I not take care of you guys?"

Sho grinned and whispered, "He's funny."

Mr. Itami continued, "What about your wife? Why didn't she come along? Isn't she worried?"

"She's got a full time job and is taking care of our two-year-old daughter. We stay in touch through e-mail and phone calls. Plus Sho and I post updates on our blog."

"I see," he said. "Still, isn't she worried?"

"Well, when I first told her about our plans to cycle across Japan, she thought I was nuts."

"Tell her there's a guy in Toyohama named Junji Itami who completely agrees with her."

"But now she thinks the trip is a great idea."

"My guess is that she just gave up arguing with you."

"Maybe. Some people tell me that a Japanese mother wouldn't let her child go on a trip like this, but then I tell them my wife is Japanese."

"Your wife isn't Japanese."

"Yes, she is. She's from Tokyo. Her family still lives there."

"No, if your wife were Japanese, she wouldn't allow her young son to be forced to ride a bike all across the country."

I couldn't argue with this logic, but countered, "Just think about what a great experience this is for Sho. He's doing something probably no other eight-year-old has ever done. And he's gaining self-confidence, learning about Japan, and getting stronger every day."

"You're getting stronger," joked Mr. Itami. "He's probably just suffering. Poor kid."

We arrived at the public bath, a nondescript wooden building, and followed Mr. Itami inside. In Japan, there's a difference between *sento* and *onsen*. *Onsen* are public bathing facilities fed by underground hot springs that are plentiful in the volcanically active country. Many of them have the feel of a high-end spa and are popular tourist destinations. *Sento* is the name for a public bathhouse that heats up regular tap water and is typically utilitarian in appearance. Usually there is one large room with many tubs of varying sizes. A tall divider down the middle of the room separates the sexes. *Sento* were more popular in Japan in previous generations, when fewer homes had their own bathtubs. But many people still use them, in part as a way to socialize.

As we entered the bathhouse, Mr. Itami was clearly among friends. Several people greeted him, and he introduced us as his "new foreign friends, one cute, the other crazy."

As we sampled the various tubs, he pointed to one that was just large enough for one person. "Want to try an electrified one?"

"*Electrified*?"

"Yes, a small current of electricity runs through the water. It's supposed to be good for the circulation."

"I doubt the science backs up the claim."

"Oh, come on! If you can ride a bike all the way across Japan, I'm sure you can handle a little electrical shock."

Chastened, I walked over to the tub. Pointing to Mr. Itami, I said, "Sho, if I die here, tell the cops he was responsible."

Sho looked up, concerned, and Mr. Itami patted his head. "Don't worry. He'll be fine. He's just wasting time because he's scared."

I dipped my right foot into the water. The current coursed up my leg and sent a tingling throughout my body. I imagined miniature lightening bolts crackling out the tips of my fingers. I wanted to jerk my foot out immediately, but didn't feel like giving Mr. Itami the satisfaction. I maintained an impassive expression and left my foot in the water for about thirty seconds. It was a bizarre feeling of imminent peril, like standing at the edge of a sharp drop, but I quickly realized that the sensation would neither increase nor decrease after the initial shock.

I returned to Mr. Itami, who said, "Myself, I never go into that one. The sensation is too weird."

We spent the rest of the evening at the batting cage, eating dinner, then enjoying a lively conversation with our friendly host before moving aside tables to make room for our sleeping mats on the community center floor. The next morning, Mr. Itami greeted us and said, "I have a surprise. I know you said you're riding to Matsuyama today, but I've decided to take the morning off and drive you to Kōchi. It's a town on the southern coast of Shikoku that's historically significant. You can't cycle across Japan and skip Kōchi. After that, I'll drive you directly to Matsuyama. It's too hot to cycle that far, anyway."

"That's very generous." I said. "I'll accept your offer to drive us to Kōchi, but let's return here by lunch time so that Sho and I can ride to Matsuyama. If you drive us there, we wouldn't be able to say that we cycled all the way across Japan."

"No one needs to know," Mr. Itami said with a wink.

"I'll know," I said firmly. "We're not cheating on this trip."

"Okay, but you're not giving us much time. Let's get moving."

Sho and I both said, "Yes, sir" at the same time and started laughing.

As he drove on an interstate interspersed with long tunnels and dramatic vistas of the gorgeous mountains of central Shikoku, Mr. Itami asked, "Have you noticed all the temples around here?"

"I guess," I said. "Although we've passed temples throughout the country. Is there something special about the ones on Shikoku?"

"Oh yes. Haven't you noticed any pilgrims walking along the roads? They wear conical sedge hats, long-sleeved white shirts and carry wooden sticks."

Sho said, "I saw a couple on our ride yesterday!"

Mr. Itami explained, "Those people are called *o-henro-san*. They walk to eighty-eight temples spread out across the island on what's known as the Shikoku Pilgrimage. It's part of their worship of a monk named Kūkai who lived around here a long time ago. They usually end their walk in the temple town of Mt. Kōya."

Sho said, "We just came from there! We learned that Kūkai traveled in China and is still alive, meditating in some cave."

Mr. Itami continued, "The route is about 1,200 kilometers long, so some of these pilgrims choose to do it by car or bus. If you ask me, that's cheating."

"Yeah, like hitching a ride during a bike trip," I said.

Mr. Itami ignored my jibe and continued, "But watch out. Not all of these *o-henro-san* are pious worshipers. A few years back, a TV channel decided to do a feature on the pilgrimage. They randomly interviewed some pilgrims, who explained how hard it is to walk for so long, but how worthwhile the experience was anyway. Blah, blah, blah. Well, a police detective in Tokyo happened to be watching the show and recognized one of the 'pilgrims' as a fugitive on the run from the law. He called his buddies on the Shikoku police force and had the criminal behind bars in a couple of days."

"Wow," Sho said. "I wonder if the wandering monk we met in Hokkaidō was actually an axe-murderer."

"Did he have a shaved head and live off handouts of food?"

"That's him!" Sho said.

"Very dangerous, that guy. You two are lucky to have survived the encounter."

Sho's eyes widened and I told Mr. Itami, "Stop joking around. You'll give him nightmares."

We spent the morning exploring Kōchi and playing on a beach before returning to Toyohama just after noon. As we loaded our bikes and prepared to ride off, Mr. Itami gave me a serious look. "The road is flat for a while, but then you have a long, hard climb up a mountain into Matsuyama. It's over ninety degrees today, and there is a lot of traffic besides. I don't think it's safe for you and Sho to ride."

"I appreciate your concern," I said, patting his shoulder. "I'll give you a call at the end of the day, so that you know we made it." I bowed to Mr. Itami and said, "Thank you for your remarkable generosity. Sho and I are lucky to have met you."

"Likewise," he said, patting the top of Sho's helmet.

Chapter 37

Shimanami Kaidō

WE CYCLED THROUGH NON-STOP SUBURBAN SPRAWL FOR 50 miles on Route 11 before the road began to meander up the side of a mountain. Convenience stores, parking lots and car repair centers were replaced by fresh green forests. I welcomed the pleasant change of scenery but suffered from climbing in the heat. The amount of sweat dripping off my body onto the searing pavement was alarming, and I worried that I would not be able to replace the fluid or sodium adequately. Exercising for many hours on a hot day always raises the risks of dehydration and the even-more dangerous metabolic condition of hyponatremia, when the body loses too much sodium. Hyponatremia could be triggered by drinking too much water. I knew the risks and mixed salt tablets into our sports drink.

"Are you doing okay back there?" I asked Sho.

"Yep, just hot."

"Make sure to keep drinking." His drinking bottle was attached to a cage on his handlebar.

"I know, Daddy. You don't have to keep reminding me."

At a pull-off ahead, I noticed a minivan come to a stop. An elderly couple climbed out of the vehicle and opened the hatchback. The man was silver-haired and wore shorts, a short-sleeved shirt and sandals. The woman wore a white blouse, blue skirt and floppy white hat. As we approached, slowly cranking the pedals up the steep climb, the couple flagged us down. "Hey! Please stop."

I pulled to the side behind their car. "Hello," I said between heavy exhalations, wiping sweat from my eyes with the back of my bike gloves.

The woman said, "We passed you back there and thought you must be awfully hot. We're just returning from filling up water bottles from a famous mountain spring nearby. This is the best tasting water in all of Japan, and it's still ice cold. We thought you might like some."

Her husband pulled out several clear half-liter bottles from the back of their car and held them out to me.

Sho jumped off his trailer cycle and said, "I'll take one!"

"That's very thoughtful of you," I said. "Maybe we'll just take one bottle."

"No, no. Take more," the woman insisted. "We have dozens."

Two of the three water bottles on my bike were empty, and I filled them with the delicious cold water. Sho and I consumed the contents of one of their bottles on the spot, and the man retrieved the empty container with a smile.

"What do you say, Sho?" I prompted, waiting for him to say thank you to the couple.

Sho handed back an empty bottle and said in English, "You guys rock!"

We took pictures together, then waved goodbye as they pulled ahead up the mountain. We made the final push into Matsuyama with renewed vigor and arrived at 7 p.m., having cycled seventy miles in six hours. We settled into a business hotel, and I called Mr. Itami.

"It's good to know you're safe and sound," he said. "I was worried about you guys all day. It's still not too late to give up and let Sho have a normal summer, you know."

I played along with his joke, "If we give up, I'm going to give you a call to pick us up."

"You just tell me the time and place, and I'll be there."

Next, I called Eiko. It was nine on a Tuesday morning in New York, and she was in her office at the United Nations Secretariat building. "Hey, sorry to bother you at work," I said. "I just wanted to check in."

"Thanks. I've only got a minute to chat. Are you and Sho doing okay?"

"Yep, we're great, although today's ride was brutal. I think the temperature hit 95 degrees by mid-morning and stayed there all day."

"I know how insanely hot and humid August can be in Japan. Growing up in Tokyo, I remember being drenched in sweat after standing outside for just a few minutes. I hope you took it easy and didn't try to ride too far."

"We were fine. I think our bodies have become accustomed to the heat." I briefly told her about Mr. Itami and the couple who gave us water, adding, "People in Japan are so nice."

"That's a pretty big generalization," Eiko said. "While there is a cultural emphasis on politeness in Japan, I think a friendly foreigner who speaks the language and has an eight-year-old boy with him brings out the good side of people. Don't discount how much your optimistic attitude and tendency to see the goodness in others actually increase the odds that you'll have so many friendly encounters."

I heard someone's voice in the background, and Eiko said, "Sorry, but I've gotta run. I'm late for a meeting. Give Sho a big kiss for me. I love you."

We spent the next morning hiking around Matsuyama Castle in the sweltering heat. The castle grounds were crowded with tourists, but the forest trail we used to reach the entrance had been nearly empty. I found out that most of the visitors had arrived on a chair lift from the opposite side of the hill. Sho and I rode it up and down for fun then hiked back down the trail to our bikes.

We set off for Dōgo Onsen, one of the oldest hot springs in Japan. I got lost on the way there and stopped a young man on a bicycle to ask for directions. He started to explain the route, then said, "Oh, it's too complicated. Just follow me."

Pedaling beside us, he said, "This bathhouse is over 1,300 years old and has been visited by many famous people over the centuries. Ever see the movie 'Spirited Away'? Dōgo Onsen was the basis for the bathhouse in the film."

Sho said, "I remember that movie!"

"It had lots of spooky spirits, right? Well, do you know the legend of Dōgo Onsen?"

We shook our heads.

"It's the Legend of the Egret. A long time ago, thousands of egrets lived in the area where the bathhouse is now located. One of these egrets hurt his leg and began soaking it in a hot spring. Day after day, he soaked his injured leg in the steaming water. The humans living in the area took notice of this curious bird. After a while, the egret flew away fully healed. People shared the legend of this hot spring's healing powers, and soon visitors from all over started showing up to take a dip. And that's why it is still popular after all these years."

Sho clapped. "Wow, all because of one bird."

"Or so they say."

It took nearly twenty minutes to get to the bathhouse, and I thanked our guide for going so far out of his way.

"It's no big deal. I'm in college and should probably be studying right now, but I enjoyed riding with you more."

Although my broken toe wasn't magically healed, and although three of my fingers remained numb, the steaming baths of the ancient *onsen* felt good on my sore muscles. Afterward, Sho and I rode four and a half hours through the afternoon from Matsuyama to Imabari. From there the next day, we planned to cycle the renowned Shimanami Kaidō, an expressway that connected nine islands between Shikoku and Honshu. The thirty-seven mile route included a bike path that crossed the world's longest series of suspension bridges and offered fabulous views. I fell asleep smiling at the prospect.

The next morning, a childhood friend of Eiko's named Saga joined us. She lived in Tokyo and flew in especially to attempt to complete the Shimanami Kaidō ride in one day. She wore a white nylon jacket to protect her from the pounding sun, a short-sleeved blue synthetic shirt, sunglasses and black exercise pants that complimented her slim figure. As we met her at the base of the first bridge, I said, "You look ready to ride!"

She shook her head, "I'm not very active, you know. I spend most days working behind a desk. And it's a very hot and humid day."

"That's okay," I said. "Just set the pace, and we'll follow you. And remember, your mantra for today's ride is 'I won't give up!' Got it?"

"Yes, sir!"

A rental shop was located at the start of this well-known ride, and we approached the owner to find a bike and helmet for Saga. He explained that she could return them at a drop-off location at the end. Looking at our bicycles, he said, "You know, your connected bikes are illegal in Japan. I wanted to rent out trailer cycles like the one you have, but there's a law against tandem bikes. Japan is one of the few countries in the world with such a ridiculous regulation."

"Yeah, I heard that," I said. "But some friends in a bike club in Tokyo told me that the police don't really enforce that law. And a trailer cycle isn't technically a tandem, because the chains are separate, so I'm not sure if it's actually illegal."

"I just hope you don't meet a police officer who interprets the law differently."

Before we cycled away, my phone rang. "*Moshi moshi.*"

"*Moshi moshi*! It's Saito."

"Hey Saito-san!" I said. "Where are you?" Over the previous few days, I had been in touch with Mr. Saito, our cycling buddy from Hokkaidō whom we had last seen at the Hakodate ferry terminal a month earlier. He had cycled down the eastern coast of Japan, while Sho and I had stayed to the west before crossing the Japan Alps. We had kept in touch over that time, hoping to ride together once our routes finally converged. "I'm about an hour away from the start of Shimanami Kaidō. I rode 120 kilometers yesterday to try to catch up with you. My legs feel like jelly today."

"Please don't rush. We're about to start riding, but we'll take it nice and slow so that you can catch up."

As I hung up, Saga said, "I like your 'nice and slow' idea. Any other tips for an inexperienced cyclist?"

I thought for a minute and said, "I'm guessing that we'll ride for around seven hours. When cycling for that many hours, especially when it's this hot, you should take in plenty of fluids and calories. I'll start drinking water or a sports drink in the first half hour of riding and eat something after an hour or so. The secret to riding all day is eating and drinking regularly."

"Got it! What should I eat though?"

"Lots of simple carbs are good, like fruit and rice balls. Sho and I are quite fond of dried squid, which is fun to chew and has lots of protein to help your muscles recover. Don't eat too much too quickly, though, or you'll get a stomach ache."

"Thanks, good advice. Have you or Sho gotten sick at all so far?"

"Nope, thank goodness. I thought we'd catch a cold early on, because we rode so often in the cold rain. But maybe the vigorous exercise boosted our immune systems."

Riding at Saga's pace was a pleasure and perfect for this route. It would have been a shame to rush past the tremendous views from the towering bridges, and we stopped frequently to take photos. Mr. Saito caught up with us an hour later. His arms and legs were deeply tanned, and his leg muscles looked even more defined than when we had last met.

"You're looking really strong!" I said.

He let out a sigh, slumped over the handlebars of his bike, and said, "Catching up with you guys over the past few days was brutal, but I'm glad I put in the effort. It's wonderful to see you. Sho looks really great."

Sho gave him a smile and asked if he wanted to have a burping contest. "I just drank a fizzy drink, and I'm currently unbeatable."

Mr. Saito laughed and said, "Ah, *tabi wa michizure!*"

I didn't know the expression and asked him to repeat it. Saga, who spoke fluent English, translated. "It's an old Japanese saying that has a dual meaning: it's good to have traveling companions on the road, just like it's good to have compassion and kinship in life."

"Well said!" I gave Mr. Saito a pat on the back. "It's good to be riding with you again."

Shimanami Kaidō was everything I hoped it would be. The skies were sunny, the views magnificent. As we cycled across massive bridges, we looked out over a shimmering sea and tree-covered islands stretching into the distance. We met a group of riders from the Onomichi Cycling Club who gave me a bumper sticker with their club name to affix to my bike and asked us to share tales of our adventures. Saga set a steady pace, but our frequent stops for photo ops and socializing slowed us down. We also missed a turn and cycled about five miles off course before realizing our mistake and retracing our steps. As the sun began to set, we had not yet reached the end of the ride. And the route became hillier. Mr. Saito peeled off to stay at a bed and breakfast where he had made a reservation. But Saga wanted to complete the entire ride in one try, and I was happy to assist.

Saga said, "I'm really suffering. My body hurts all over. But I remember the mantra you gave me. I promise not to give up."

Sho joined in. "Don't worry, Saga. You'll be fine. We've ridden in the dark lots of times. And up mountains. And in the rain. And without food."

"I think she gets the point, buddy," I said.

"No," Saga said. "It's good for me to hear. If an eight-year-old can handle this, then so can I."

We reached the town of Onomichi well after nightfall, exhausted but happy. Saga took us out for a celebratory meal and said, "I never thought I'd be able to do something like this. But I did it. I really did it."

Chapter 38

Hiroshima

SAGA, STILL GLOWING FROM HER TRIUMPH, FLEW BACK TO Tokyo the next day. Mr. Saito caught up with us in Onomichi, and Sho and I rode with him along a busy route into Hiroshima. He found a hotel, while Sho and I spent the night in the home of a TV Japan announcer, whose job was to host us and take video that could be used in the next TV spot about our ride. She filmed us cycling up to her house, eating a home-cooked meal, shooting off fireworks, and reading in futons at bedtime.

The next morning, Sho and I set out to explore. Like all major cities in Japan, Hiroshima sprawls over many miles. Quaint, densely packed neighborhoods built around narrow roads and alleys spilled out onto a collection of major arteries belching traffic in and out of the modern downtown area, built after its destruction in World War II. We rode over bridges, through under passes, past factories and shops, crawling ever deeper into the city, whose population numbered well over a million.

I gripped the handlebars firmly to keep the bikes from veering out and tried to remain relaxed in the midst of the traffic. After seven weeks of daily cycling, we were comfortable navigating even the most heavily traffic-choked byways, but we still needed to be cautious. The key was to maintain a line close to the edge of the road and to ride at a safe speed. A big mistake cyclists make when riding in traffic is swerving out quickly to avoid a pothole, squirrel, car door or other unexpected obstacle. It's an easy way to get hit by a car, and I remained focused on anticipating such potential dangers.

But I was distracted, struggling over our plans for the day. We were headed into the heart of the city to the Hiroshima Peace Memorial Park, a collection of monuments and memorials to the 140,000 people who are estimated to have died as a result of the atomic bomb that was dropped here in the final days of World War II. I pondered whether to take Sho to the Peace Memorial Museum. Full of graphic displays of the horrifying impact the bomb had on the people of Hiroshima, it would be a disturbing place for anyone to visit, let alone a child. Our TV Japan host had advised me against taking him.

"We were required as elementary school students to go there on a field trip," she said. "It gave me nightmares. They shouldn't make young children see it." She added that growing up in Hiroshima in the 1960's and 70's, she often saw bomb survivors, known in Japanese as *hibakusha*, many with grotesque scars. "I always looked away when I saw *hibakusha* on the street. It was terrifying as a child to think about what they had been through and what happened here."

Her experience gave me pause. I had planned to take Sho to the museum, thinking that, despite his young age, it was a rare opportunity for him to learn about this important historical event. I also thought that it wasn't a bad idea for him to witness the consequences of war, countering the simplistic glorification common on TV and in movies.

The museum emphasized the importance of promoting the peaceful resolution of differences among nations and advocated for a world without nuclear weapons. The night before, while mulling over whether to take Sho to see it, I had read through a Hiroshima guide, highlighting the following passage:

> The Peace Memorial Museum collects and displays belongings left by the victims, photos, and other materials that convey the horror of that event, supplemented by exhibits that describe Hiroshima before and after the bombings and others that present the current status of the nuclear age. Each of the items displayed embodies the grief, anger, or pain of real people. Having now recovered from the A-bomb calamity, Hiroshima's deepest wish is the elimination of all nuclear weapons and the realization of a genuinely peaceful international community.

A world without nuclear weapons was an unlikely hope, perhaps, but a worthy vision to encourage in my child. Still, did an eight-year-old need to be introduced to the horror of nuclear war? Did I need to traumatize my son with images of burning children for him to figure out that it would be better for humanity not to have these weapons?

We were getting close to the museum, and I checked the GPS to keep from getting lost. After a few more turns, we rolled into the outer edge of the Peace Park. A broad rectangular open plaza filled with various monuments, it was full of people walking about in the hot sun. The museum, a modern two-story marble building, stretched along one end of the park. As we locked up our bikes, Sho asked, "Daddy, this is the city that got bombed in the war, right?"

"Yes, the U.S. dropped an atomic bomb on Hiroshima at the end of World War II, in August 1945. We are standing in the place where it hit."

Sho looked around warily, as if expecting another bomb to appear from the sky. "It doesn't look like a bomb was dropped here."

"Well, that happened a long time ago . . ."

"Hold on!" Sho interrupted, holding up his finger and squinting in thought. After a moment, he declared triumphantly, "That was sixty-four years ago."

"Nice job doing math in your head. But Sho, the museum has some scary pictures from the war. Do you want to go in or skip it and just walk around this nice park?"

Sho looked at me for cues as to how I wanted him to respond. Then he asked, "Do you think I should see it?"

I paused, imagining him as a grown man talking to me about this bike ride. Perhaps he would tell me of his many wonderful memories from the trip, "except for the museum in Hiroshima. I wish you hadn't taken me there. It was traumatic. I had nightmares for a long time afterward." Hell, *I* expected to have nightmares. But I felt that this was important to share with him, that it was better to let him learn about this sad reality now and to process it together.

Finally, I said, "It will be tough, but yeah, I think it's an important place for you to visit."

"Then let's go." As we walked toward the entrance, I hoped it was the right decision.

I had arranged to meet Mr. Saito here, and he was waiting for us at the entrance. We exchanged pleasantries then entered the museum. We soon separated, tacitly agreeing to experience the exhibits on our own, and would meet outside later. A crowd of visitors filled the opening hall, whispering to one another in respectfully somber tones. Sho and I slowly made our way along the exhibits. The ground floor included two large models of 1945 downtown Hiroshima, one showing the city before the bomb, the other showing the city after the explosion. Sho shuttled between the two, noting the differences. "Dad, this part is just totally gone." He pointed to the area marked with a red ball that represented the atomic bomb's hypocenter. "And so many of the other buildings are really damaged."

We walked along a wall of exhibits describing Hiroshima's role in Japan's wartime preparation and the decision by the

U.S. to drop the bomb. As I read, I wished the museum had included more historical context for the war. It did not delve into the history of Japan's expansionistic policies, the bombing of Pearl Harbor, the many atrocities carried out by Japanese forces across Asia, the Rape of Nanking, or other examples of human suffering caused by Japan during the war. The overwhelming impression was of Japan as a victim and the U.S. as a remorseless destroyer. I couldn't help but feel that the museum was missing an important opportunity to provide greater context to the bombing.

But discussing World War II remains a divisive issue in the country. Many Japanese friends told me that their high school history teachers conveniently ran out of time before reaching the major events of the twentieth century, presumably in order to avoid discussing the war.

Sho stayed close to my side as we moved through the increasingly disturbing exhibits. There were horrific life-size models of people who had been burned in the blast, walking with their arms outstretched like zombies, skin dripping down. There was a wall with the clearly visible shadow of a man who had been incinerated in the blast, a photo of a woman whose kimono had burned its patterns into her skin.

"Look Dad, a tricycle." Sho pointed to the small bent and rusted frame on display. "What happened to it?"

I read the description to him quietly, struggling to stay composed. The tricycle had belonged to a young boy who loved to ride it for hours on end. The child was killed by the bomb blast, and his father buried the tricycle in their yard in memory of his lost son. Later, the father dug it up for the museum to put on display. A wave of despair washed over me. I wanted to wrap my arms around Sho and envelope him in a protective bubble. He looked up to see a tear run down my cheek.

We held hands in silence.

Over the next hour and a half, we read story after story of human suffering. Every so often, Sho asked a question in a quiet voice. We finished by watching a video interview of a survivor who described what happened to him that day. He had been a junior high student when the atomic bomb exploded, and his school had collapsed on top of him. Most of his classmates were crushed, but he and a few others trapped under the rubble survived. As they waited to be dug out, the students sang their school song to keep up their spirits.

As we emerged onto the memorial plaza to a gloriously sunny day, I was emotionally and physically drained. A few wisps of alabaster clouds hung in the sky, and we found a place to rest beside the statue of Sadako Sasaki, a young girl who died from exposure to radiation after surviving the blast. As she grew sicker, she attempted unsuccessfully to fold 1,000 origami cranes, believing that such a feat would result in a miracle cure. For decades, children from around the world have sent folded cranes in her memory that are displayed near the statue. Her arms stretched out to the sky, a look of serene confidence belying her fate. The large shell of the six-story A-Bomb Dome loomed in the distance, the blasted out remains of a building now surrounded by tourists taking photos. From this distance, we could not see the forms of children's bodies that had been burned into the sidewalks as they walked to school at 8:15 a.m. on August 6, 1945.

I watched Sho closely, fearing that the museum had been too much. His face was calm, though, as he held my hand. We sat in the shade, watching passersby stroll along the pleasant plaza. Finally, Sho broke the silence. "Daddy, did Ojii-chan fight in the war?" he asked, referring to his Japanese grandfather, Eiko's dad.

"No, he was too young to fight. But just barely. He was fifteen when World War II ended and had been in cadet school in Tokyo, preparing to defend Japan from the invading Americans. He's still in touch with friends he made in that school."

"What about Obaa-chan?"

"Your grandmother was also a kid during the fighting, but had to work in a factory in Tokyo, along with most of her friends, to support the war effort. At that time, the men were off fighting, the boys were learning to be soldiers, and the women and girls were working in factories to support the war machine. Everyone was required to do something to help Japan win. Near the end of the war, Tokyo was fire-bombed, and much of it burned down. But your grandmother's house survived. It's the one we go to on New Year's to celebrate with family. Obaa-chan was a good student, but she never got the chance to go to college. She told your mom to study hard and take advantage of opportunities to learn."

"What about Granddad? Did he fight in the war?"

"No, my father was around your age and living in Oklahoma when the war ended."

"Did he want to fight?"

"I don't think so, but he certainly wanted the U.S. to win the war. You have family and friends in Japan, so you know a lot about the country and people. But when Granddad was your age, many people in the U.S. thought all Japanese were cruel savages. This was in part due to propaganda put out by the U.S. Government. But part was based in reality. Japanese soldiers did terrible things in Korea, China and other countries they invaded. These stories made many people think that all Japanese were cruel."

I paused, wondering if I should continue. Then I told Sho, "During the war, Japanese people who lived in the United States were rounded up and put into internment camps, basically prisons. It was strange, because the U.S. was at war with Germany and Italy too, but almost all of the people put into camps were Japanese."

"They would have put *Mommy* into a camp?"

"Probably. But I don't think the U.S. and Japan are going to fight each other again any time soon, so I'm sure Mommy will be fine."

Sho mulled over what I had said, and pronounced with great determination, "I wouldn't let them take her away."

I gave him a hug and looked out at a group of children chasing one another nearby, dodging back and forth and giggling as they bounded in and out of the shadows of Sadako's statue.

Chapter 39

Endings

THE NEXT FEW DAYS PASSED QUICKLY. TRAVELING WITH MR. Saito took some of the pressure off me: he called in advance to find accommodations for us each day, suggested more cycling-friendly routes and with his pleasant banter made the many hours on the road less monotonous. The trip began to feel almost too easy.

We visited the famous Shrine Island of Itsukushima, its towering vermillion "floating" *torii* gate emerging from the waters of the Inland Sea of Japan. With a horizontal wooden beam across the top curving up at either end and supported by two broad pillars, *torii* were a common sight throughout the country. They marked the entrance into the sacred space of a Shinto shrine. To non-Japanese, they offered the easiest way to distinguish a Shinto shrine from a Buddhist temple, for Japan incorporated both religions into its culture. I had seen many *torii* on this ride, but Itsukushima's was the most dramatic. Its image graced the cover of many guidebooks about Japan, typically alongside a shot of Mt. Fuji.

While at the "floating" gate, Sho made an announcement. "Daddy, I want to dance like Billy Elliot. When we get home, can I start taking tap and ballet classes?"

I did not see that one coming. No one in our immediate family was a dancer, and I had never imagined Sho wanting to dance. I paused for a moment, feeling that old prejudice: dance, especially ballet, was for girls. But just as quickly, I realized I had outgrown that bias. I was proud of Sho for having set himself an ambitious goal and following his own path, and I wondered if this trip might have helped give him the confidence to do so.

"Sure. Let's talk with Mommy and find a dance studio back home."

We spent the rest of the afternoon listening to the Billy Elliot soundtrack over and over as we cycled to Iwakuni. After the third time through, I had enough. "I love your enthusiasm, Sho, but let's turn off the music for a while." Sho agreed, but a few minutes later, he began to belt out the songs on his own.

We saw rare albino snakes housed in a glass cage next to the Kintai Bridge in Iwakuni and happened across the filming of a kids' TV show featuring super heroes battling a green alien bug monster with Samurai swords. The actors wore ridiculous costumes and fought with plastic weapons, but Sho was enthralled. Mr. Saito told us about his time as an elementary school teacher and about his hometown of Yamagata, where winter snows can bury the town in meters of drift. He taught Sho how to turn a long narrow leaf from a roadside plant into a squeaky instrument, and we spent each night shooting off fireworks and pointing out brilliant constellations hanging like artwork far overhead.

When we disembarked from a ferry onto the eastern shore of Kyushu, the southernmost major island of the Japanese archipelago, I felt both relief and sadness at the looming end of our grand adventure. In less than a week of riding down the coast, Sho and I would reach our destination, Cape Sata. The thought of seeing my wife and daughter was sweet, but I was ambivalent about returning to my old job at Intel. As we took a break on the Kunisaki Peninsula on our way to the town of

Beppu, Sho explored the beach, while Mr. Saito and I stood by the roadside admiring the ocean view.

He picked up on my mood and asked, "Are you sorry that the trip will end so soon?"

"I miss Eiko and Saya very much and am looking forward to seeing them. But I feel like this journey has shaken something loose, that I've changed. I think I should do more with my life than climb a corporate hierarchy."

Mr. Saito nodded and said, "I know you only from this trip, but it's hard for me to picture you as a businessman. The image doesn't seem quite right. I can see you as a teacher, like I was. You are good with kids and certainly a loving father."

"Thanks for saying that. Speaking of which, have you noticed that Sho's knees are starting to bump into the handlebars of the trailer cycle? He's grown in the past two months."

"Not just physically," Mr. Saito said. "He's more mature than when I first met him at the beginning of your trip. He seems more confident and certainly knows how to deal with adversity. Instead of whining, he just laughs it off. That's remarkable for an eight-year-old."

I smiled and said, "Sometimes when we cycle past a shop window, I glance over to see our reflection. Sho looks so small on the trailer cycle. The image is there and gone in the blink of an eye as we rush past, and it reminds me of how fleeting all this is, how quickly childhood ends and how soon we grow old. Like a cherry blossom that blooms so beautifully in the spring but falls to the ground after just a week or two."

Mr. Saito said, "You're starting to sound Japanese! Well, you're giving Sho a precious gift—time with his dad. He will always have memories from this trip, and I suspect that they will only become more meaningful to him as he grows older. When my mother was dying, she was hospitalized. On the last day of her life, she asked the doctors to send for me. As she waited for me to arrive, she held on and stayed conscious until I got there. When I came in the room and our eyes met, she began to cry. And within minutes, she was gone. She had held off death in order to see me one last time. The secret of life became very clear to me in that moment. It was so simple: spend as much time as you can with the people you love and don't be afraid to truly live."

Sho climbed up from the beach and announced, "I was just thinking—I wish I could go back in time."

"I've often imagined that scenario," I said. "There are so many interesting historical places I'd love to see, like ancient Greece or China when the Great Wall was being built. You could visit family members who have died, meet yourself as a kid, maybe even travel back far enough to see the dinosaurs."

"I guess," he said with a furrowed brow. "I was just thinking, if a friend gave me a birthday present I didn't like, I could turn back time and maybe they'd choose a better present the second time around."

We spent the final few days of the ride sweating beneath a brutally hot sun but enjoying the incredible beauty of Kyushu's coastline. As we crossed a bridge on the way out of Miyazaki, Sho spotted movement in the water below. We stopped the bikes and witnessed a show worthy of Sea World. Individual fish, maybe five or six inches long, flew out of the water in tight arcs before plunging back in a splash. This happened dozens of times in two or three minutes.

"What kind of fish are those?" asked Mr. Saito.

"Let's call them the Flying Fish of Miyazaki," I said, taking out my video camera to capture the performance.

Sho said, "I want to fish here! We won't even need a fishing rod. Just row out in a boat, and they will jump right in. All you need to do is whack the fish on the head with a paddle and you've got dinner."

"Great idea, buddy. Why do you think the fish are jumping like that anyway?"

Mr. Saito said, "I'm baffled."

Sho said, "Maybe they're trying to impress the girls."

Later that day, we visited Aoshima Shrine, which was constructed on a peninsula made up entirely of shells deposited over the past twenty-four million years. The surrounding swirling water had carved complex wavy patterns into the rock floor that stretched out in a large shallow bank, making it a perfect spot for Sho to explore. The unusual pattern here was known as *oni no sentaku ita*, or "the giant's washboard." It was easy to imagine a giant rubbing his clothes back and forth over the naturally corrugated formations.

After cycling a little further down the coast, we tested our throwing skills at Udo Shrine, which was built into the rock ledge of a seaside cliff. A railing in front of the shrine looked out over a large boulder a hundred feet below. The monks had laid out a rope in a circle around the perimeter of the boulder, and a sign read, "Men throw clay pebble with left hand. Women throw with right hand. 5 balls 100 yen. If the ball lands in the rope circle, you will have good luck." Mr. Saito and I missed all five shots with our left hand, but we gave Sho permission to throw with his right, and he made one in.

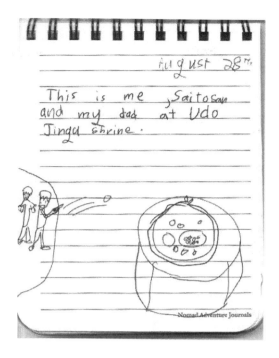

"I'm sorry you guys aren't going to have any good luck," he said consolingly. "I'll share some of mine if you need it."

Sixty-seven days after our start, Sho and I pedaled beside Mr. Saito an hour outside of Cape Sata, the southernmost point of mainland Japan.

We had all but completed our journey! I felt elated, proud and relieved. We had cycled 2,500 miles, persevering through violent rainstorms, stubborn winds, accidents, intimidating mountains, and oppressive heat. And we were still going strong. I imagined calling the naysayers and saying triumphantly, "Guess where we are?" We had long grown accustomed to the day-to-day experience of cycling for many hours: sometimes Sho and I talked, sometimes he talked to himself, sometimes we sang along to music, sometimes I just pedaled, not thinking of anything. The novelty of cycling

本土最南端
佐多岬
Cape Sata
↑
12Km

hours each day had worn off, and I looked forward to spending some quality time away from my bike.

The triumph of completion was tempered by a sense of loss. I had spent so much effort planning, preparing for and embarking on this adventure that I began to grieve its end even before we reached Cape Sata. A wonderful memory does not hold the power of an adventure yet to come, and I was left with a void.

I also wondered about my professional life. I wasn't ready to quit Intel, but I knew that it would not be healthy for me to continue working in a corporate environment. The money and prestige did not outweigh the stress and the need to meet goals set by others. I decided that my next major task would be to come up with a vision for a professional identity after Intel. I would not leave my job immediately after returning, but I would begin to lay the groundwork for a change, perhaps in another year or two. I wanted to be present for my kids as they grew up, keep my body strong and healthy, and make enough money to meet my commitments. It would take some time for me to figure it out, but I was determined to make it happen.

The final hour took us on rolling climbs through forests and beside a glistening sea. The air was humid and hot, and the area had a tropical feel. Deep green, large-leafed plants spread all around us, and the hanging limbs of mangrove trees reached down over us like giant fingers. We passed several male sago cycads, their monstrous cones jutting out of symmetrical fern-like leaves. Sho was amazed by their size and said, "Daddy, that pine cone is almost as big as me!"

Mr. Saito said, "That's a very slow-growing plant. The one you are looking at might be 100 years old. And don't eat it— every part of that plant is extremely toxic."

The road ended in a parking lot beside an official visitor's entrance. We would have to leave our bikes behind, pay a modest fee, and hike a bit to reach the end of our journey. As I locked up my bike beside a gnarled banyan tree, I noticed remains of the green industrial sludge from the Hakodate ferry still spread across the tire tread, still faintly gleaming after thousands of miles. Mr. Saito, Sho and I passed through a short tunnel then began to follow a cracked concrete path through the forest. The humid air clung to my throat, and I appreciated the canopy's shade. The trail was disintegrating in places, and I took care not to stumble.

As we hiked those last few hundred yards, I asked Sho, "So did you think riding across Japan for sixty-seven days was hard?"

"Kinda."

"Too hard for an eight-year-old?"

"Nah. But can I ride my own bicycle on the next trip?"

"Next trip?" I said, raising my eyebrows. "You're up for more?"

"Sure."

"Let's talk with Mommy about that."

"Daddy, if we do another trip, can we make sure that there are at least some game rooms?"

"Perhaps. That reminds me, did you ever decide which was the greatest game room in all of Japan?"

Sho frowned. "Not really. Some are bigger than others, but they're all kinda the same after a while. One thing's for sure: they're a lot better than what we have in the U.S. If I ever become president, the first thing that I'll do is order that all game rooms in the U.S. have Pokemon Battorio and Kyoryu Kingu. Those games rock, and you can't find them anywhere in America! It's really not acceptable."

Mr. Saito, who had been walking a few yards ahead, suddenly stopped and said, "Sho, look up in the tree!"

A Japanese macaque, nibbling on a leaf, crouched on a branch twenty feet overhead and stared down at us. We froze, and Mr. Saito whispered, "Where there's one, there are usually others."

Sho scanned the trees overhead and shouted, "There's another one!" The macaques bounded off their branches and disappeared, their chattering echoing through the forest. Sho gave Mr. Saito a sheepish look and said, "Sorry about that. I scared them away."

"Don't worry about it," Mr. Saito responded, mussing his hair. "We're not here to look at monkeys anyway. We're here to visit the southern cape, which looks to be just ahead."

We followed Mr. Saito out of the forest and emerged onto a ridge that offered a stunning view of the sparkling intersection of the East China Sea and Pacific Ocean spread out all around us. From this vantage point, some of the islands of the Osumi Archipelago were visible, the most dramatic of which, Iojima—known as Sulfur Island—stained the surrounding water yellow from the constant eruption of its namesake Mt. Io.

And then I saw the white lookout tower jutting out from the cape's promontory.

"There it is, buddy," I said, putting my arm around Sho and letting out a deep, satisfied breath.

Sho said, "I hope they have ice cream. I'm melting in this heat."

We reached the official tip of Cape Sata and took pictures next to a signpost at the edge of a cliff, the sea stretching out in the distance behind us. Up close, the lookout tower was in obvious disrepair. Its white paint was peeling and stained, and the underside of the observation deck had lost chunks of masonry. Many of the windows on the upper floor had been blown out, and the entranceway was missing a number of tiles. But to me, it was perfect, the final prize of a long sought goal.

Standing beside Sho, I suddenly recalled the final miles of the marathon I had run in Jackson, Tennessee with my father at age thirteen. As I approached Mile Twenty-Four at a pace I decided to call "jog-walking," I saw a familiar shape ahead running steadily toward me. My father. He had finished the marathon over an hour earlier, and had returned to the course to run the final two miles with me, the last place finisher.

"You're really close now, buddy," he said as he settled into an easy jog next to me. "You're definitely going to finish this thing."

With him by my side, I felt a surge of energy. The heaviness in my legs lifted, and my posture straightened with confidence. I began running at a strong pace, something that had seemed impossible just a few moments earlier. I knew then that I would complete my goal.

"You know those westerns, when the good guy and bad guy are fighting over a gun, and it gets knocked out of their hands and slides across the floor?" I said, breathing heavily from my renewed effort.

"Yeah?"

"Well, in the movies, the good guy reaches for the gun and just has to stretch out a few more inches to get it. You're not sure if he's going to make it, but he always does in the end, and shoots the bad guy just in time. In real life, sometimes, you just can't make those last few inches."

My dad smiled and said, "I know what you mean. In the last hour of the marathon, I kept wishing that a truck would come down the road and just run me over and put me out of my misery."

"I had fantasies of a helicopter swooping down and a guy with a machine gun filling me with bullets, so that I could just lie down on the side of the road."

"You'll be able to lie down in just a few more minutes. Look there!" Several hundred yards ahead, I could see the finishing banner draped over the road, stretched between two tall poles. Volunteers were taking down the race tents when I crossed the finish line, five hours and twenty-one minutes after starting.

My father gave me a hug and said, "You did it, and I'm really proud of you for not giving up. It's a great achievement."

I said, "Sometimes you need someone to help you with those last few inches."

Back in Cape Sata, where I was now the father, powerful waves crashed far below, swirling the sun's shimmering rays into white foam. I draped an arm over Sho's shoulders and said, "I'm really proud of you, Sho. You did it."

He nestled his head into my side.

It would soon be time to say goodbye to Mr. Saito. Sho and I would take a train back to Tokyo to be reunited with Eiko and Saya. Mr. Saito would continue cycling up the western coast of Kyushu.

"Well, Saito-san. It was a privilege to travel with you," I said, bowing to him.

He reached out and shook my hand. "You and Sho were the biggest surprise of my ride around Japan. It was wonderful to get to know you. You were actually my first American friends."

Sho fished out three Pokemon coins and handed them to Mr. Saito. "These are for you. They are my strongest Pokemon. I want you to have them."

"Are you sure?" Mr. Saito said, and Sho nodded. "Thank you for such a thoughtful gift. You're a special kid. As I continue on by myself, I won't truly be alone. I will look at these and feel like you are still traveling with me."

I took out my journal, hoping to capture every detail from this moment. Sho asked, "Daddy, why do you write in your journal all the time?"

"I want to remember this trip, and it's best to write things down while they are still fresh. Also, I'm thinking about writing a book about our adventures."

"Can I read it?"

"Of course you may. The book will be for you. Kinda like a long letter from me explaining how much I love you."

"You could just tell me that. It would be a lot easier than writing a whole book."

"Well, I imagine that some day—a long time from now, after I've died—you might enjoy having the book around. Whenever you miss me, I'll be waiting for you right there in the pages."

Sho said, "I wish it was impossible to die, because then I wouldn't have to say goodbye to you or Mommy."

I nodded and said, "Yeah, I feel that way too. You know, I used to travel all over the world for work. It was interesting, but after you were born, I realized that I preferred spending time with you while you were growing up. I remember returning from a business trip that had lasted three weeks. You were only six months old and waiting for me in the airport with Mommy. When I held you in my arms, I promised that I wouldn't stay away from you that long again."

"But we just spent two months away from Mommy and Saya. What about them?"

"Good point. I've learned a lesson on this trip: that I don't want to be away from Eiko and Saya for a long time again, either, even if I'm on an incredible journey with you. You know the answer, right?"

Sho gave me a big smile. "They'll have to come along on our next adventure!"

I laughed and wrote down his words. I had to note every detail, had to record what we had done together, Sho and I, on our glorious trip down the length of Japan.

The End

Acknowledgments

WHEN SHO AND I CAME UP WITH THE IDEA TO CYCLE ACROSS Japan, I knew we would need help. As we prepared for and embarked on our trip, friends, family members and strangers stepped in time and again. Writing this book was another major challenge and, once more, my friends offered much needed support and advice.

Thank you to:

- The many people in the United Nations who promoted our ride and who spend each day trying to make the world a better place: Maaike Jansen, Georgios Kostakos, Wambui Munge, Leah Wanambwa, Lisa Rolls Hagelberg, Lucy Jasmin, Achim Steiner, and Juanita Castano.

- Dr. Irv Rubenstein, exercise physiologist and co-founder and president of S.T.E.P.S. personal training center in Nashville, TN. Irv helped me develop a training plan for the ride that kept me healthy throughout the 67 days of cycling.

- Eric Marcos and his team at Bicycle World in Mt. Kisco, NY, who spent many hours tuning up our bikes and helping improve my bike repair skills (which came in handy in the wilds of Hokkaido).

- The teachers and administrators at the United Nations International School, who invited us to speak to the students and hosted several events promoting the ride: Jacquee Novak, Junko Saito, Deb Karmozyn, Vanessa Go, Jackie Jenkins, and Jon Gage.

- The crew at TV Japan, who televised news accounts of our ride from start to finish, including Yoshi Sugishita, who arranged for us to stay with his family in Matsumoto. Sho and I have fond memories of his brother Yuki and were honored to have spent time with him before he died.

- The friendly folks at Japan Cycling Navigator, who gave us routing tips and advice on touring Japan by bike: Eiichi Watanabe, Osamu Naganuma, Hideo Tomita, Kenichi Ikeda and Koizumi Shigehiro.

- Anand Chandrasekher, who sponsored the ride on behalf of Intel Corporation, and Ben Seab at Intel, who provided technical support.

- Bicycle expert and enthusiast Ed Cangialosi, founder of Reparto Corse, who highlighted our ride on his website.

- Dana Ostomel, founder of Deposit a Gift, for support with fund raising and for publishing an article about our family adventures.

- Joe "Metal Cowboy" Kurmaskie, who offered tips on cycling long distances with kids.

- Shuichi Kameyama, Yuki Yamagishi and the rest of the staff at Japan National Tourism Organization, who promoted our ride around the world. Shuichi's parents were generous hosts when Sho and I rode through Seki City, Japan.

- Jessica Daniels, who spread the word about our ride within the far-flung but close-knit community of the Fletcher School of Law and Diplomacy.

- My training partners in the Westchester Triathlon Club, who challenged me to get into better shape than I thought possible: Rich Izzo, Kevin Cunningham, Christine Dunnery, Tom Bookless, Pete Preston, Deirdre Hopkins, Heather Stewart, Mimi Boyle, Mark Golab, Adam Derechin, Sandy York, Carl Curran, Martin Avidan, Ed Beusse, Jim Irvine.

- Paul Descloux, who shared his deep knowledge of cycling and took me on many training rides up and down the hills of Westchester County.

- Dee Dee De Bartlo and her staff at February Partners, for expertise and advice on how to share *Rising Son* with the world.

- Andrew Nahem and Veronica Zhu for artistic input on the book jacket.

- Bill McKibben, author, environmentalist and founder of 350.org, who inspired my interest in working to protect the environment and who helped me in the subsequent ride across Iceland with my kids.

- Catherine Hiller, accomplished author and editor, who served as the development editor for *Rising Son* and taught the writing class in which I reviewed each chapter. This book is much improved thanks to her work.

- My writing group classmates, who patiently told me when the narrative just wasn't working: Jennifer Warner, Sally Weinraub, Mark Thompson, and Lisa Ahmad.

- The readers of the first draft of the final manuscript, who made many helpful suggestions: Hiroko Miyamura, Rainer Jenss, Brad Graff, Sanjyot Dunung, Jennifer McFadden, and Bryan Harris.

- Akira Saito (aka "Mr. Saito" or "Saito-san" in the book), who was a wonderful traveling companion and so kind to Sho. It is an honor to have become your first American friends.

- My brother-in-law and sister-in-law, Aki and Akemi Ikegaya, who traveled many hours to give Sho and me some much-needed family support in the middle of the bike ride.

- My parents, for teaching me to seek out a meaningful life. My brother Stuart and sister Becky, who always look out for their little brother. My niece and a gifted writer, Bonnie Scott, who provided a helpful teenager's perspective on the book.

- My father-in-law, Naotoshi Ikegaya, who checked on us regularly throughout the ride and accepted me with love into his family long ago.

- My daughter, Saya, who reminds me to get at least one hug each day and knows my big secret.

- Eiko, my wife, fellow family adventurer and love of my life.

- And finally, Sho. I can't wait for our next adventure.

18115195R00205

Made in the USA
Charleston, SC
17 March 2013